Here's what a few famous Brooklyn residents and fans told the authors:

"A nice place to visit, a great place to live."
—Howard Golden,
Brooklyn Borough President

"Brooklyn is homes and neighborhoods with caring, loyal people who proudly take their Brooklyn roots with them wherever they go. It's mostly a quiet place where you can see the sky, travel on wide, tree-lined streets, hear the sounds of life, and smell the culinary diversity."
—Franklin Thomas,
President, The Ford Foundation

"Brooklyn, there really are great restaurants there. And with deep dish apple pie and (Gage & Tollner's) Miss Edna, I may never go back to Virginia."
—Willard Scott

"You can take the kid out of Brooklyn, but you can't take Brooklyn out of the kid. Kickin' the can. Ring-a-leevio. Stoop ball, potsy. Punch ball! Playing marbles along the curb. Hearing my mother call me from the third-floor window telling me it was time to eat. Brooklyn! The cosmos!"
—Julius La Rosa

"If I'm gonna live in the city, Brooklyn is where I'd live forever. When I saw it I flipped. It's very unpretentious—nobody cares who you are until you can shoot a basketball. Until I scored three points in a game the cats in the neighborhood wouldn't speak to me. When I moved here the only thing I wanted to do was find Ebbets Field. At least the wall was left. BAM is a beautiful place, my favorite place to play. It sounds great and the decor is fantastic."
—Branford Marsalis

"I simply love Brooklyn—everything from stickball to Bungalow Bars to Ebbets Field. I often return to my former neighborhood on President Street. Unlike my present neighborhood in Manhattan, I knew every merchant by first name. I remember attending the movies on the roof of the Kaneo Theater, where dishes and glasses were awarded to lucky winners. Culture was personified by the Brooklyn Museum, Brooklyn Library, and Brooklyn Academy of Music, where I saw my first opera. All of this was warm, lively, middle class, and fun."

> —Arthur Levitt, Jr.,
> former Chairman, American Stock Exchange

"Culturally, the most happening borough in New York is Brooklyn."

> —Mze Moyo,
> Coordinator, African Street Festival

"When the Dodgers left Brooklyn, they left Gold's to supply the heat."

> —The Golds, Gold's Horseradish

"We sell our beer in Tokyo and London and Berlin. People all over the world know and love the name Brooklyn."

> —Steve Hindy, Brooklyn Brewery

"For the real Yiddishe *gefeel*, Brooklyn is the original."

> —Rabbi J. J. Hecht, radio personality

BROOKLYN

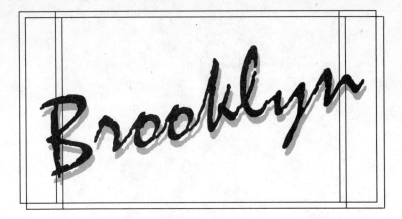

WHERE TO GO,
WHAT TO DO,
HOW TO GET THERE

Ellen Freudenheim
with Daniel P. Wiener

St. Martin's Press   New York

To our children, David and Anna

BROOKLYN: WHERE TO GO, WHAT TO DO, HOW TO GET THERE. Copyright © 1991 by
Ellen Freudenheim and Daniel P. Wiener. All rights reserved. Printed in the
United States of America. No part of this book may be used or reproduced in any
manner whatsoever without written permission except in the case of brief
quotations embodied in critical articles or reviews. For information, address St.
Martin's Press, 175 Fifth Avenue, New York, N.Y. 10010.

Maps copyright © 1991 by Florence A. Neal.
Design by Judith Dannecker

Library of Congress Cataloging-in-Publication Data

Freudenheim, Ellen.
        Brooklyn : where to go, what to do, how to get there / Ellen
Freudenheim and Daniel P. Wiener.
                p.   cm.
        Includes index.
        ISBN 0-312-05395-9 (pbk.)
        1. Brooklyn (New York, N.Y.)—Description—Guide-books.   2. New
York (N.Y.)—Description—1981–   —Guide-books.   I. Wiener, Daniel
P.   II. Title.
F129.B7F74   1991
917.47'23—dc20   90-19120
                                                            CIP

10 9 8 7 6 5 4 3 2

NOTE: All information listed in this book, including prices, is subject to
change. To the best of their ability, the authors have verified the accuracy
of the information at the time *Brooklyn: Where to Go, What to Do, How to
Get There* was written.

CONTENTS

ACKNOWLEDGMENTS

First and foremost, we wish to acknowledge the hundreds of shopkeepers, Brooklyn community district managers, and Brooklyn residents who cooperated in our research for this book. Thanks also to the celebrities who took a moment to contribute their thoughts about Brooklyn.

In the course of our research, we gleaned a great deal from the publications issued by the Fund for the Borough of Brooklyn, from the late Elliot Willensky's *AIA Guide to New York* and *When Brooklyn Was the World*, and from the invaluable *WPA Guide to New York*. While we cannot acknowledge everyone by name, we would like to express our appreciation to those who either helped with our research or reviewed the manuscript in part: Diane Robinson Frazier, Greg Gardner, Jean Halloran, Diane Johnson, Elaine Kronenberger, Khadija Matin, Bernie McDonald, Bob Ohlerking, Pat Smith, Elizabeth White, Mary Yrizirry, and staff members Claire Lamers, Jane McDonough, and Matilda McKellen of the Brooklyn Historical Society. Justin Ferate deserves particular mention for his generous assistance. Thanks are due to Marshal Beil and Marya Yee for their legal expertise and to the various Goldens in our lives—Sharon, Jeff and Judy, and Maggie, and to Peter and Martha Davis for their encouragement. Thanks also go to cover photographer Curtis Willocks, and to mapmaker Florence Neal. Our editor, Anne Savarese, has been nothing short of wonderful to work with. To our families and in particular our children, David (six) and Anna (three), a special hug for their patience through many hours of work and for their constant reminder of what is important in life. Last, each to our respective spouse, an acknowledgment that two heads are better than one—usually.

INTRODUCTION

It'd take a guy a lifetime to know Brooklyn t'roo an' t'roo. An' even den, yuh wouldn't know it all.

—Thomas Wolfe, 1935

BROOKLYN! A GUIDE TO BROOKLYN?

Yes, Brooklyn. This is the first nationally distributed guidebook to Brooklyn in more than fifty years. Although Brooklyn is New York City's largest borough, for too long now it has been overlooked by New Yorkers and out-of-towners alike. We're not sure why, although we think it has something to do with Manhattan's bright lights and skyscrapers—and the fact that so few journalists bother to venture across the East River.

But it's also possible that Brooklyn has been overlooked because its many neighborhoods seemed inaccessible, even to those who live here. New residents struggle to find their way around this borough of 2.5 million people—a place big enough to rank as one of the five largest cities in the United States. Ex-Brooklynites aren't quite sure how their old neighborhoods have changed—or what to go back to if they visit. As for foreign tourists and Manhattanites, well, Brooklyn just isn't a known quantity.

This guide sets out to make the best of Brooklyn *accessible*. It is not another book about Dodger nostalgia. It is a practical guide to Brooklyn in the 1990s:

restaurants, shops, cultural sites and history, and children's activities in more than a dozen neighborhoods. It will take you not only to well-known Brooklyn institutions like the Brooklyn Academy of Music (BAM) but also beyond BAM, to the historic Victorian brownstone neighborhood of Fort Greene, home to leading jazz musicians. It will lead you to restaurant row in Bay Ridge and to an authentic Russian meal in "Little Odessa," Brighton Beach, where vodka continues to flow even after you're dancing on the tabletops. We will take you to a first-class children's museum and to a tiny Norwegian shop where the wares are as wonderful as the people who sell them.

For many people Brooklyn is forever stuck in the past. It was the home of the Brooklyn Dodgers, Ralph Kramden, and the old Coney Island amusement park, all long gone. And Brooklyn was where Woody Allen, George Gershwin, and Walt Whitman *came* from. But today, whole sections of Brooklyn have been revitalized by new waves of immigrants—from across the oceans and across the East River. Ironically, some of these new Brooklynites are the children or grandchildren of people who grew up in Brooklyn and moved away.

The reason behind Brooklyn's popularity is not just lower rents than those in Manhattan plus handsome housing and a few great cultural institutions. It runs deeper. If Manhattan is the thumping heart, then Brooklyn is the elusive soul of New York City. Brooklyn's got personality because it is so ethnically diverse, because it is human-scaled, and because there are roots here in the many neighborhoods—Italian, Jewish, Chinese, Middle Eastern—that somehow maintain their ethnic authenticity. Brooklyn is still New York City, but it has a lot less concrete and fewer high rises. In neighborhoods with buildings only three or four stories high, and some with suburban-style homes, you can actually see the sky while strolling along a tree-lined street. Only fifteen minutes from Wall Street, it is quieter here than in Manhattan, and the pace is slower. What's more, for residents and visitors alike, Brooklyn is a treasure chest of history, culture, and family fun.

We discovered Brooklyn because we had to. Intrepid ex-Manhattanites with two small children, we went in search of discount furniture, that elusive knish, and a great place to take the kids on a rainy day. Our guide in this foray was our neighbor, Sharon Golden, who tossed off suggestions that we visit a hitherto-unknown "Avenue J" or "McDonald Avenue" as though they were as familiar as Madison or 5th. To our astonishment it was hard, short of word of mouth, to find out about Brooklyn.

So, after years of exploration and hours of conversation, we can tell you that Brooklyn offers an incredible array of things, places, and cuisines. You can't beat the Brooklyn Museum, the Brooklyn Botanic Garden, BAM, or the Children's Museum for culture and entertainment. There is enough left of "old Brooklyn" (that is, from before World War II) for good reminiscing: Peter Lugers, Junior's, the boardwalk, Gargiulo's, Alba's, Gage & Tollner, and more. If you want, you can eat huge strawberry pancakes for breakfast, Middle Eastern couscous chicken for lunch, and Polish potato pirogi for dinner, while shopping for designer clothing at blue-jeans prices. And you'll still have time to take a ride on Coney Island's famous roller coaster, the Cyclone, visit the nation's first museum for children, or play nine holes of golf.

Possibly the best thing about Brooklyn is its people. The vast majority of Brooklynites are hospitable and friendly folk who are proud to show off the neighborhoods in which they live and work. In fact, you may find that as a visitor in Brooklyn you'll have more fun, and feel better appreciated, than you would as a tourist in Manhattan. So don't be afraid to ask questions or simply strike up a conversation with a "native." More than likely the response will delight you.

HOW TO USE THIS BOOK

There are several ways to tour Brooklyn.

Pick a neighborhood. The introductions to each chapter will highlight what you can expect to find there. Then set your priorities—food, fun, or fashion—and take it from there.

Or, use the Where to Find It index (see page 258) to pinpoint the particular cuisine, shop, cultural or historical site, or entertainment you want. Then consider the surrounding neighborhoods yours to explore.

Parents can turn directly to the Brooklyn's Best Bets for Children section (page 240) or the Kidstuff section in each chapter, or look for the symbol ✳ throughout the book, which signifies points of particular interest to children.

What's Included (and What's Not)

Brooklyn's a big place, so by definition this guidebook is incomplete. Brooklyn is dynamic, changing overnight as new businesses pop up and some old ones bow out. Unless you are content to explore, call ahead before setting out to a particular destination.

Brooklyn purists may take issue with the way we've stretched the boundaries on some neighborhoods and lumped others together in this book. To them we apologize. But to make the borough accessible, it sometimes pays to bend the rules a bit. In fact, where certain special points of interest lie in residential neighborhoods lacking other remarkable destinations, we've taken the liberty of placing such listings with those of the nearest neighborhood.

Each listing met at least one of several criteria: businesses had to either be in existence for five years or have something unique to offer; membership organizations, clubs, and courses in which you must enroll are not listed; and we omitted most of the national franchises and chains that operate in Brooklyn. Because one can never really know every nook and cranny in a city this big, we encourage readers to send us their own picks and pans for future editions. A form is included in the back of the book for just that purpose.

Transportation

Cabs. Yellow cabs are rare on Brooklyn streets. A reliable and slightly cheaper alternative is the numerous neighborhood car services, licensed by the Taxi and Limousine Commission. Several are listed in each neighborhood section, but almost any car service will take you wherever you wish to go. If the local car service is busy, try calling one based in an adjoining neighborhood. Prices are set by a dispatcher instead of registering on a meter. When you call a car service, the dispatcher should give you a price for your trip before sending a car for you. Expect to wait about five to ten minutes for a car, or longer during rush hour or in bad weather. Car services are a good way to get around Brooklyn or to get from Brooklyn back to Manhattan.

Unbeknownst to many Manhattanites, car services are also considerably cheaper than yellow cabs when going from Manhattan to Brooklyn, particularly when you are headed for distant points. Call at least a half hour in advance and most services will pick you up in Manhattan for a flat fee of about $20 or less.

Subways. The subways that run to Brooklyn from Manhattan are the 2, 3, 4, 5, and the A, B, C, D, F, G, J, L, M, N, Q, and R. Three stations where many lines intersect are Borough Hall in Brooklyn Heights and Atlantic Avenue and DeKalb Avenue near Fort Greene. For information on the subway and bus routes, call the hotline operated from 6 a.m. to 9 p.m. daily by the New York City Transit Authority at (718) 330-1234. Be prepared to wait a few minutes to get through.

LIRR. The Long Island Railroad stops at the Atlantic Avenue station, at the intersection of Atlantic and Flatbush Avenues. The terminal, just a stone's throw from the Brooklyn Academy of Music, connects with a number of subway lines.

Maps

The maps preceding each chapter should be adequate for most casual expeditions in Brooklyn. Or you can pick up a detailed street map of Brooklyn in bookstores, many drug stores, and often from sidewalk book merchants. A subway map, free at token booths, is also helpful.

Credit Cards

While many establishments take credit cards, some mom-and-pop stores and restaurants do not. When a listing in the book says "Major credit cards," you can assume that you'll be able to use one or more of the following cards: American Express, Visa, MasterCard, and Diner's Club. If you're worried about getting stuck with the wrong card, call ahead.

Safety and Style

The neighborhoods listed in this book are, we feel, friendly to visitors. Still, since this is New York City, you should make sure to pack your street smarts. A few tips: Wandering around during the day is always better than a nighttime stroll. Two is always safer than one (it's more fun to bring a friend anyway). Brooklyn is a practical place; you generally are better off dressing down in casual clothes. All but the fanciest restaurants will seat and serve anyone who looks presentable, regardless of whether the men are wearing jackets and ties or the women fancy clothes.

Phone Numbers

All of the phone numbers listed here are in the 718 area code unless otherwise noted.

Mail Order from Brooklyn

If you don't live in Brooklyn but still want to shop here, you'll find that many stores will ship by UPS. You can also obtain a small catalog listing nostalgic Brooklynabilia, from T-shirts to knishes to mugs: write P.O. Box 106, 328 Flatbush Avenue, Brooklyn, NY 11238.

Also available is a Special Entertainment '92 leisure discount book featuring Brooklyn and Staten Island. It contains coupons for discounts of up to 50 percent at more than 350 restaurants, retail shops, and amusements. The 1992 edition is priced at $30. For further information or to order a copy, write Entertainment Publications, Inc., 375 86th Street, Brooklyn, NY 11209.

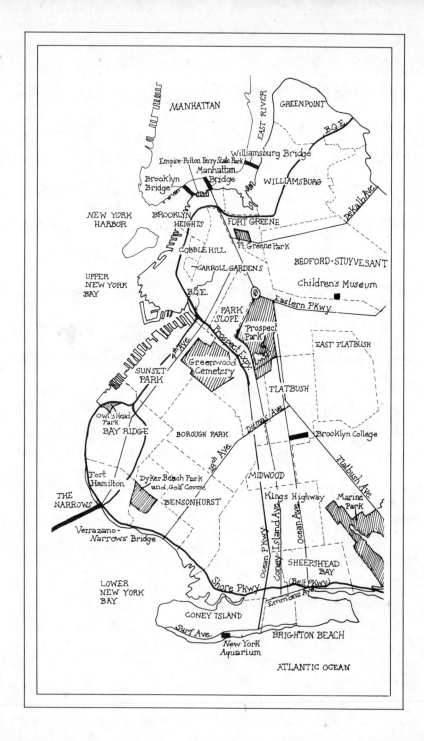

BROOKLYN

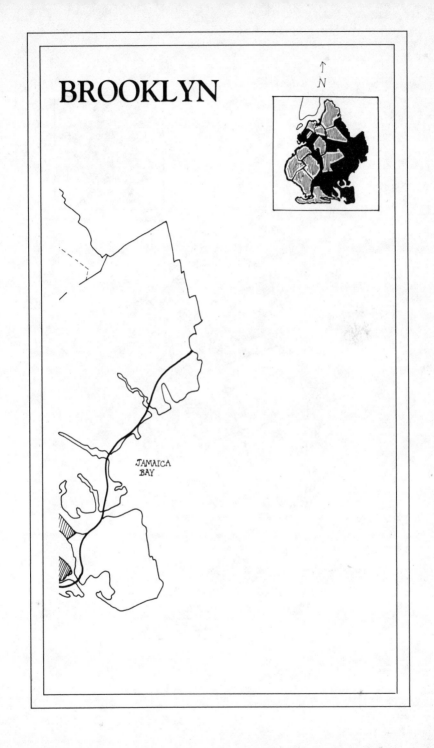

N

JAMAICA
BAY

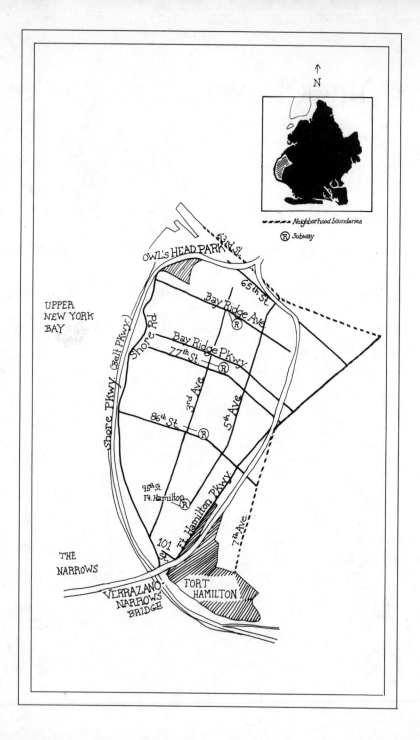

N

Neighborhood boundaries
Ⓡ Subway

OWL'S HEAD PARK

UPPER
NEW YORK
BAY

Shore Pkwy (Belt Pkwy)

Shore Rd.

65th St.

Bay Ridge Ave.
Ⓡ

Bay Ridge Pkwy.
77th St. Ⓡ

3rd Ave.

5th Ave.

86th St. Ⓡ

95th St.
Ft. Hamilton Ⓡ

101 St.

Ft. Hamilton Pkwy.

7th Ave.

THE
NARROWS

VERRAZANO
NARROWS
BRIDGE

FORT
HAMILTON

BAY RIDGE

Where it is: 65th Street to 101st Street, Belt Parkway to Fort Hamilton Parkway.

What's nearby: Bath Beach, Bensonhurst, Borough Park, Dyker Heights, Staten Island, and Sunset Park.

How to get there:

By car: Take the Brooklyn-Queens Expressway (BQE) to the Gowanus Expressway toward Staten Island. Exit at 86th Street (and 7th Avenue). If you arrive at the Verrazano-Narrows Bridge, you've gone too far.

By subway: R train to 86th Street (at 4th Avenue).

Cab services: About $20 from Grand Central Station; $15 from Brooklyn Heights. Apple Car Service (363-9000) or Harborview Car Service (748-8800).

Special events: Norwegian Constitution Day Parade along 5th Avenue between 67th and 90th streets (first Sunday after May 17); annual Ragamuffin Parade, a gala event for families and kids in costumes, on 3rd Avenue (last Saturday of September).

How it got its name: Known first as Yellow Hook for the yellow clay in its soil; the infelicitous name was changed in 1853 after New York City suffered a bout of yellow fever. The spectacular views from a ridge overlooking the entrance to New York Bay gave Bay Ridge its current name.

ABOUT THE NEIGHBORHOOD

It would be impossible to take in all of Bay Ridge in one visit. The neighborhood is just too big. You'll find large name-brand shops along 86th Street and smaller, intimate family-run shops on 5th Avenue. Third Avenue is restaurant row, with many good restaurants along a twenty-five-block stretch. Because this is also a residential, family neighborhood, there are plenty of ways to combine a shopping expedition with a family outing.

Bay Ridge is not the place for high fashion, fine antiques, or silver-and-crystal dining. Its shops and restaurants reflect the solid middle-class values of the local populace. What that means is good, moderately priced home furnishings, clothing, gifts, food, and hobby items as well as a wide range of restaurants that serve tasty, reasonably priced meals.

While wave upon wave of European immigrants have moved into and then out of Brooklyn's many neighborhoods, a mix remains comfortably settled in Bay Ridge. The shops, restaurants, and community events in Bay Ridge celebrate its ethnic diversity. The early Scandinavian settlers' presence is still felt in the neighborhood bakeries and food shops. The Norwegian weekly newspaper *Nordisk Tidende* is published here, and the annual Norwegian Constitution Day Parade culminates with the crowning of Miss Norway in Leif Ericson Park. The sizeable Italian population is reflected in the many excellent Italian restaurants and cappuccino and espresso cafés. At Christmas, fourth- and fifth-generation Italians in the Dyker Heights section of Bay Ridge bedeck their homes with thousands of lights and decorations. The Irish, and more recently the Greek, Lebanese, and Syrian, presence is reflected in small specialty shops that sell food, clothing, and gift items from the old country.

Historical Notes

The area now called Bay Ridge was purchased from the Nyack Indians by the Dutch West India Company in 1652. A rural farming area until the late 1890s, Bay Ridge, like Brooklyn Heights, was developed as a retreat for wealthy Manhattanites. The spectacular views from a ridge overlooking the entrance to New York Bay gave Bay Ridge its name and attracted a number of industrialists who built summer estates along the bluffs of Shore Road. But with the extension of the 4th Avenue subway in 1915, the exclusivity of the area was destroyed. The neighborhood's population changed as Manhattan workers seeking more suburban surroundings began to settle in the area.

The long history of Bay Ridge remains visible in its homes and churches. Elegant turn-of-the-century houses more typical of Westchester than Brooklyn line Colonial Road and Shore Road between 80th and 83rd streets. The land on which Fort Hamilton was built played a role in George Washington's failed

Battle of Long Island against the British in 1776. Nearby Saint John's Episcopal Church at 99th Street and Fort Hamilton Parkway, known as the "church of the generals," was frequented by such military leaders as Stonewall Jackson and Robert E. Lee.

Visitors love looking at the so-called **Gingerbread House**, a whimsical cottage with a mock thatched roof, located at the corner of 82nd Street and Narrows Avenue. Local legend suggests that it was built as a country getaway for a young homesick British bride. The home at the intersection of Colonial Road and Wakeman Place is also a point of local historical interest. It was on the estate known as Owl's Head, belonging to Henry Murphy, the first editor of the *Brooklyn Eagle* newspaper, that the construction of the Brooklyn Bridge was authorized.

Standing guard over the neighborhood's one- and two-family homes and dominating many of the views is the **Verrazano-Narrows Bridge**. Named after Giovanni da Verrazano, first explorer of New York Harbor, the bridge's opening in 1964 linked Brooklyn to Staten Island and New Jersey. At that time it was the world's longest suspension bridge.

Shopping Areas

There are three main shopping areas: 3rd Avenue, 5th Avenue, and 86th Street.

86th Street: Major chain stores. This two-lane street between 4th and 6th avenues is home to many national and regional retail chains, including Benetton, Newmark and Lewis, Lane Bryant, Lerner's, Woolworth's, and Century 21.

5th Avenue: Specialty retail. From 75th to 88th streets, the stretch of speciality stores, ethnic delis, gift shops (such as the top-notch **The Hutch**), and cafés is "Main Street" for the families in the adjacent neighborhood of tree-lined streets and two-story homes. The block from 82nd to 83rd streets could be called the "wedding center" of Brooklyn. Along with a number of bridal boutiques, this is the home of **Kleinfeld's**, New York City's most famous prenuptial retail operation.

3rd Avenue: Restaurant row. Bay Ridge has so many good restaurants, it's hard to know when to stop eating. No fewer than eighteen are located on a one-mile stretch of 3rd Avenue between 70th and 95th streets. The choices vary, from one of the best Indian restaurants in Brooklyn, **India Passage**, to great Italian food at **Areo**, to huge portions of barbecue chicken and ribs at **Short Ribs**, to music, dancing, and dinner at **T. J. Bentley**. In addition there are some trendy clothing shops, such as **Mango's**, along with cafés and two outstanding bakeries, both of which supply their goodies to top-tier Manhattan restaurants.

Kidstuff

While Bay Ridge has a number of good playgrounds, the best and most interesting is the two-and-a-half-mile stretch known as **Shore Road Park** along the waters of upper New York Bay, a favorite spot for kite flying, fishing, and biking. **Dyker Park** is a large area with athletic fields and tennis courts. **Owl's Head Park**, overlooking the harbor, is great for picnics. (For more information on parks see pages 13–14.)

For kids interested in guns and things military, a visit to the **Harbor Defense Museum** is a must. Around Christmas, an evening drive past the bright, elaborately decorated homes in **Dyker Heights** would put a smile on any Scrooge's face.

Even the most impatient youngster will stop and stare at the wonderful items sold in some of Bay Ridge's youth-oriented shops. From **Craft Cottage** and **Walt's Hobby Shop** to the gear sold at **Panda Sport**, there is plenty to entertain and stimulate. And for growling stomachs or sweet tooths an abundance of pizza and ice-cream parlors, including a few old-fashioned spots, such as **Hinsch's**, is available as well.

ENTERTAINMENT

Cineplex Odeon Alpine Theater. 6900 5th Avenue, at 69th Street, 748-4200. ✴

A small, friendly, seven-screen first-run movie theater located at the beginning of the 5th Avenue commercial strip in Bay Ridge. Walk two blocks through a middle-class residential area to lots of great restaurants on Third Avenue. There's easy local parking and bargain matinees.

Lee Mark Lanes. 423 88th Street, between 4th and 5th avenues, 745-3200. Daily, 9 a.m.–6 p.m. No credit cards. ✴

This two-floor, thirty-six-lane renovated bowling alley is a popular neighborhood spot for birthday parties and league play. Babysitting is available. If you're going to have a children's party, you can arrange for inflatable bumpers to be installed so that every ball stays in the lane.

Pastels. 437 88th Street, between 4th and 5th avenues, 748-1002. Wed., Fri., and weekends, 10 p.m.–4 a.m. Admission is $5 on Fri., Sun., and Wed.; $10 on Sat.

This is a nice disco that draws well-dressed locals. The decor is contemporary: shiny metallic bars, video screens, and a big central dance floor.

PARKS AND PLAYGROUNDS

5th Avenue playground. 84th Street, on 5th Avenue. ✳

This is your basic urban playground, complete with swings and other necessary equipment. Nothing fancy, but it is conveniently located near 5th Avenue shopping. For a greener setting, check out the 79th Street and 95th Street playgrounds on the other side of Bay Ridge (see listing below).

Leif Ericson Park. 4th Avenue, between 66th and 67th streets. ✳

Reflecting the neighborhood's early Scandinavian roots, this sixteen-acre park is the site of the annual crowning of Miss Norway during Bay Ridge's Norwegian Constitution Day Parade in May.

Owl's Head Park and **Shore Road Park.** Shore Road, between 68th Street and Colonial Road, 965-6524.

With almost thirty acres of lovely green space on a bluff overlooking the harbor, this breezy point is a popular place for family picnics. Get here early to watch the Tall Ships sailboat flotilla on the fourth weekend in July, or enjoy the summer concerts sponsored by the Brooklyn arts association, BACA (see page 108). At 69th Street a footbridge crosses the Belt Parkway to the waterside promenade, where the walking, jogging, and biking path starts. The 97th Street ball fields are popular for amateur baseball games. Nearby there are two lovely playgrounds, lots of open space, and tennis courts (call 965-8993 for permit information). Take a stroll along the sidewalk from 100th Street back down to 69th Street for fresh breezes, views of the Verrazano-Narrows Bridge, and some lovely old homes. At John Paul Jones Park, at 4th Avenue and 101st Street, adjacent to the entrance to Fort Hamilton, there are frequent summer concerts.

Russell Pederson Playground. Colonial Road, at 84th Street. ✳

A nice-sized playground located in one of the neighborhood's wealthiest residential sections, this is a lovely place to stop with little ones on a fine day.

79th and 95th Street playgrounds. Along Shore Road, 965-6528. ✳

Here are two lovely, breezy playgrounds. The 79th Street playground is newly renovated and only a few long blocks from the heart of Bay Ridge's 3rd Avenue restaurant area. The 95th Street playground, also pleasant, is near a popular ball field at 97th Street.

Shore Parkway Promenade. From Owl's Head Park at 69th Street to Bensonhurst Park at Bay Parkway. ✳

Running along Brooklyn's western-most edge, this long, narrow band of asphalt and benches between the Belt Parkway and the water connects Owl's Head Park at 68th Street to Bensonhurst Park and passes under the Verrazano-Narrows Bridge. Bikers, joggers, and walkers love this stretch on warm days. You can cross over the Belt Parkway at the exits or stop and park in one of the parking areas just to the side of the parkway. When you get near the bridge, keep your eyes open—you might see some of the peregrine falcons that nest in its superstructure.

POINTS OF CULTURAL INTEREST

Brooklyn Public Library. 73rd Street, between 3rd Avenue and Ridge Boulevard, 748-3042. Call to check hours. ✳

Located at the edge of a lovely residential area off tree-lined Ridge Boulevard, this large, pleasant library has a children's room on the second floor with a wide selection for preschoolers through teens. There are occasional movies and special programs for youngsters. For Brooklynites: any book you borrow here can be returned to your local Brooklyn branch library.

Fontbonne Hall Academy. 9901 Shore Road, corner of 99th Street.

Life was tough for the industrial barons of the nineteenth century, as you can see from this extraordinarily lovely mansion, built as a getaway from the noise and bustle of Manhattan. Lore has it that this home, the sole remnant of a district once filled with gracious plantation houses and mini-castles, was purchased by Diamond Jim Brady for Lillian Russell. Party guests would boat down to this bucolic retreat—which sure would beat the subway! Today the halls are filled not with party guests but with young female students. No tours are available.

"Gingerbread House." 82nd Street, near Narrows Avenue. ✳

Thatched cottages in England dating back to the 1600s were considered so quaint by the turn of this century that some whimsical wealthy folks used the thatched cottage as a theme for their second (or third) homes. This house dates from the era when Brooklyn was full of rolling green hills, meadows, and the sounds of nature. It is a private home, so no tours are available.

Harbor Defense Museum at Fort Hamilton, Fort Hamilton Parkway at 101st Street, 630-4349. Mon., 1–4 p.m.; Thurs.–Sat., 10 a.m.–5 p.m.; Sun., 1 p.m.–5 p.m. Free admission. ✳

Housed in a 160-year-old wedge-shaped stone building used to protect Fort Hamilton from a rear-guard attack, the Harbor Defense Museum chronicles the development of the guns, mines, cannons, and missiles used to defend New York Harbor. The museum building, called a *caponier*, is listed in the National Register of Historic Places, as is the adjacent fort, now an officer's club. Kids will love the exhibits of guns, medals, uniforms, and paintings. There's also a ten-stop, self-guided walking tour that takes you past a block of cannons, Robert E. Lee's house, the barracks, stable, and commissary, as well as the officers' quarters. The B-63 bus or the B-16 bus will get you within a couple of blocks of the fort. Ask the driver to let you off at the nearest stop. Part of Fort Hamilton is actually under one of the ramps for the Verrazano-Narrows Bridge.

Poly Prep Country Day School. 92nd Street, corner of 7th Avenue, 836-9800. Call for a schedule.

Poly Prep is nestled in a vast greenbelt of a campus, complete with duck ponds, swimming pools, and tennis courts. Founded in Brooklyn Heights in 1854, today it is a highly regarded private school whose distinguished alumni roster includes Richard Perry, a leading producer of hit records; Arthur Levitt, ex-chairman of the American Stock Exchange; and Ken Duberstein, former president Ronald Reagan's chief of staff. The school offers continuing education courses and evening adult instruction. Occasional special events, such as performances by the Harvard Glee Club and the Alvin Ailey Dance Theater, are open to the public.

Verrazano-Narrows Bridge. Shore Parkway and Fort Hamilton Parkway. ✳

Visible from many Brooklyn neighborhoods, the Verrazano-Narrows Bridge celebrates Giovanni da Verrazano, the first European to see Staten Island (in 1524). Designed in 1964, the steel bridge is 4,260 feet long and is the starting point for the New York City Marathon each fall. The bridge connects Brooklyn with Staten Island and is a quick route to southern New Jersey and Pennsylvania. Driving across it toward Staten Island will cost you $5; the return trip is free.

NOTABLE RESTAURANTS

There are many good restaurants in Bay Ridge. For tips on where to find quick snacks and ice-cream parlors, see the separate listing at the end of this section (page 21).

Al Hubbard's Steak House. 6925 3rd Avenue, near 69th Street, 833-4500. Mon.–Thurs., 4:30–11 p.m.; Fri. and Sat., 5 p.m.–midnight; Sun., 3–10 p.m. Major credit cards.

Bay Ridge may boast more steak houses than any other neighborhood in Brooklyn. If meat and potatoes are your thing, try this moderately priced restaurant for its good steaks, pork chops, and roast beef. Aficionados swear that the potato pie is outstanding. Weekend reservations are recommended.

Areo Ristorante Italiano. 8424 3rd Avenue, corner of 85th Street, 238-0079. Tues.–Sun., 11:30 a.m.–11:30 p.m. Major credit cards.

It's easy to see why this is such a popular local spot—modern decor, big windows, usually busy, always noisy, with excellent Italian food at moderate prices. The antipasti are superb, as are specials such as sliced filet mignon marsala, *zuppa di pesce*, and such vegetable dishes as spinach in garlic. Entrées average under $15 and the atmosphere is festive, young, and fun.

Bally Bunion, an Irish house. 9510 3rd Avenue, near 95th Street, 833-2801. Daily, 11:30 a.m.–11 p.m. Major credit cards.

It could be any time of day, but the warm publike glow of Bally Bunion is timeless. This informal restaurant, with green decor, a green menu, and a long, inviting bar, serves up a bit of Irish schmaltz with menu items ranging from shepherd's pie to shrimp teriyaki. Prices for entrées are in the $10 to $15 range.

Canedo's. 7316 3rd Avenue, between 73rd and 74th streets, 748-1908. Mon.–Sat., 5–10:30 p.m.; Sun., 2–10:30 p.m. Major credit cards.

You won't need a guide to find this small, romantic restaurant, but you will need the address; there's no sign out front. Just look for a beautiful wooden facade marking a fourteen-table Italian eatery where the chef and the ambience—soft lighting, framed 1890s-era posters, and mirrors—are top-tier. The *scampi i carciofi salsa bianca con riso* (shrimp and artichoke in white sauce with rice) is out of this world. You can order from the menu or the kitchen will prepare any of your favorites. The service is good: after eating a juicy, garlic-laden artichoke appetizer, you are given a lemon slice and a steaming towel to wipe your hands. Yet for all the fancy trappings, dress ranges from fancy to casual and dinner entrées are under $15. Weekend reservations are recommended.

Embers. 9519 3rd Avenue, near 95th Street, 745-3700. Mon.–Sat., noon–11 p.m.; Sun., 2–9 p.m. Major credit cards. ✳

This is a family restaurant, crowded and noisy, where you can get great fresh steaks and chops in big portions. That's not surprising, though, because it is run by the folks who own the meat market next door. Experts say the

T-bone is T-best. You'll get great food, excellent value, and friendly service. The casual atmosphere is great for kids. Since Embers does not take reservations, there may be a wait during busy times. Dinner entrées run from $7 to $15.

Greenhouse Cafe. 7717 3rd Avenue, near 77th Street, 833-8200. Daily, lunch, 11:30 a.m.–4 p.m., and dinner, 4–11 p.m.; Sun., noon–10 p.m. (brunch noon–3 p.m.) Major credit cards.

This excellent Italian restaurant serves its food in a slightly more elegant setting than some of its neighbors and has a good, inexpensive wine list as well. Prices are moderate. There's also a stomach-filling brunch on Sundays. With so much going for it, you must make reservations to make sure you'll get a table. After your meal, head next door and linger over espresso and the wicked desserts at the **Cappuccino Cafe.**

Hamilton House. 10033 4th Avenue, near 101st Street, 745-6359. Mon.– Sat., 5–11 p.m.; Sun., brunch, noon–2:30 p.m., and dinner, 3–8 p.m. Major credit cards.

Definitely a place for a special event (or to take fussy in-laws), the Hamilton House, at the foot of the Verrazano-Narrows Bridge, has good continental cuisine and a piano bar. In the winter, when the leaves have fallen, there are views of New York Harbor. Dinner entrées, which include fish, broiler, and pasta items, range from $10 to $16. You'll need a reservation for Saturday nights.

India Passage. 7407 3rd Avenue, between 74th and 75th streets, 833-2160. Mon.–Fri., lunch, 11:30 a.m.–3 p.m., and dinner, 5–11 p.m.; weekends, noon–11 p.m. Major credit cards.

Like New York's other boroughs, Brooklyn has its share of mediocre Indian restaurants, but India Passage is different. The decor is classy, the prices are reasonable, and the food is fantastic. Kids will love the tandoori chicken which literally falls off the bone into your mouth. Faruk, the owner, serves up traditional favorites from the clay oven and also has added a few new ones, such as mangoed chicken with crispy broccoli and some southern Indian specialities. Dinner entrées start at about $12.

Lorelei's. 9404 4th Avenue, corner of 94th Street, 238-8899. Daily, 11:30 a.m.–11 p.m. Major credit cards.

The atmosphere in this German restaurant is lovely, with antique furnishings, stained glass, a working fireplace, and a long, friendly bar filled with local residents. German and continental dishes plus steaks and seafood are featured on the menu. The price is right: a three-course dinner of smoked salmon, Wiener schnitzel or sauerbraten, and dessert costs about $20.

Lum Chin. 9110 4th Avenue, between 91st and 92nd streets, 238-1822. Mon.–Sat., 11:30 a.m.–midnight; Sun., 12:30 p.m.–1 a.m. Major credit cards.

This may be the biggest and fanciest Chinese restaurant in Brooklyn. What's it doing in Bay Ridge? It is part of a chain of Lum Chins that started about twenty years ago across the Verrazano-Narrows Bridge in Staten Island. (The most recent one opened in Manhattan's Gramercy Park.) Dinner entrées run about $12 per person.

Martini's Bay Ridge Seafood Restaurant. 8616 4th Avenue, near 86th Street, 748-2070. Daily, 11:30 a.m.–11 p.m. Major credit cards.

Here is where you can see old Bay Ridge. Very good, fresh, basic seafood dinners and a conservative decor of seascape murals attract an older crowd at this longstanding local favorite. Martini's is a lovely place to come for a quiet meal with family or friends. Service is friendly but not always speedy, so plan to come and relax. The early bird dinners on Tuesday through Thursday from 3 to 6 p.m. are a bargain at $9.95; dinner entrées and Sunday brunch both range from $10 to $14. Weekend reservations are recommended.

Mr. Tang. 7523 3rd Avenue, near 76th Street, 748-0400. Weekdays, noon–11 p.m.; weekends until 12:30 a.m. Major credit cards.

This good-size, fancy Chinese restaurant has a broad menu whose Cantonese and Szechuan dishes have received good reviews by restaurant critics. Chicken entrées cost $9 to $11; seafood dishes range from $9 to $15. Tang is actually part of a small chain of several restaurants by the same name in Brooklyn. The others are at 86th Street and 19th Avenue, Nostrand Avenue and Avenue T, Avenue T between 58th and 59th streets, and Coney Island Avenue at Avenue X.

New Corner Restaurant. 7201 8th Avenue, near 72nd Street, 833-0800. Daily, noon–11 p.m. Major credit cards. ✳

You won't find the New Corner just around the corner. This large yet personable Italian restaurant is hidden in a residential section (call for directions). But it's worth searching for, particularly if you've never had out-of-this-world lobster fra diavolo or french-fried broccoli. The portions are beyond huge: one bowl of minestrone is a full meal. Sambuca liqueur is automatically served with coffee. The menu is a la carte and most entrées are $10 to $13. Weekend reservations are recommended.

Nightfalls. 7612 3rd Avenue, near 76th Street, 748-8700. Daily, 11:30 a.m.–11 p.m.; later on Sat. and Sun. Major credit cards.

You'd hardly expect to find an indoor waterfall in Brooklyn, but there's one here in a modern, elegant setting. The ambience at Nightfalls has made it a long-standing favorite, and with a new renovation the restaurant appears to have recovered admirably from a recent fire. There's piano music on Saturday nights. Entrées, such as chicken with spinach and peppers, lemon sole, and broiled tuna, range from about $11 to $19. Reservations are recommended.

The Pasta House. 7215 3rd Avenue, near 72nd Street, 748-2268. Mon.–Thurs., 5–11 p.m.; Fri. and Sat., 5 a.m.–midnight; Sun., 2–10 p.m. Major credit cards. ✳

Kids like pasta, and this is a good place to bring them if you're looking for something a little classier than the local pizzeria. The service is good and the ambience is clean and modern. Entrées are about $9. Pasta dishes start at about $7 and are available in half portions. Weekend reservations are recommended.

Peggy O'Neal. 8121 5th Avenue, between 81st and 82nd streets, 748-1400. Daily, 10 a.m.–4 a.m. Major credit cards.

Stainte! ("Cheers" in Irish). A favorite among New York's finest, this very Irish pub draws police officers from all over the city—some on their way home to Staten Island and New Jersey across the nearby Verrazano-Narrows Bridge. With shepherd's pie, corned beef and cabbage, and great Irish soda bread, it's no surprise that this is also a favorite place among local Irish immigrants and Irish Americans. Tuesday is Nurses' and Policemen's Night—first drink is on the house. Thursday is Oldies Night, and Irish Night is on Wednesday and Sunday. Dinner ranges from $9 to $14.

Pete's. 8727 4th Avenue, corner of 88th Street, 745-1444. Mon.–Sat., 11 a.m.–2:30 p.m. and 4:30–11 p.m.; Sun., 1–9 p.m. Major credit cards. ✳

When your local Italian butcher tells you to try his favorite restaurant, there's bound to be a reason. Either his son owns it or the food is really good. At Pete's it's reason number two. The food is terrific, the prices are extremely reasonable (entrées are under $15), and the service is friendly and quick. Penne with garlic, olive oil, and fresh chopped tomato is spicy, tasty, and filling. The shrimp in garlic, cream, and vodka is also a treat. Ask for the roasted peppers and olives as an appetizer. The front windows open onto the sidewalk, so on a summer evening when a breeze is blowing the restaurant is pleasantly airy.

Sally's Place. 7809 3rd Avenue, near 78th Street, 680-4615. Tues.–Sun., lunch, noon–3 p.m., and dinner, 5:30 p.m.–11 a.m. Major credit cards. ✳

Middle Eastern residents are among the most recent immigrants to Bay

Ridge. Good Middle Eastern food in a white-tablecloth ambience provides an alternative to the American and Italian restaurants that predominate here. Entrées range from $7 to $15, and there is a children's menu. Try the omelette, which is like a mini-soufflé. Weekend reservations are recommended.

Short Ribs Restaurant & Bar. 9101 3rd Avenue, corner of 91st Street, 745-0614. Sun.–Thurs., noon–11 p.m.; Fri.–Sat., noon–1 a.m. Major credit cards. ✳

Barbecued ribs, chicken, seafood dishes, and gumbos are the highlights at this free-standing multistory restaurant with an exterior outlined in white lights. The portions are huge and tasty. The combination dish—half a rack of ribs, barbecued shrimp, and chicken—is easily food enough for two, and that's not counting the salad and fries that come with it. Two people can order one appetizer and one main course and come away more than satisfied. Order with abandon; doggie bags are a common request here. There's also a kids' menu. Because of the crowds, you should make reservations; try for a table on the second level. Sunday brunch is also popular, and you can order for takeout. A full rack of baby back ribs is $9.95; a barbecued chicken is just $6.95.

SideStreet's Cafe. 275 71st Street, just off 3rd Avenue, 833-3759. Daily, 5–11 p.m. Major credit cards. ✳

This popular, intimate café has a New England feel with its exposed brick and wood walls, simple chairs, and friendly staff. The menu favors Italian dishes, such as shrimp *fra diavolo*, pastas, and veal parmesan, but there is a wide variety of American specials as well for about $13. Weekend reservations are recommended.

T. J. Bentley. 7110 3rd Avenue, near 71st Street, 745-0748. Tues. and Thurs., 11:30 a.m.–11 p.m.; Fri.–Sun., 11:30 a.m.–midnight. Major credit cards.

This comfy wood- and brass-decorated restaurant is packed with a twenty-to-forty crowd for dinner and Sunday brunch. There's live music, dancing, and lots of action nightly. No cover charge; you can come for a moderately priced American-Italian meal at about $20 per person and wait until the music starts, or just have a few drinks at the long bar (which used to be in Luchow's on 14th Street in Manhattan). Friday and Sunday from 5 to 9 p.m., there's a big band sound with a fifteen-piece live band; on Saturday, the disc jockey starts spinning discs at 10 p.m. There's also live music during Sunday brunch, from 11 a.m. to 1 p.m. Various lunch specials are featured during the week. Casual attire is acceptable, but on weekends no sneakers, jeans, T-shirts, or sweatshirts are allowed. Weekend reservations are recommended.

Ice Cream Parlors and Quick Meals

Classy Coffee. 7716 3rd Avenue, near 77th Street, 238-9502. Mon.–Thurs., 9 a.m.–8 p.m.; Fri. and Sat., 9 a.m.–11 p.m.; Sun., noon–10 p.m. Major credit cards.

Coffee lovers take note: here is an attractive café and shop specializing in more than seventy-five different kinds of coffee beans, reputed to be chemical-free and water processed. Try one of several dozen flavored coffees with names that sound more like ice cream (but have virtually no calories!), such as chocolate cherry, butter rum spice, and Hawaiian coconut. A few tables are available for customers to enjoy their pastries and candy.

Elysee Cafe. 8002 5th Avenue, corner of 80th Street, 238-0777. Daily, 9 a.m.–midnight. No credit cards.

Cappuccino, espresso, and pastries are served in this appealing new café decorated in modern Italian style with sleek chrome and Lucite tables and chairs. Characteristic of the ethnic mobility of the neighborhood, this French-named restaurant was started by Italians and at the time of this writing is run by a Middle Eastern family.

Hinsch's. 8518 5th Avenue, between 85th and 86th streets, 748-6650. Mon.–Sat., 8 a.m.–7 p.m. No credit cards. ✳

For over eighty-five years there has been an ice-cream parlor at this location, and Hinsch's makes a point of keeping tradition alive. As soon as you walk in the door, the old-fashioned soda fountain and booths will remind you of your childhood—no matter where you grew up. Hinsch's makes their own ice cream and candies and sells a line of candy cigarettes and solid chocolate crayons. This is a good place to come with the kids, as are the Logue family's other eateries in Bay Ridge, **Once Upon a Sundae** and **Logue's Confectionery** (see below).

Lento's. 7003 3rd Avenue, near Ovington Street, 745-9197. Daily, noon–11:30 p.m.

Thin crust lovers, this bar-cum-pizzeria is heaven! Just make sure you eat on the premises, or the thin crust gets hard. Lento's is near shopping and parks.

Logue's Confectionery. 6922 3rd Avenue, corner of 77th Street, 748-6650. Mon–Sat., 8 a.m.–7 p.m. Closed Sun. No credit cards. ✳

The real attraction here at Logue's is homemade chocolate candy and ice cream served in an old-fashioned setting. Locals frequent Logue's for easy meals—burgers, sandwiches—with the kids.

Mother Hubbard's. 7017 3rd Avenue, near 71st Street, 921-0988. Daily, noon–11 p.m. Major credit cards. ✳

Good burgers, espresso, and a kiddie menu make this a good place to stop for lunch. Locals claim these are the best burgers on 3rd Avenue. You can get away with a meal for under $10.

Once Upon a Sundae. 7702 3rd Avenue, between 77th and 78th streets, 748-3412. Mon–Fri., 8 a.m.–10 p.m.; Sat., 8 a.m.–11 p.m.; Sun., 9 a.m.–11 p.m. No credit cards.

In 1980 the Logue family, which has been in the Bay Ridge ice-cream business for more than twenty-seven years, transplanted the turn-of-the-century furnishings of Brooklyn's oldest ice-cream parlor from Fulton Street in Bedford-Stuyvesant to new lodgings in Bay Ridge. The results are, well . . . go see for yourself!

Samira's International Kitchen. 6916 4th Avenue, near 69th Street, 745-2416 or 745-3504. Mon–Sat., 9 a.m.–7 p.m. No credit cards.

Don't be put off by the lonely five tables here; Samira's is really a gourmet Middle Eastern catering shop whose major clients include United Nations dignitaries and several large delis at the World Trade Center. Restaurant guests get whatever is freshly cooked for the day or standard appetizers, called *mazza*, such as excellent kibbe meat or pumpkin pies, *hummus*, and pita. Other items include stuffed cabbage, chicken and broccoli, lentils and rice, and apple crumb pie. Call twenty-four hours ahead if you want something special. They will deliver if you pay cab fare.

SHOPPING

Specialty Food Shops

A&S Greek American Meat Market. 7918 5th Avenue, near 79th Street, 833-1307. Daily, 8 a.m.–9 p.m.

Queens, not Brooklyn, is the center of the Greek immigrant population in New York. However, Bay Ridge has a sizeable Greek population, and alongside the tuna and chicken salads this Greek deli sells traditional large, crusty loaves of bread, several kinds of feta cheese, olives, phyllo dough, squid salad, and such ethnic items as Greek incense.

Fredricksen & Johannesen. 7719 5th Avenue, near 77th Street, 745-5980. Mon.–Sat., 9 a.m.–6 p.m. Major credit cards.

This spacious, clean, and well-stocked store is dedicated exclusively to Scandinavian cuisine. The display case features homemade lean pork sausages, fish pudding, *fenalar* ("the same meat that kept Leif Ericson alive on his explorations"), a range of pâtés, and imported cheeses. There are condiments, crackers, herrings, anchovy paste, dehydrated fruit soups, meatballs, and fish balls. Cooks who don't know a potato *fefsa* from a *spekeskinke* will be aided and abetted by a variety of cookbooks and interesting utensils, such as Danish wafflers, *krumkake* pans, cookie presses, and Swedish pancake pans. It has been said that customers come from a seven-hundred-mile radius, particularly for the meat products. A mail-order catalog is also available.

Leske's Bakery. 7612 5th Avenue, near 76th Street, 680-2323. Mon.–Fri., 6 a.m.–6:30 p.m.; Sat., 6 a.m.–5:30 p.m.; Sun., 6 a.m.–2:30 p.m.

Part of Bay Ridge's Scandinavian scene, Leske's sells a mouthwatering array of authentic Danish pastries, breads, cakes, and cookies, also known as *kringlers, yulekarger, vortkarger, limpa* bread, and *kransekagge*.

Martini's Bay Ridge Seafood Center. 8618 4th Avenue, near 86th Street, 748-2070. Daily, 11:30 a.m.–10 p.m. Major credit cards.

This large and well-established seafood store delivers fresh fish and fresh oven-ready dinners such as shrimp creole or lemon sole with side orders of pasta. Local delivery only. Take-out available until 8 p.m. Call for daily menu.

Nordic Delicacies. 6909 3rd Avenue, near 69th Street, 748-1874. Mon.–Sat., 9 a.m.–6 p.m. Checks accepted.

If it's a Nordic feast you want, then this is the place—and they deliver hot dinners. Monday's special is meatballs, Tuesday it's fish pudding with white shrimp sauce, Wednesday it is *komper* (potato dumplings; one is enough for dinner), Thursday it is beef stew, Friday it is baked codfish, and Saturday *komper* again, with rice pudding. In addition there are potato cakes, a Norwegian version of pita bread that you can turn into a dessert or top with tuna; open-face sandwiches of roast beef, smoked salmon, and other cold cuts; homemade waffles; *krumkake*; and apple cakes. You'll also find lots of packaged goods, such as fish cakes, fish balls, assorted flatbreads, and a full line of imported chocolates. Delivery is available until late afternoon; call in advance. This is one of the few Norwegian-run local shops. Co-owner Arlene comes from Norwegian stock, although, typical of the area, her married name is Italian. Call for a menu.

Pierrot. 7515 3rd Avenue, near 75th Street, 748-5840. Tues.–Thurs., 8:30 a.m.–7 p.m.; Fri. and Sat., 8:30 a.m.–8 p.m.; Sun., 8 a.m.–6 p.m.

It won't take long to figure out why this tiny shop does a regular business with fancy-food emporiums like Balducci's in Manhattan: the pastries are tasty and beautiful. The most intriguing are pie crusts shaped like covered earthen bowls and bird's nests filled with balls of homemade sorbets.

Quattlender's Pastry Shop. 9300 3rd Avenue, corner of 93rd Street, 748-6535. Mon. and Tues., 10 a.m.–7 p.m.; Wed.–Sat., 7 a.m.–5 p.m.

The appealing facade of this fifty-year-old pastry shop just begins to tell the story of what's inside: good, old-fashioned pastries filled with goodies such as fruits or nuts and chocolate. Quattlender's is famous for its muffins, carrot cake, and black bottom cupcakes, which are filled with cream cheese and chocolate chip bits. Locals swear that this is one of the places that make Bay Ridge home.

Interesting Neighborhood Shops

All By Hand Studio. 7810 3rd Avenue, near 78th Street, 745-8904. Mon.–Sat., 10 a.m.–5 p.m. Closed Sun. Major credit cards.

Given its strong family orientation, Bay Ridge has a fair share of shops dedicated to crafts and hobbies. Among the many items displayed here are a big selection of jewelry in the $25 range, wooden pieces from bread boards to recliners, and reproductions of Victorian parlor clocks. The stained glass in the Tiffany-style lamps is made on the premises.

All Irish Import Store. 8515 3rd Avenue, near 85th Street, 748-9240. Mon.–Fri., 10 a.m.–6 p.m.; Sat., 10 a.m.–6 p.m.; Sun., 1 a.m.–5 p.m. No credit cards.

This little shop proudly sells things for which an Irish expatriate might yearn, from Aran sweaters to Irish bacon and soda bread. It is also a source for tickets to concerts by such Irish folk singers as Pat Noonan.

Bianco's. 409 Bay Ridge Avenue (69th Street), between 4th and 5th avenues, 748-3020. Mon., Tues. and Thurs.–Sat., 10:30 a.m.–6 p.m. Closed Wed. and Sun. No credit cards.

A treasure hunter's heaven—but not inexpensive—Bianco's three-generation family business specializes in appraisal and resale of estate jewelry. The display cases feature sterling silver picture frames and gold jewelry, but the interesting stuff is in individual envelopes in the boxes kept behind the counter. On any given day there may be antique watches, star sapphire earrings, Art Deco watch fobs, jade bracelets, and diamond rings. Prices start at $100. There is no pressure to buy, and the stock changes weekly. On Saturday dealers return unsold items, so go early on Monday to see the latest selection.

Choc-Oh-Lot-Plus. 7911 5th Avenue, near 79th Street, 748-2100. Mon.–Wed. and Fri., 10 a.m.–6 p.m.; Thurs., 10 a.m.–8 p.m.; Sat., 10 a.m.–5 p.m.; Sun., noon–4 p.m.

Bay Ridge is a neighborhood that appreciates good old-fashioned family fun. This mom-and-pop specialty store sells more than five hundred plastic candy molds and several dozen Wilton cake molds in the form of Superman, Batman, Sesame Street characters, and other popular figures. There are bins of inexpensive cake toppings and over 250 varieties of Mylar balloons.

Harry's P & G Furniture. 241 Bay Ridge Avenue, between 2nd and 3rd avenues, 745-0730. Daily, 8 a.m.–5:30 p.m.; Mon. and Thurs., 8 a.m.–8:30 p.m. No credit cards.

Every ten days new merchandise arrives at this large warehouse which handles overstocks and sometimes slightly damaged furniture. Most of the merchandise comes from large department stores or straight from the North Carolina manufacturers. Sofas, chairs, tables, and bedroom sets are 30 percent to 50 percent less than at retail outlets. Selected armchairs are available in more than fifty different fabrics. And the staff is friendly, too.

High Knees. 8406 3rd Avenue, near 84th Street, 680-9279. Tues.–Sat., 11 a.m.–5 p.m. Major credit cards. ✳

For little girls who are sugar and spice and everything nice, here is a lovely selection of imported and designer clothes and shoes for dressy occasions. Sizes range from newborn to age ten. The selection for boys to size 6x is smaller. Outfits start at $25.

The Hutch. 8211 5th Avenue, near 82nd Street, 748-4574. Mon.–Sat., 10 a.m.–6 p.m. Major credit cards.

Catering to customers throughout the tri-state area, the Hutch has carried a large selection of fine gift items, including crystal, silverware, place settings, imported ceramic bowls, glassware, and silver picture frames, for more than two decades. The store carries brands such as Ginori, Baccarrat and Christofle, and Waterford.

I. Kleinfeld and Son. 8206 5th Avenue, between 82nd and 83rd streets, 833-1100. Tues. and Thurs., 11 a.m.–9 p.m.; Wed. and Fri., 11 a.m.–6 p.m.; Sat., 10 a.m.–6 p.m. Major credit cards.

One of New York's most famous specialty stores, Kleinfeld's is a magnet for thousands of brides each year. They come from all over the U.S., Europe, and China for the enormous selection of gowns, accessories, and evening and dress wear for the bridal party that includes major names, such as Caroline Herrerra, Priscilla of Boston, and Pat Kerr. The main store has evening dresses, clothes for the mother of the bride or groom, formal wear, and over a thousand wedding gown samples. The average gown costs between $1,500 and $2,500. An appointment is required. Allow six months for the gown to be measured, fitted, and sewn. A second store on 3rd Avenue at 82nd Street specializes in gowns for bridesmaids.

Jenny Lynne. 7015 3rd Avenue, near 70th Street, 745-8748. Mon.–Sat., 10:30 a.m.–6:30 p.m.; open late Wed.–Fri. Major credit cards.

From aerobics outfits to office and evening wear, these stores offer a selection of moderately priced women's wear. Check out the shoes down the street at 7011 3rd Avenue and the specialty shop for sizes 14 and above at 7021. Brands include Calvin Klein, Multiples, Guess, and other favorites.

Lilliput. 8024 3rd Avenue, near 81st Street, 833-3399. Mon.–Fri., 10:30 a.m.–6 p.m.; Sat., 10 a.m.–6 p.m. Closed Sun. Major credit cards. ✳

This upscale toy store has some beautifully displayed, unusual imported items for preschool and elementary schoolchildren. Educational toys are the specialty here; there are no war toys or games based on TV shows. Helpful sales staff will direct you to fold-up doll carriages, expensive wooden wheelbarrows or less expensive plastic ones, wind-powered cars, and an impressive collection of dolls. Inexpensive items include books and musical tapes. Watch for sales in February and August.

Mangos. 7115 3rd Avenue, near 71st Street, 680-6329. Mon.–Sat., 10 a.m.–10 p.m.; Sun., 11 a.m.–7 p.m. Major credit cards.

Fun, colorful, sexy clothes at affordable prices are the ticket at this shop, founded by two renegade Wall Streeters. For young-at-heart women who like the look created by Betsy Johnson, Gordon Henderson, and Urban Outfitters, this is the place.

Hobby and Sports Shops

Brooklyn Gallery of Coins and Stamps. 8725 4th Avenue, near 87th Street, 745-5701. Mon.–Fri., 9 a.m.–5:30 p.m.; Sat., 9 a.m.–4 p.m. No credit cards. ✳

This small, twenty-year-old shop is a wonderful resource for beginners to experienced collectors of stamps, coins, antique toys, world's fair items, trains, military items, and baseball cards. They have some seven hundred reference books for every level and interest. You would not believe the traffic here, even on a rainy Saturday afternoon—people come from all over the tristate area to buy and sell.

Craft Cottage. 8818 3rd Avenue, near 88th Street, 745-7578. Mon.–Sat., 10 a.m.–6 p.m.; Wed. and Fri., 10 a.m.–9 p.m. No credit cards. ✳

As wholesome as apple pie, the craft supplies you'll find here will remind you of your youth—lanyard cord, ribbon, paints, basket material, blank banners, and many wooden items, such as trains and figurines, for painting. Classes and kiddie birthday parties are held here.

Fifth Avenue Bait and Tackle. 6718 5th Avenue, between 67th and 68th streets, 748-1911. Daily, 10 a.m.–6 p.m. No credit cards. ✳

This store is a true hole-in-the-wall, but if you're looking for basic fishing equipment, they've got it—from a kid's $15 starter fishing rod to a $300 rod for experts. Live bait is usually available and artificial worms (great gifts for little boys) go six for a buck.

Panda Sport. 311 77th Street, near 3rd Avenue, 238-4919. Mon.–Sat., 11 a.m.–6 p.m.; winter hours are 11 a.m.–8 p.m. Major credit cards. ✳

Forget bats and balls and other standard sports paraphernalia—Panda's got that stuff, but the real fun here is, well, *fun*. For instance, in the summertime they've got huge wildly colored rafts, wet suits, kid-size life vests, goggles, and surfboards. In winter you'll find a full line of ski equipment (including rentals). They also arrange ski trips.

Royale Sporting Goods. 8102 3rd Avenue, corner of 81st Street, 836-5601. Mon., Wed., and Fri., 10 a.m.–7 p.m.; Tues. and Sat., 10 a.m.–9 p.m.; Sun., 10 a.m.–5 p.m. Major credit cards. ✳

In true suburban style, this sprawling sporting goods store has great inventory on full display for browsers or shoppers: more than 180 baseball mitts, dozens of football helmets, home exercise equipment, footwear, and clothing.

Sports World. 8023 5th Avenue, near 80th Street, 680-4887. Mon.–Sat., 11 a.m.–7:30 p.m. Major credit cards. ✳

Has Brooklyn ever recovered from the departure of the Dodgers? Collectors of baseball memorabilia will love the huge selection of baseball cards, signed baseballs, bats, banners, and more crammed into this friendly, cozy, well-organized shop. Call to put your name on the mailing list for the thrice-yearly catalog.

Walt's Hobby Shop. 7909 5th Avenue, at 79th Street, 745-4991. Daily, 10 a.m–6 p.m.; Thurs. and Fri., 10 a.m.–8 p.m. Closes early on Sun. Major credit cards. ✳

Veterans come here to buy model World War I and World War II planes and boats, while the younger set goes for do-it-yourself plastic racing cars and the large selection of Dungeons and Dragons books and materials. Prices range from $10 for models of space shuttles and Model Ts to $150 for engine-powered airplanes and racing cars. The store, which has been in Bay Ridge for twenty-five years, sponsors summertime competitions for racing car enthusiasts and has a repair service as well. It recently introduced a special section with dollhouse furniture, weaving and loom kits, and other traditional "girls' toys."

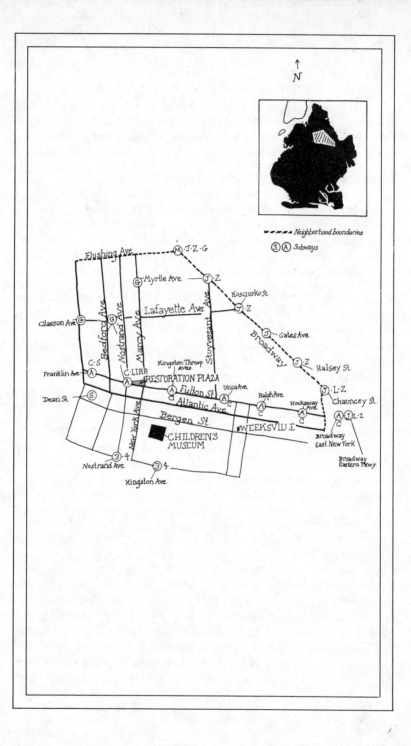

BEDFORD-STUYVESANT

Where it is: Bounded by Myrtle Avenue on the north, Eastern Parkway to the south (although some call Atlantic Avenue the southern boundary), Classon Avenue on the west, and Broadway on the east.

What's nearby: Crown Heights, downtown Brooklyn, Fort Greene, Park Slope.

How to get there:

By car: Take Fulton Street from Flatbush Avenue through Fort Greene to Restoration Plaza. Turn left on Marcy, Throop, or Lewis streets to get to the brownstone district.

By subway: A train to Nostrand Avenue for Restoration Plaza, or to the Utica Avenue–Fulton Street stop for the Stuyvesant Heights brownstone area.

Cab services: White Top (774-6660) or Black Pearl (493-4959). Cost is about $13 from Brooklyn Heights, $20 from Grand Central Station.

Special events: Fulton Art Fair, three consecutive weekends at Fulton Park (June and July). African Street Festival at the new Boys and Girls High School, featuring one week of children's and evening entertainment and hundreds of vendors (July). Weeksville Family Festival (August). Fall house tour, organized by Brownstones of Bedford-Stuyvesant (October).

How it got its name: Bedford and Stuyvesant were two separate communities until the middle of this century. While they still retain some of their original differences, the combined name has been in use since the 1930s. Some experts say it gained prominence in 1931 when the *Brooklyn Eagle* reported on racial conflict between blacks in Bedford and whites in Stuyvesant; others suggest that it was coined by the Brooklyn Con Edison Company.

ABOUT THE NEIGHBORHOOD

Go take a look: you may be surprised at how lovely much of Bedford-Stuyvesant is. Indeed, the existence in Bedford-Stuyvesant of a sturdy middle class is one of Brooklyn's best-kept secrets. The well-maintained twelve-block landmarked district of Stuyvesant Heights is typical of any other tree-lined brownstone neighborhood of Brooklyn, with the important distinction that the caring, proud owners of these homes are African-American. The architectural variety of this area, with the largest stock of Gothic, Victorian, French, and other classic brownstones in New York City, is stunning. Equally impressive is the commitment of Bedford-Stuyvesant's middle class to improving the quality of life in the nation's second largest African-American community, which is second in size only to the South Side of Chicago. Homeowners here include lawyers, judges, businesspeople, teachers, and civil servants. One visit will show you that the stereotype of Bedford-Stuyvesant as a model of inner-city decay simply does not hold true in Stuyvesant Heights along such dignified streets as Chauncey, Macon, Decatur, Bainbridge, MacDonough, Hancock, Jefferson, and Stuyvesant.

Historic Bedford–Stuyvesant's brownstones and churches are an architectural feast. For a look at the history of African-Americans in Brooklyn, visit the reconstructed nineteenth-century houses and museum at **Weeksville**, a free black community well before emancipation. Contemporary cultural highlights include the **Billie Holiday Theater**, which produces shows written and performed by African-American playwrights, and the magnificent gospel choirs at Sunday church services. The week-long **African Street Festival** in July is famous for the three hundred vendors it attracts from all over the world and the continuous entertainment by Africans and African-Americans that lasts for the entire week.

Both Bedford and Stuyvesant Heights have been undergoing a quiet renaissance for well over a decade. Many young black professionals have bought and renovated brownstones. Some grew up in Brooklyn; others hail from Manhattan, New Jersey, and the southern United States. Certainly one big attraction stimulating the rejuvenation of Stuyvesant Heights and nearby streets is the housing stock—brownstones of the same vintage as those in Fort Greene and Park Slope are a fraction of the price. Family also exerts a pull; many people live near their close relatives on the same block.

It would be hard to overestimate the importance of the many churches in Bedford-Stuyvesant. They provide a historical memory and continuity for the community, create social service programs to fill the vacuums left by inadequate government programs, and help knit together the area's social fabric. Among several outstanding institutions, the **Bridge Street African Wesleyan Methodist Episcopal Church** is the oldest African-American church in Brooklyn, dating from 1818. The pre–Civil War era **Siloam Presbyterian Church** was one of several stops in Brooklyn for slaves fleeing north via the Underground Railroad. The activist **Concord Baptist Church** has the largest black congregation in the United States, estimated at about twelve thousand.

First-time visitors may wish to get oriented by car or even take a guided tour, as the neighborhood's most interesting spots are far apart. (See tour listings in the appendix, page 255.) A pleasant time to visit is midday Sunday, when well-dressed families, with many women sporting fabulous hats, are on their way to or from church. A trip to Bedford-Stuyvesant is not primarily for shopping (although there is a hub of West Indian shops at the intersection of Nostrand Avenue and Fulton Street, plus a smattering of national chains, banks, and small businesses around Restoration Plaza). Rather, a foray into Bedford-Stuyvesant gives visitors an appreciation for the historic and contemporary accomplishments of as well as the challenges faced by New York's African-Americans.

Historical Notes

The two communities that comprise Bedford and Stuyvesant Heights today have very different histories. Bedford was originally a Dutch hamlet established in 1663. Even before the 1827 abolition of slavery in New York State, a free black community thrived in the area. Bedford was also home to the Brooklyn Howard Colored Orphan Asylum (1866) and the Zion Home for the Colored Aged (1869).

To the east of Bedford, Stuyvesant was a fancier community built during the 1890s by the staunch upper middle class. F. W. Woolworth, the dime store titan, lived here at 209 Jefferson Avenue. The architecture is lavish, and many remaining structures recall Stuyvesant's high-rolling past: the **Masonic Lodge**, the fabulously decorative **Boys High School**, the **Renaissance** and **Alhambra** apartments, and **Fulton Park**, designed to be reminiscent of London's Bloomsbury Square.

Through the 1930s Bedford, along with Harlem, was a major destination for rural southern blacks and West Indians. Many bought homes in the area.

When the Brooklyn Navy Yard expanded during the 1940s, a huge influx of workers created intense housing pressure in both Bedford and Stuyvesant Heights. Many of the area's new residents were African-American or Caribbean islanders, and the now-familiar syndrome of fright and flight occurred. Racist scare tactics used by unscrupulous realtors in a blockbusting campaign led to the diminishing white population. In the wave of inner-city riots that occurred across the nation in the 1960s, Bedford-Stuyvesant "blew up" in riots twice, following the killing of a young boy by a policeman and following the assassination of Reverend Martin Luther King, Jr. After a tour of the area, Robert Kennedy helped establish the Bedford-Stuyvesant Restoration Corporation, the nation's first community development corporation. Some New Yorkers who have never been to Bedford-Stuyvesant still may view it as a fearsome place, but its residents tell a different story twenty-five years after those riots—of a community determinedly on the mend, of neighbors working together toward common goals.

Kidstuff

The Brooklyn Children's Museum in nearby Crown Heights is one of the best places in all of New York City for preschool and grade school–age children. (See page 241 for a full description.) The **Magnolia Tree Earth Center** and **Weeksville** are naturals for an educational family visit. There are also several parks and playgrounds in the neighborhood. The **African Street Festival** in July is a huge attraction, with contests, performances, crafts, and other special entertainment for children. If your kids appreciate architecture, history, and soul food, there is plenty here for them to enjoy.

ENTERTAINMENT

Flamingo Lounge. 259A Kingston Avenue, between Saint John's and Lincoln Place, 493-7200. Thurs.–Sat., 10 p.m.–4 a.m.

One of Brooklyn's best but least-known jazz bars, the ten-year-old Flamingo has attracted such artists as Eddie Stout, vocalist Irene Reid, Percy France, and trumpeter Walter Kelly. Many of these performers also play gigs at Manhattan hot spots. Some have jazz pedigrees, like veteran saxophonist Cecil Payne, who played with Dizzie Gillespie back in the 1940s. Given the hours and the club's location in a rundown residential section off Eastern Parkway, your best bet is to take a local cab service both to and from the club.

PARKS AND PLAYGROUNDS

Fulton Park. Fulton Street, between Stuyvesant and Lewis avenues. ✴
Many cultural events are held in this renovated neighborhood park, including jazz concerts and the **Fulton Art Fair** during the summer. There is a play space for children here, too. While the kids are playing, take a long look at the lovely nineteenth-century houses along Chauncey Street. In the middle of this quiet park note the old statue of Robert Fulton holding a replica of his steamboat *Nassau*, the first to ferry between Brooklyn and Manhattan's Nassau Street.

POINTS OF CULTURAL INTEREST

Bedford-Stuyvesant Restoration Corporation at Restoration Plaza. 1368 Fulton Street, at New York Avenue, 636-6900 or 636-6906.
The enclosed mall and office complex called **Restoration Plaza**, which is located in the renovated Sheffield Farms milk bottling plant, is an important piece of recent Bedford-Stuyvesant history. The nation's first community development corporation, the Bedford-Stuyvesant Restoration Corporation was founded in 1967 with the bipartisan support of senators Robert F. Kennedy and Jacob K. Javits. Constructed with private and public capital and community resources, it has been a visible force in improving the neighborhood's business and residential communities. Among its achievements: restoration of the exteriors of forty-two hundred homes, underwriting of home mortgages, creation of jobs and assisting local entrepreneurship, improved health services, and a range of cultural and recreational programs. Restoration Plaza is the unofficial "downtown" of the neighborhood, with its concentration of utilities, banks, shops, and post office. The **Billie Holiday Theater** and the **Marie Brooks Caribbean Dance Theater** are located within the complex, as is the **Skylight Art Gallery** on the third floor and a commercial recording studio in the basement.

Billie Holiday Theater. 1368 Fulton Street at New York Avenue, 636-0918. Performances are on Wed.–Sat., 8 p.m.; weekend matinees. Call for a schedule and to be put on the mailing list.
Described as a "theater with a soul and a mission," the Billie Holiday Theater is home to one of New York's professional resident black theater companies. For nearly twenty years the "Billie" has been the artistic arm of the Bedford-Stuyvesant Restoration Corporation. There are three major productions a year,

totalling about two hundred performances that usually play to capacity crowds. The shows, which are written by African-American playwrights and showcase Equity actors, get consistently good reviews from critics in the major New York dailies. The programs run the spectrum of comedies, dramas, and musicals. The theater is located in Restoration Plaza a block and a half down Fulton Street from the Nostrand Avenue stop on the A train.

Boys and Girls High School. 1700 Fulton Street, near Utica Avenue, 467-1700. The interior may be viewed by appointment.

Across from Fulton Park and near Atlantic Avenue, this 1974 building has a special significance to Bedford-Stuyvesant. It is the largest school in the neighborhood and the site of many important community events, including the annual African Street Festival in July. In 1990 this was Nelson Mandela's first stop during his three-day visit to New York in 1990. The exterior artwork includes a powerful mural done by Ernest Crichlow depicting the struggles of African-Americans from slavery to present times. Inside, works by such African-American artists as Norman Lewis line the corridors. The original Boys High School was in a fabulous building that still stands on Marcy and Putnam. The original Girls High, now a New York City Board of Education building, was located at nearby 475 Nostrand Avenue.

Brooklyn Public Library, 496 Franklin Avenue, off Fulton Street near Hancock Street, 638-9544. Call to check hours.

Close to Fulton Street, this library is a good spot for a respite and a read. For Brooklynites: any book you borrow here can be returned to your local library.

Brownstoners of Bedford-Stuyvesant house tour, 452-3226.

On the third weekend in October the volunteers of Brownstoners of Bedford-Stuyvesant conduct a house tour of the interiors and gardens of several restored nineteenth-century brownstones in the area. These homes represent some of the most handsome in all of New York City. The activist Brownstoners group, which includes a judge, an airline executive, a lawyer, and other professionals committed to the neighborhood, also organizes a "discover your neighborhood" fair to promote Bedford-Stuyvesant as a viable place to live. Their motto: "Come home to Bedford-Stuyvesant."

Magnolia Tree Earth Center Grandiflora. 679 Lafayette Avenue, opposite Herbert Von King Park, 387-2116. Mon.–Thurs. and Sat., 10 a.m.–5 p.m. Closed Fri. and Sun. ✳

This environmental education center, established in 1972, is famous for its lovely magnolia tree transplanted from North Carolina and now an official NYC landmark. With environmentalism on the rebound, the Earth Center continues to provide good programs on recycling and conservation to more than two thousand school children a year. The staff also can provide assistance to community groups on greening projects and care of street trees. The center is located on a well-kept block of brownstones facing a large park, Herbert Von King Park (previously known as Tompkins Park). While Magnolia is intensely committed to improving the quality of life in African-American communities, people come from all over to enjoy the various exhibits at the George Washington Carver Gallery. Call for an appointment first.

Medgar Evers College. 1650 Bedford Avenue, near Montgomery Street (Crown Heights), 270-4991.

The only black-oriented college in the City University of New York system is located on a new campus in nearby Crown Heights. Call for information on services and activities of the Center for Women's Development, the Caribbean Research Center, and the Center for Law and Justice.

Simmons African Arts Museum. 1063 Fulton Street, between Classon and Grand avenues, 230-0933. Weekends, noon–6 p.m. Call to check hours. ✳

An unusual collection of contemporary African art and masks from twelve West African nations forms the nucleus of this neighborhood art gallery. The pieces are part of the private, nonfunded collection of the owner, who has traveled and collected in Africa for more than twenty years. He presents educational exhibits designed primarily for community residents, but all visitors are welcome.

Weeksville (Hunterfly Road) houses. 1698–1708 Bergen Street, between Rochester and Buffalo roads, 756-5250. Call for hours. ✳

Use your imagination when you make the pilgrimage here. These lonesome frame homes are remnants of nineteenth-century Weeksville, one of Brooklyn's most prominent free black areas. The houses date from the period immediately before and after the American Civil War. To learn about Weeksville is to learn about the proud and difficult odyssey that American blacks made from slavery to freedom. The figures associated with Weeksville include Moses R. Cobb, a black policeman born into slavery in North Carolina who is said to have walked from North Carolina to New York City after emancipation; Major Martin Delaney, grandson of an enslaved West African prince, who became active in the Underground Railroad and wrote for the Weeksville newspaper, *Freedman's Torchlight*; and Dr. Susan Smith McKinney-Steward, the third black female physician in the nation, born in Weeksville in 1847.

The Weeksville houses were discovered in 1968 when historian James Hurley set out on an aerial exploration over an area that nineteenth-century documents indicated had been a thriving black community. He and pilot Joseph Haynes noted an oddly situated lane that did not coincide with the modern block layout. What they found were four frame houses, circa 1840 to 1883, located on the old Hunterfly Road. Since that exciting moment, the houses have been restored and declared landmarks, a small museum has been installed, and the Society for the Preservation of Weeksville and Bedford-Stuyvesant History has produced award-winning films, traveling exhibits, and educational materials dedicated to the rediscovery of black cultural roots in Brooklyn. Their excellent booklet on Weeksville is a must read for people interested in historic Brooklyn.

Churches

Churches are an important part of everyday life and a community focal point in Bedford-Stuyvesant. And there are a lot of them. The **Bridge Street African Wesleyan Methodist Episcopal Church** at 273 Stuyvesant Avenue is Brooklyn's oldest African-American church, founded in 1818. A hundred years later, the first black church to move into Bedford-Stuyvesant during the great northward migration of rural blacks was **Bethany Baptist Church** at 460 Sumner Avenue. Among many other churches of architectural significance are **Saint Mary's Church** at 230 Classon Avenue, built in 1858, and **Saint George's Episcopal Church** at 800 Marcy Avenue, built by architect Richard Upjohn in 1887; both have original Tiffany windows.

Concord Baptist Church of Christ. 833 Marcy Avenue, at Madison Avenue, 622-1818.

Concord Baptist Church boasts the nation's largest African-American congregation, numbering about twelve thousand and including many of Bedford-Stuyvesant's most prominent residents. A leader in community affairs, the church organizes scholarships, nursing home care, and other services. Founded in 1848, this is one of a handful of extant churches built by the early black residents of Brooklyn.

Our Lady of Victory Roman Catholic Church. 583 Throop Avenue, between Macon and MacDonough streets, 574-5772.

The bright red fences and window trim, well-tended shrubbery, and black stones give this stunning Gothic Revival 1895 church a striking appearance. Almost a half block in size, it is within walking distance of attractive brownstone blocks.

Washington Temple Church of God in Christ. 1372 Bedford Avenue, between Bergen and Dean streets, 789-7545. Sun. services are from 11:30 a.m. to 1:30 p.m.; music, 11:30 a.m.–12:30 p.m.

Music lovers, take note! To hear a traditional gospel choir accompanied by keyboards and percussion instruments, come to Sunday services here. The music director is Timothy Wright, known both for his live concerts and for almost a dozen recordings of his gospel choir. Washington Temple has not one, but seven different choirs. Other churches with gospel choirs are the Institutional Church of God in Christ in Fort Greene and the Brooklyn Tabernacle in Park Slope (see pages 179 and 214).

NOTABLE RESTAURANTS

Auggie's Brownstone Inn. 1550 Fulton Street, between Albany and Kingston avenues, 773-8940. Mon.–Sun., 4 p.m.–11 p.m. No credit cards.

This is the oldest black-owned bar in the neighborhood. Though its location is on a run-down block, there's a garden area for eating, TV, and a notable oldies-but-goodies selection on the jukebox. Thursday night is fish and crab night. Dinners cost less than $10.

B's West Indian American Restaurant. 1188 Fulton Street, corner of Nostrand Avenue, 638-6687. Daily, 8 a.m.–1 a.m. No credit cards.

It looks like a fast-food chain, but this Trinidadian spot just a few blocks from Restoration Plaza serves goat *roti*, goat curry, cow's foot soup, and a full range of West Indian specialties. There's another B's at 875 Utica Avenue, at the corner of Church Avenue.

Gill's West Indian. 627 Classon Avenue, between Atlantic Avenue and Pacific Street, 783-4524. Mon.–Sat., 11 a.m.–11 p.m. Closed Sunday. No credit cards.

This little restaurant is in the middle of nowhere, in an area bereft of any other commercial activity, but just an eight-minute car ride from the Manhattan Bridge. The food and decor are authentic West Indian. The spirit of the place is captured by its lengthy slogan, "Come discover at reasonable prices truly tempting and tantalizing varieties of West Indian cuisine and exotic drinks without the cost of a trip to the Caribbean." The food is inexpensive, and you can order to take out or stay.

Harvest Manor Restaurant. 1040 St. Johns Place, between Kingston and Brooklyn avenues, 756-0200. Mon.–Thurs., 11:30 a.m.–9 p.m.; Fri.–Sat., 11:30 a.m.–10 p.m.; Sun., 1–9 p.m. No credit cards.

This huge restaurant offers fish cakes, fried chicken, veggies and grits, and a legendary peach cobbler. At high noon there's a blue-collar crowd; dinner draws more professional types. Lots of tour groups stop here. There is parking on the premises and you can take out or eat in. Lunches cost about $5, dinners about $12.

McDonald's Dining Room, 327 Stuyvesant Avenue, at Macon Street, 574-3728. Daily, 8 a.m.–10 p.m. No credit cards. ✱

A stop here is mandatory if you truly want to "see" Bedford-Stuyvesant. McDonald's Dining Room, established in 1948 and now a landmark, looks like many an old eatery in the Deep South: a simple, decent place with a counter, some booths, and a back room with plastic-covered tables. However, McDonald's holds a special spot in the heart of local residents. A well-dressed Sunday crowd comes here for a dose of nostalgia and to enjoy salmon cakes, chicken livers, and grits for breakfast, or fried whiting and breaded pork chops for dinner. For people who grew up in the neighborhood, this seventy-five-seat restaurant seems to provide a hotline back to childhood memories. Owner Clara Walker sponsors a scholarship fund and hosts many special events, honoring people who have worked to improve race relations or local economic development. The food is also delicious and inexpensive, with most meals under $10. Needless to say, this is *not* part of the fast-food chain.

North Carolina Country Kitchen. 1991 Atlantic Avenue, corner of Saratoga Avenue, 498-8033. Daily, 7 a.m.–10 p.m. (the store closes at 8 p.m.). No credit cards.

From Flatbush Avenue go three miles east on Atlantic Avenue (it's a big six-lane highway) to a most unlikely country-style building. This handsome new pine-fronted restaurant was built on a gas station site by the woman who also owns the food store across the street. The kitchen serves up grits, biscuits, bacon, and eggs cafeteria style for breakfast. The big lunch and dinner menu includes chicken, chitterlings, black-eyed peas, cornbread, and great sweet potato pie and cobblers. There are a few outdoor tables. The twenty-year-old food store sells hard-to-find items that spell home to the traditional southern palate, including hams and sausages, fresh greens, and canned goods, such as King Syrup, old-fashioned molasses, grits, chow-chow condiment, pickled okra, hominy, boiled peanuts, chewing tobacco, and more.

Three blocks further down Atlantic Avenue is the Tower Isles Jamaican beef patty plant, which has a small retail outlet on Hopkinson Avenue. There you can buy a patty to eat on the spot or get a case of frozen patties for under $30.

Pleasant Grove Kitchen. 1927 Fulton Street, near Howard Avenue, 773-8049. Mon.–Sat., 7:30 a.m.–7 p.m. No credit cards.

Run by the Pleasant Grove Baptist Church, this small restaurant six blocks from Restoration Plaza serves up classic southern fare: sweet potato pies, peach cobbler, salisbury steak, oxtails, pork chops, and three kinds of chicken: fried, smothered, and baked. Inexpensive and good, but located in an economically depressed section of Fulton Street.

SHOPPING

Kinapps Primitive Country Store. 1213 Fulton Street, near Bedford Avenue, 636-5520. Tues.–Sat., noon–7:30 p.m.; Sun., noon–5 p.m. Closed Mon. Major credit cards.

Kinapps has made a mark in natural hairstyling for African-Americans. Kinapps is a combination hair salon and clothing store that sells active-wear clothing, one-of-a-kind jewelry, painted T-shirts, and colorful hats, some patterned with African motifs. Check out the fliers and announcements left in piles here by local non-profit groups for listings of cultural events and performances.

St. John's Bakery. 1501 Fulton Street at Kingston Avenue, 778-9341. Mon.–Sat., 8 a.m.–8 p.m. Closed Sun. No credit cards.

Just a few blocks from Restoration Plaza, St. John's sells a range of Caribbean and Jamaican specialties, including fresh spicy vegetable and meat *roti*, Jamaican beef patties, and *hardo* bread. Exotic and wonderful drinks, such as *sorrel*, *mauby*, and ginger beer, can also be found here.

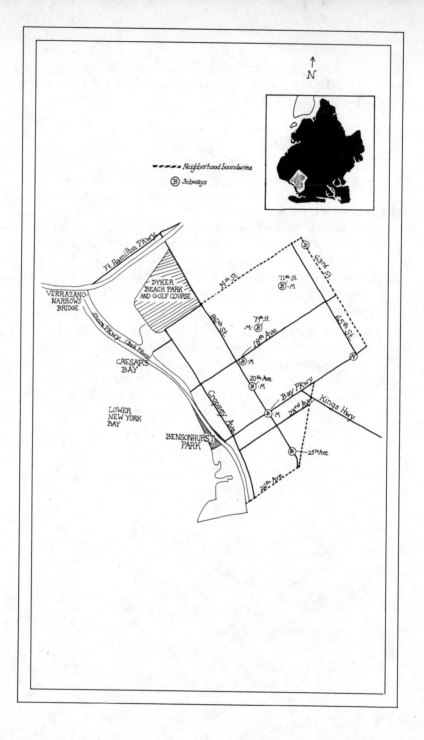

N

Neighborhood Boundaries
Ⓑ Subways

Ft. Hamilton Pkwy.

DYKER
BEACH PARK
AND GOLF COURSE

VERRAZANO-
NARROWS
BRIDGE

Shore Pkwy. (Belt Pkwy)

CAESAR'S
BAY

LOWER
NEW YORK
BAY

BENSONHURST
PARK

14th St.

86th St.

Cropsey Ave.

71st St.
Ⓑ · M

77th St.
M · Ⓑ
18th Ave.

Ⓑ · M

20th Ave.
Ⓑ · M

Ⓑ · M 23rd Ave.

Ⓑ 25th Ave.

26th Ave.

Bay Pkwy.

Kings Hwy.

63rd St.

65th St.

Ⓑ

Ⓑ

Ⓝ

BENSONHURST

Where it is: Bounded by 14th Avenue to the northwest, 61st Street and MacDonald Avenue to the northeast, Avenue U and 26th Street to the southeast, and Gravesend Bay to the southwest.

What's nearby: Bay Ridge, Borough Park, Brighton Beach, Coney Island, Sheepshead Bay, Staten Island.

How to get there:
By car: Take the Belt Parkway to the 86th Street exit.
By subway: N train to the 18th Avenue Station.
Cab services: New York Car Service (745-0001) or YES Car Service (492-9300). Cost is about $10 from Brooklyn Heights, $18 from Grand Central Station.
Note: Check a map before you go. Bensonhurst's street grid is confusing. The streets called "Bay 6" or "Bay 7" exist only in Bensonhurst and are woven into a grid that includes plain numbered streets, as in "86th Street," and numbered avenues as well.

Special events: Procession of Saint Fortunata (July); Santa Rosalia Festival, celebrated by immigrants from Palermo, Sicily (September).

How it got its name: Bensonhurst was named after the Benson family, resident cabbage and potato farmers in the mid-1800s.

ABOUT THE NEIGHBORHOOD

Bensonhurst is Brooklyn's Little Italy. You'll find some excellent Italian restaurants here plus several traditional Italian bakeries that rival the best of Manhattan's Mott Street. You'll find good local opera at the **Regina Opera Company** (see page 44) and plenty of outdoor activities as well. **Dyker Beach Golf Course, Nelly Bly Amusement Park**, and **Bensonhurst Park**, with its three-mile waterside promenade for jogging, biking, fishing, and kite flying, are all major attractions.

Everywhere you look in Bensonhurst are visible clues to local culture. The half-mile stretch from about 65th Street to 78th Street along 18th Avenue is lined with Italian food shops—pork stores selling homemade sausages; *focacceria* (selling pizza, rice balls, and other Italian fast foods); *fornio* (bread bakeries); *pasticieria* (pastry bakeries); and *latticini* (dairy shops)—along with shops specializing in imported Italian records, linens, and toiletries. **Caffè Mille Luci** and **Caffè Italia** and other espresso bars are the genuine article—straight out of an Italian town or railway station, they serve a mostly male clientele. Elderly gents sit on sidewalk chairs and watch the passing street scene while chatting in Italian. Looking somewhat mysterious from the outside are a half dozen or so private social clubs whose unadorned signs bearing the names of Italian towns punctuate the avenue; if you peek inside you'll see just tables and chairs. The scene at 86th Street on weekend evenings is a flashback to the 1950s: local teenagers cruising up and down the street in big fancy cars, radios blaring. The names of the clothing stores along here also are suggestive: Passion Boutique, Oh La La Fashions, and Male Ego. There are innumerable bridal shops and big wedding halls. Residents follow Italian soccer matches as closely as they do baseball's World Series. On almost every summer weekend you'll find a feast honoring a patron saint, culminating in the huge ten-day **Santa Rosalia Festival** in September.

The sense of humor born of working-class Bensonhurst has helped some residents fulfill the American dream. Local-boys-made-good include Phil Silvers, Dom DeLuise, and Abe Burrows. Bensonhurst was also the home of television's most beloved bus driver, "Honeymooner" Ralph Kramden.

Where you go in Bensonhurst depends on what you want to do. There is excellent Italian food at a number of restaurants and you have your choice of environments, from the intimate grottolike **Il Grottino**, to **Tomasso's** where you can hear opera or Gershwin, to a garden setting at **Villa Vivolo**. You'll find bakeries like the **Alba** and **Angelo's** which are worth a long journey. **Spumoni Gardens**, one of Brooklyn's best pizzerias, is off the main drag but worth a visit if you're a pizza fanatic or you're traveling with kids. **Bensonhurst Park** offers joggers, skaters, bikers, and romantics a great view of barges, sailboats, and the beautiful Verrazano-Narrows Bridge. Bargain hunters will revel in the display of everyday items, from cheap wristwatches to garbage pails, sold from outdoor stalls on two blocks along 86th Street.

To see how very distinct neighborhoods meld into one another—a true Brooklyn phenomenon—drive down 17th Avenue, a well-kept residential street, all the way from Bensonhurst to Borough Park. Italian pork stores give way to kosher butchers; teenagers in form-fitting clothing yield to demurely dressed girls and boys wearing yarmulkes.

Historical Notes

Little remains of Bensonhurst's early years as a rural farming area. One interesting remnant of the Revolutionary War is a "liberty pole" at the **New Utrecht Reformed Church**, which marks the site where colonial rebels taunted English soldiers by hoisting the American flag.

In the 1890s, when Coney Island was a world-famous seaside resort, a competitive complex called Bensonhurst-by-the-Sea was built. Although it tried to lure customers with new hotels, an amusement park, and racetracks, Bensonhurst-by-the-Sea never succeeded. Unfortunately, none of its grandeur remains.

The growth of Bensonhurst as a middle- and working-class community followed the extension of the subway lines in 1915. The 4th Avenue subway (now the R and N trains) provided an escape for Italian and Jewish immigrants stuck in Manhattan's cramped and dirty Lower East Side. Many descendants of the neighborhood's original families still live here. Successive generations of Italian immigrants also have settled here, seeking out members of their extended families to help them adjust to a new country. Some have made their fortunes in America and returned to Italy; others have homes in both Italy and America. These multigenerational, bicultural ties contribute to the neighborhood's conservative, slightly Old World flavor.

Bensonhurst is not exclusively Italian. A long-standing Jewish community remains here, along with Irish, Polish, and most recently Asian residents. Typical of so much of Brooklyn, there are layers upon layers of different cultures even in this relatively concentrated Italian neighborhood.

Kidstuff

Families can easily spend the better part of a day in Bensonhurst, but to cover everything you'll need a car. Parents of young children will find in Bath Beach Mall one of Brooklyn's two huge **Toys "Я" Us** department stores, and nearby, **Nellie Bly Amusement Park**, and a playground. It is easy to grab a bite at one of the numerous pizza parlors, and in warm weather, outdoor stands sell Italian ices. In the summer you may stumble upon a weekend street festival.

For outdoor fun plan a picnic near the bike path and fly a kite in **Bensonhurst Park**. Of all the small shops in the area, girls will appreciate the doll houses and furnishings at **Mini Mansions**, and all kids are fascinated by **Zak's Fun House**, which is crammed with magic tricks and costumes year-round. Across the street from Zak's, the **86th Street outdoor stalls** offer plenty of cheap toys and games to delight a child.

ENTERTAINMENT

Maple Lanes. 570 60th Street, near 15th Avenue, 331-9000. Daily, 9 a.m. –1 a.m. *

For great people-watching, roll a ball or two down Maple Lanes. For outings with little kids call a day in advance so they can set up bumpers in the gutters. These almost guarantee that your tot will get a strike.

Nellie Bly Amusement Park. 1824 Shore Parkway, near Toys "Я" Us. 996-4002. Open Easter to Halloween (weather permitting), from noon to dusk. Rides average $1; there is no admission or parking fee. *

This petite, relatively clean amusement park is just a couple minutes' drive from Toys "Я" Us. Not only is it a little bit of heaven for toddlers and preteens, but it's also not too much of a headache for parents. The park features more than a dozen kiddie-sized rides, including a miniature roller coaster, ferris wheel, carousel, and train, plus a petting farm, an eighteen-hole miniature golf course, and an arcade of games. This park is not nearly as hectic or as tacky as Coney Island, but note that aside from the small ferris wheel, batting cages, and go-carts, Nellie Bly is strictly for young children. A family-owned business, it has operated for more than twenty years.

Regina Opera Company, Regina Hall. Corner of 12th Avenue, at 65th Street, 232-3555. Performances are at 8 p.m. on weekdays and 3 p.m. on weekends. Call for a schedule.

For opera buffs on a budget, this is one of the better small opera bargains in New York City. Performing for nearly twenty years, the company has helped launch the likes of Dolora Zajic, now with the Metropolitan Opera. The operas are staged with thirty-five-piece orchestra and elaborate scenery and costumes. The Regina also hosts concerts throughout the year. At $8 for adults and no charge for kids twelve and under, the price is right.

United Artists Marboro Quad. 6817 Bay Parkway, near 69th Street, 232-4000. Call for show times. *

This four-screen theater in the heart of Bensonhurst shows the usual gamut of first-run movies. Although it has been overshadowed by the newer United

Artists complex at Sheepshead Bay, the lines may be shorter here. It is also near **Torre's Restaurant**, a definite plus (see page 48).

PARKS AND PLAYGROUNDS

Bensonhurst Park. Bay Parkway, at 21st Avenue, 996-2752. ✳
  The largest of Brooklyn's eighteen municipal neighborhood miniparks, this combination promenade and park stretches for over three miles along the Belt Highway and is a favorite for jogging, roller-skating, and biking. You'll get views here of Staten Island's wooded shore from one end of the promenade and the Statue of Liberty from the other. Summer concerts are held at the Cropsey Avenue end. You can go kite flying and fishing at Bay 8th Street, just before exit 5 on Belt Parkway.

Bensonhurst Park Playground. Cropsey Avenue, at Bay Parkway and 21st Avenue, 996-2752. ✳
  Do you and your little ones need a breather after Toys "Я" Us? Leave your car in the store lot and take a walk to this lovely playground. Just a few blocks away, it is right next to the entrance to Belt Parkway west.

Bensonhurst Playground. 14th Avenue, at 86th Street. ✳
  This well-maintained, safe space is just a five-minute drive from the 86th Street shopping area. There is plenty of room for running around, plus modern wooden climbing equipment and swings.

Dyker Beach Park and Golf Course. From 86th Street to Shore Parkway, between 7th and 14th avenues, 965-6594.
  Less than half the size of Prospect Park, Dyker nonetheless has 216 acres of grassy space that includes a soccer field, tennis courts, and the Dyker Beach Golf Course, a public course. It's located past the Verrazano-Narrows Bridge on the south side of Fort Hamilton. For golf information call 836-9722. The first tee is near 86th Street and 7th Avenue.

Garibaldi Playground. 18th Avenue, at 84th Street. ✳
  This small urban playground, across from the lovely **New Utrecht Reformed Church** (see page 46), is a place for the kids to let off some steam while you sneak a nibble of one of Bensonhurst's dreamy Italian pastries.

POINTS OF CULTURAL INTEREST

Beth Hatalmud Yeshiva. 2127 82nd Street, at 21st Avenue, 259-2525.
  Jewish and Italian immigrants have lived side by side in Brooklyn for about

a hundred years. This nationally known Orthodox boys' school is one of many local institutions, including nearly two dozen synagogues, that have been supported for decades by the small Jewish community that still lives in Bensonhurst.

Brooklyn Public Library. 86th Street, near Bay 17th Street, 236-4086. Call to check hours. ✳

Just a few blocks away from the commercial shopping strip on 86th Street, this branch of the library offers a well-equipped children's room, movies, and, of course, a quiet break.

New Utrecht Reformed Church. 1828 83rd Street, at 18th Avenue, 236-0678.

The oldest church in the area, this lovely, well-kept landmark was constructed in 1828. The stones come from a church built in 1700 that once stood in what is now the New Utrecht Cemetery, also a landmark, located nearby at 16th Avenue and 84th Street. The liberty pole in the front marks the site where the American flag was first raised at the end of the American Revolution.

Regina Pacis. 65th Street and 12th Avenue, 236-0909.

This is the largest church in Bensonhurst, with about four thousand congregants. During Easter, Christmas, and other festivals there are huge turnouts—on Good Friday, for example, about seven thousand people participate in a candlelit procession carrying large statues as far as a mile and a half. The **Regina Opera Company** (page 44) is a spin-off of this church.

Santa Rosalia Society. 18th Avenue, at 70th Street, no phone.

Social clubs like this one dot 18th Avenue in Bensonhurst. Named after a hometown in Italy by new immigrants from that town, these modest storefront clubs provide friendship and an opportunity to engage in what Americans now call "networking." People from (in this case) Santa Rosalia meet here to talk, to reminisce, and to get help in finding jobs and housing contacts. In the summer the social clubs celebrate the festival of their town's patron saint, and Italians from the town gather from all over New York City for the festival. The biggest of these is the Santa Rosalia Festival, organized by the Santa Rosalia Society.

NOTABLE RESTAURANTS

Caffè Italia. 6917-21 18th Avenue, near 70th Street, no phone. Mon.–Sat., noon–11 p.m.; Sun., noon–9 p.m.

The scene here is straight out of Italy. On summer nights, local men hang around on the street and in the café, talking, gesticulating, laughing. The fare includes homemade gelati spumoni, espresso, cappuccino, and Sambuca.

Caffè Mille Luci. 7123 18th Avenue, near 72nd Street, 837-7017. Mon.– Fri., 7 a.m.–2 a.m.; Sat.–Sun., open twenty-four hours.

A trip to this truly authentic Italian café is cheaper than a plane ticket to Italy, and it will transport you to the same place. Try the outstanding coffee and choose from a wide assortment of Italian pastries and sweets. Women's travel advisory: forget coming without a male companion. Below the café is an excellent restaurant, **Il Grottino**, owned by the same family.

Il Grottino Ristorante. 7123 18th Avenue, corner of 72nd Street, 837-7017. Mon.–Sun., 5 p.m.–midnight. Major credit cards.

Nestled below ground under the **Caffè Mille Luci**, this intimate restaurant is a grottolike room with a small bar, visible kitchen, and about a dozen tables. Patrons come from New Jersey, Long Island, and all of the New York City boroughs for the authentic Italian cuisine made from the freshest ingredients. Everything—from the appetizer, served compliments of the house before you order, to killer Italian cream desserts like *tirami su*—is impeccable, including the service. Entrées average about $14; pasta dishes cost less. There's live music on Friday and Saturday nights.

L and B Spumoni Gardens. 2725 86th Street, near West 11th Avenue, 372-8400. Sun.–Thurs., 11:30 a.m.–midnight; Fri.–Sat., 11:30 a.m.–2 a.m. No credit cards. ✳

This old pizzeria serves a pie that is nothing less than splendid, as the local clientele will attest. The crust is light and crisp, the toppings fresh. A large outdoor seating area makes the place as much fun as the food is tasty: you can eat in the sunshine and the kids can run around. Homemade spumoni ice cream is sold next door if you haven't filled up on pizza. For "real food" try the restaurant inside. Pasta or seafood entrées cost less than $10.

Taste of the Tropics. 6702 18th Avenue, corner of 67th Street, 236-3643. Mon.–Sat., 10 a.m.–6 p.m.; Fri.–Sun., 10 a.m.–11 p.m. ✳

Caribbean ice cream is not what you would expect to find in this neighborhood. For a real treat try the Brooklyn-made orange pineapple, peach mango, and other exotic flavors.

Tommaso's. 1464 86th Street, between 14th and 15th avenues, 236-9883. Daily, noon–11 p.m. Major credit cards.

The food is good, but the singing is the reason people travel here. Loud, exuberant opera with piano accompaniment is performed Thursday through

Saturday nights from 7:30 until closing. On Thursday night, Juilliard-trained Tommaso himself sings Verdi and Puccini favorites. Sunday night features Gershwin-era favorites. The staff is friendly, there's an excellent wine selection, and there are even balloons for the kids. For about $32 per person you'll get a complete dinner that will satisfy the heartiest appetite. Worth noting is the unusual ten-day pre-Lent *Carnevale*, the Italian equivalent to Mardi Gras, which is celebrated here in grand style with huge portions.

Torre's Restaurant. 6808 Bay Parkway, near 68th Street, 256-1140. Mon.–Thurs., 11:30 a.m.–11:30 p.m.; Fri. and Sat., 11:30 a.m.–12:30 a.m.; Sun., 11:30 a.m.–10 p.m. No credit cards.

Good Neapolitan cuisine at moderate prices make this a terrific local restaurant. The best dishes are the barbecued jumbo shrimps lathered with garlic, olive oil, and lemon juice for $12.50, lobster tail *fra diavolo*, and a heaping plateful of veal marsala for just $8.75.

Villa Fiorita. 7720 18th Avenue, between 77th and 78th streets, 837-7950. Daily, noon–midnight. Major credit cards.

If ravioli is your thing, note that the daily homemade version here is worthy of Manhattan's best restaurants, but at very moderate prices. The restaurant's simple, intimate ambience and fresh Italian fare make this the kind of restaurant visitors wish they had in their own neighborhoods. A full meal comes to less than $20 a person. After dinner, visit one of several authentic Italian espresso bars a few blocks away.

Villa Ruggiero. 2274 86th Street, between 23rd Avenue and Bay 32nd Street, 373-2590. Tues.–Sun., noon–11:30 p.m. Major credit cards.

If you want a good but inexpensive Italian meal near Shore Park, try this local favorite. Southern Italian cuisine is the specialty. Sample freshly prepared spaghetti, veal parmigiana, shrimp scampi, and other entrées for about $12 or less.

Villa Vivolo. 8829 26th Avenue, near 88th Street, 372-9860. Mon.–Fri., 11:30 a.m.–midnight; Sat.–Sun., 12:30 p.m.–midnight. Major credit cards.

This fifty-year-old restaurant may be off the beaten track, but it serves wonderful homemade pasta and veal dishes, stuffed artichokes, and other Italian specialties at about $20 per dinner. Located in an attractive old home on a pleasant residential street, the patio garden will have appeal for claustrophobic New Yorkers. Along with good food, there's romance and history: Rudolph Valentino (one of many Bensonhurst-based entertainers) is rumored to have worked here before he became a cinema heartthrob. Parking is available on the premises; call for directions. Weekend reservations are recommended.

SHOPPING
Specialty Food Shops

Alba. 7001 18th Avenue, corner of 70th Street, 232-2122. Daily, 8:30 a.m.–8 p.m.

"Internationally famous for four generations" is what Alba's card says. With pastries this fabulous, it is easy to see why this bakery has been in business since 1932. The specialties are cream-filled confections. Everything is artfully done. One of the best products is a strawberry layer cake with whipped cream.

Angelo's Bakery. 2482 86th Street, near 25th Avenue, 372-3866. Daily, 8 a.m.–7 p.m.

Angelo's is a few minutes' drive away from the center of Bensonhurst, but customers have been taking the extra time to shop here for more than twenty-five years. The selection includes artful marzipan, cookies, and semolina bread, as well as Italian cheesecake, luscious strawberry shortcake, and banana cream pie. Along traditional lines, they make *pipatelle* (biscuits); *tirami su* (made with *mascarpone*, Italian cream cheese); *sanguinaccio* (a folk dish with mysterious ingredients); and *gelati di campana* (which comes in the red, white, and green colors of the Italian flag).

Bari Pork Store. 7119 18th Avenue, near 71st Street, 266-9300. Mon.–Sat., 8 a.m.–7 p.m.; Sun., 8 a.m.–2 p.m.

In this era of lean cuisine, the words *pork store* (and there are many such stores throughout Brooklyn) can evoke flashing red lights for health-conscious consumers. However, this store also sells low-cholesterol, low-sodium meats and cold cuts. The traditional southern Italian foods are fresh and truly tasty: fresh mozzarella and *scamorza* cheese, *pizza rustica* (which looks like apple pie but is filled with dried sausage and cheeses), homemade veal, pepper-onion and broccoli-rabe sausages. Bari, by the way, is the name of a province in the Apulia region of Italy from which many of the local residents hailed. The place is especially crowded on Saturday.

18th Avenue Bakery. 6016 18th Avenue, at 60th Street, 256-2441. Daily, 8 a.m.–7 p.m.

Beautiful big loaves of raisin bread, semolina, lard bread, and more come out of the ovens here. Already forty years old, this bakery is here for keeps.

Pastosa Ravioli. 7425 New Utrecht Avenue, near 75th Street, 236-9615. Mon.–Sat., 8:30 a.m.–6 p.m.; Sun., 8:30 a.m.–3 p.m.

Headquarters of a small pasta empire, Pastosa has four stores in Brooklyn alone and about a dozen in the tri-state area. Each store makes pasta daily. With twenty-five years of experience, they've got their recipes right for homemade ravioli, prosciutto balls, artichoke salad, stuffed mushrooms, meatballs and sauces.

Prodotti Alimentari Italiani, Giordano and Sons. 7614 17th Avenue, between 76th and 77th streets, 837-7200. Mon.–Sat., 8 a.m.–7 p.m.; Sun., 8 a.m.– 2 p.m. No credit cards.

You could go to other specialty food stores and spend twice as much on Italian imported goods, but don't bother—the owner here prides himself on selling absolutely nothing American-made. This is a great source for imported Italian cheese, Italian salami, Italian olives, and lots of Italian-made pasta. For people who've just arrived from Italy, it's the closest thing they'll find to their hometown supermarket.

Queen Ann Ravioli. 7205 18th Avenue, near 72nd Street, 256-1061. Tues.–Sat., 9 a.m.–6 p.m.; Sun., 8 a.m.–2 p.m. Closed Mon.

The pasta sold here is made in the huge modern facility visible at the back of the store. Pasta doesn't come any fresher unless you make it yourself. Condiments and bottles of strained fresh tomatoes are also available to round out the menu.

Sbarro. 1705 65th Street, corner of 17th Avenue, 331-8808. Mon.–Fri., 8 a.m.–7 p.m.; Sat. and Sun., 8 a.m.–8 p.m.

Most folks know Sbarro as a pizza and pasta shop in their local mall, but this is Sbarro's original store, still in the same location since it opened in 1959. This excellent shop sells salads, pasta, gift packages, and a roster of prepared foods for catering. A display of photos and news clippings tells the proud family's story of success.

Tony's Focacceria. 2313 86th Street, near 23rd Avenue, 946-5700. Daily, 9 a.m.–9 p.m. ✳

Locals swear by Tony's, an eat-in pizzeria and *tavola calda*, a kind of Italian deli. They have a large menu of delicious Italian foods—hot and cold hero sandwiches, baked clams and mussels marinara, broccoli *rabe*, spinach rolls, lasagna, and Sicilian ricotta rice balls. Cold buffets can be arranged for parties of ten or more. Delivery is also available.

Trunzo Brothers. 6802 18th Avenue, corner of 68th Street, 331-2111. Mon.–Sat., 8 a.m.–7 p.m.; Sun., 8 a.m.–2 p.m.

This is a one-stop-shopping source for Italian foods. Imagine all of those little mom-and-pop Italian food shops rolled into one *latticina frescha*-grocery-dairy-deli-*salumeria*. The sandwiches are mouthwatering. Also try the mozzarella rolled with spinach, the *soppressa*, and the ready-to-bake homemade minipizzas.

Villabate. 7117 18th Avenue, between 71st and 72nd streets, 331-8430. Daily, 7 a.m.–9 p.m.

If you love the pastry shops on Mott Street in Manhattan's Little Italy, then you've come to the right place for dreamy, creamy pastries, including cannoli, zabaglione, and other delights.

Virabella Bakery. 2278 86th Street, near 23rd Avenue, 449-3384. Daily, 7 a.m.–9 p.m.

An espresso bar in this bakery is a welcome sight, since you'll want some coffee or gelati to wash down the extraordinary cannoli, *bocconcini*, and other pastries. The beautifully shaped marzipan in the form of fruits and animals get high marks on both looks and taste.

Food for an Italian Pastry Tray
Where there's an Italian neighborhood, there are great bakeries. Try the following:
gelati di campana—rich ice cream
marzipan—almond paste molded in shapes of fruits
pipalette—cookies
zabaglione—a sweet froth made of eggs, sugar, and wine
tirami su—light, sweet pudding of *mascarpone*, Italian cream cheese
zucotto—a soft cake made with cream
cannoli—rich cream-filled rolled pastry

Interesting Neighborhood Shops

Anchor Point Archery and Fishing. 7217 18th Avenue, between 72nd and 73rd streets, 256-8576. Mon.–Fri., 10 a.m.–7:30 p.m.; Sat., 10 a.m.–6 p.m. Closed Sun. Major credit cards.

Surprise! About the last thing you'd expect to find in Brooklyn is an indoor archery range. Longtime neighborhood resident John Sarlo has turned a hobby into a business, selling a line of sophisticated hunting and sporting bows by PSE and Pearson Oneida, plus camouflage clothing. Courses in safety and instruction for children are available. There is also a small line of fishing gear.

Arcobaleno. 7306 18th Avenue, near 73rd Street, 259-7951. Daily, 10 a.m.–10 p.m.

From compact discs to videotapes, this store stocks a full line of imported Italian music and movies. Many customers are locals and recent arrivals from Italy who like to keep in touch with Italian popular culture.

Berta 67. 6510 18th Avenue, near 65th Street, 232-4084. Mon.–Wed., 9:30 a.m.–7 p.m.; Thurs. and Sat., 9 a.m.–9 p.m.; Sun., 10 a.m.–6 p.m. Major credit cards. ✱

Prices at this department store are cheap, cheap, cheap. Shelves and racks are jammed with women's and children's wear, housewares, dishes, sheets, and luggage. Brand names include French Toast, Gitano, and Ocean Pacific. A few doors down, at 6708 18th Avenue, Berta's sells discount housewares, such as toasters, blenders, and microwave ovens by Hamilton Beach, Corning, and Wearever; discount bed and bath items by Fieldcrest, Springmaid, and Martex; plus gift items by Lenox, Murano, and Studio Nova. Berta 67 has stores throughout Brooklyn, at 2151 86th Street, 712 Brighton Beach Avenue, and 1120 Kings Highway.

Dalmazio. 7116 18th Avenue, near 71st Street, 951-9500. Mon.–Sat., 10:30 a.m.–7 p.m. Major credit cards.

Top-of-the-line fine Italian imported items are featured in this store and its cousin across the street, **Centro de Corrido**, at 7109 18th Avenue. Dalmazio carries Ginori china, Morano crystal, Cortese porcelain giftware, silver flatware, and unusual wedding favors. A spectacular line of cookware by Inoxriu sells in sets of twenty-one pieces starting at $850. Centro de Corrido sells lovely items for the home, including linens, lacey trousseau items, and flatware, plus adorable gifts for newborns. The store is closest to the 18th Avenue stop on the N train.

Finishing Touches. 7013 18th Avenue, near 70th Street, 837-7223. Mon.– Sat., 10 a.m.–5 p.m.; Thurs., 10 a.m.–8 p.m. Major credit cards.

Weddings are serious business here. The loveliest of several bridal specialty stores in the neighborhood, this small shop specializes in custom headpieces, dyeable shoes, and accessories for the bride and bridesmaid. An appointment is recommended.

Festival. 6412 18th Avenue, near 64th Street, 259-3811. Mon.–Fri., 10 a.m.–7 p.m.; Thurs., 10 a.m.–8 p.m.; Sat., 10 a.m.–6 p.m. Major credit cards. ✱

Better children's wear for both boys and girls from layette to size 14 is sold here. Special items include boys' $200 white silk communion suits, $200 imported Italian christening gowns of organza and satin, and the Chico line, in addition to a good selection of everyday clothes.

George Richland. 2183 86th Street, corner of Bay Parkway, 372-1210. Mon.–Sat., 10 a.m.–6 p.m.; Thurs., 10 a.m.–8 p.m. Major credit cards.

Head to toe, you can get the whole look here: soft calf slip-on shoes, gold or silver cufflinks, trimly tailored Italian suits, and brand names like Le Baron,

Louis Roth, and Rubin of Canada. Shirts start at $25 and ties at about $15, while suits run from $300 to $800.

Maggio Music. 8403 18th Avenue, corner of 84th Street, 259-4468. Mon.–Fri., 1–9 p.m.; Sat., 10 a.m.–6 p.m.; closed Sun. Major credit cards.

This father-son business has been in the Maggio family for thirty-five years, but that doesn't mean it is old-fashioned. Electronic instruments are crammed into this small space, from electric guitars and beginner keyboards to top-of-the-line synthesizers. They also give lessons to kids ages six and up. Come with a sense of humor for amiable banter with the owners.

Male Attitude Clothing. 2084 86th Street, near 20th Avenue, 449-7518. Mon.–Fri., 10 a.m.–6 p.m.; Thurs.–Fri., 10 a.m.–8 p.m.; Sat., 10 a.m.–7 p.m.; closed Sun. Major credit cards.

Tired of looking like a trout fisher, a tennis pro, or a buttoned-up Wall Street lawyer? The fashionable, high-quality men's sports clothes here are sharp, sexy, and Italian. These moderately priced to expensive items won't be found in most brownstone Brooklyn clothing stores, which tend more toward T-shirts, khaki, denim, and unisex clothes.

Mini Mansions. 1710 86th Street, near 17th Avenue, 331-7992. Daily, 11 a.m.–6 p.m. ✳

Brooklyn's largest independent dollhouse store, run by a husband and wife team, is a treasure trove of miniatures for both children and adult collectors. A range of large, unusual dollhouses, including mock Brooklyn brownstones, start at $350. Any accessory you can think of, from people to pool tables to chandeliers, is sold here starting at about $5. Carpeting, linoleum, electrical lighting, furniture of any period, and even landscaping, can be installed in your model house. Work is done on the premises, and the prices are lower than those in Manhattan.

Peter Pan Yarn/King Arthur Yarn. 7618 18th Avenue, near 76th Street, 232-9001. Mon.–Fri., 9 a.m.–6 p.m.; Sat., 9 a.m.–5 p.m.; Sun., 11 a.m.–3 p.m.

Knitting and crocheting are traditional, time-intensive arts, so while some customers may just want to browse (or wistfully collect a few skeins of great-looking yarn), plenty of grandmothers and moms who have time to create their own sweaters come here for the raw materials. Afficionados will appreciate the wide range of yarns available, some at a discount.

S.A.S. Italian Records. 7113 18th Avenue, near 71st Street, 331-0539 or 331-0540. Mon.–Sat., 10 a.m.–9 p.m.; Sun., 10 a.m.–8 p.m. Major credit cards.

If you want the sounds, sights, and smells of contemporary Italian life, pop in here to pick up Italian popular music, videotapes, soaps, and toiletries. Great for expatriates, and not a bad bargain for other New Yorkers who, for the price of a subway token and a tape, can imagine themselves on the Spanish steps in Rome.

Something Else. 2051 86th Street, near 20th Avenue, 372-1900. Tues.–Sat., 10 a.m.–6 p.m.; Thurs., 10 a.m.–8 p.m. Major credit cards.

Trendy casual clothing for women is the specialty here and at the sister store in Bay Ridge (8402 5th Avenue). The look is young, with lots of cotton shorts and slacks, appliquéd denim jumpsuits, and party dresses. Prices are moderate, ranging from $40 for pants to $130 and up for cocktail dresses.

Street stalls. Along 86th Street, at Bay Parkway. ✳

This is not exactly a street market, but the stalls put out by the shopkeepers on one side of the street create a crowded, marketlike ambience. People come as much for the festive atmosphere as for the bargains. Fresh fruit and vegetable stands have low, low prices. Housewares; kids' clothing; flowers; racks of T-shirts; rows and rows inexpensive sunglasses, earrings, and hair ornaments; crates of toilet tissue, soda, and ketchup; shoes for under $10; plastic hangers; handbags; toys; and seasonal items (Christmas cards, chocolate Easter bunnies, Halloween supplies) are just some of the items on display. Behind the stalls are shops: an Italian butcher, a pizza parlor, a hardware store, and other neighborhood establishments.

Toys "Я" Us. 8793 Bay Parkway, at 87th Street and the waterfront, 372-4646. Mon.–Sat., 9:30 a.m.–9:30 p.m.; Sun., 10 a.m.–6 p.m. Major credit cards. ✳

Toys "Я" Us needs no introduction; Brooklyn has two. You can easily get lost in this chain store's warehouse of toys, clothing, games, layette equipment, and more. Many people come here to load up on heavily discounted essentials, such as disposable diapers and jars of baby food, and for big ticket items, such as bikes. The other Brooklyn store is in Mill Basin.

Val Con's American Bridal Center. 8402 18th Avenue, corner of 84th Street, 236-0344. Tues.–Thurs., 11 a.m.–9 p.m.; Fri., 11 a.m.–5 p.m.; Sat., 10 a.m.–5 p.m.

Weddings are big business in Bensonhurst, judging from the number of bridal shops. Young couples planning their nuptials will find the whole shebang here: bridal gowns and bridesmaid's dresses, tuxedos, rings, and the full compliment of floral, travel, and photography services.

Zak's Fun House. 2214 86th Street, between Bay Parkway and Bay 31st Street, 373-4092. Mon.–Sat., 9:30 a.m.–9 p.m.; Sun., 10 a.m.–5:30 p.m. Major credit cards. ✷

One of New York City's larger costume rental outfits, Zak's sells and rents costumes year-round, along with theatrical makeup and all sorts of magic tricks, from $2 squirting flowers to real Houdini stuff. Having an identity crisis? Among the three thousand costumes you will find the Three Musketeers, an executioner, Cinderella, the Empress of Evil, an Easter rabbit, a mermaid, a king, even a knight in shining armor. Adult costumes can be rented for $25 for three days. Kids costumes start at $15 (no rentals). Accessories include more than three hundred masks, one hundred wigs, and hats: crowns, sailor hats, construction hats, derbys, and jesters' and firefighters' hats. Zak's also sells party goods and arranges party entertainment. Come early for Halloween; there are lines out the door. The store is named after Zakerlee, a 1970s late-night TV host of mysteries and murder movies. A catalogue is available.

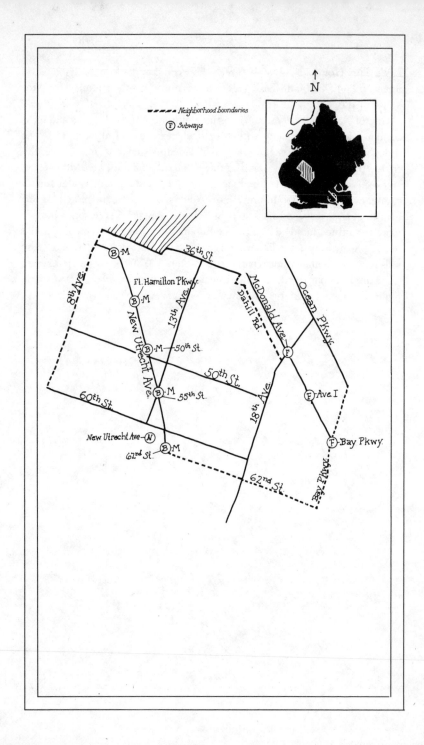

BOROUGH PARK

Where it is: Bounded by Fort Hamilton Parkway and 18th Avenue and by 38th Street and New Utrecht Avenue.

What's nearby: Bay Ridge, Bensonhurst, Flatbush, Midwood, Park Slope, Sunset Park.

How to get there:
By *car:* Take the BQE to the Prospect Expressway. Stay in the left lane (do *not* follow the signs to Staten Island) and exit at Fort Hamilton Parkway. Follow the cross streets (40th to 65th streets) to 13th, 16th, or 18th avenue.
By *subway:* B or M train to Fort Hamilton Parkway.
Cab services: Simcha (436-2448) and Punctual (972-6100). Fares are about $17 from Grand Central Station, $9 from Brooklyn Heights.

Special events: The neighborhood is colorful during holidays. Stand on a busy street corner and watch the passing scene at the springtime holiday of Purim; the celebration is as close as Orthodox Jews get to a carnival. Locals dress in costume, perform clownish skits, and deliver baskets of food, called *schlach-monos,* to neighbors and friends. During the autumn holiday of Sukkoth, stroll past the many sukkahs, small thatched-roof huts in which meals are eaten. Prior to Passover, Borough Park stores sell all kinds of provisions, from hand-made matzohs to silver seder plates.

How it got its name: This area was named after a large real estate development, Borough Park, east of New Utrecht Avenue.

ABOUT THE NEIGHBORHOOD

If we could use a single word to describe Borough Park's main attraction for most visitors, it would be *discount*. You can find just about anything, from housewares to top-of-the-line silver, linens, and fine china, at 10 to 50 percent below department store prices. From top-quality children's clothing at **Rachel's Boutique**, to women's undergarments at **Underworld Plaza**, hats and accessories at **Gold's Trimmings**, suitcases at **A to Z Luggage**, and designer sheets at **D'Rose Linen's**, Borough Park is a discount shopper's heaven.

Those with an interest in things Jewish couldn't find a more authentic Orthodox community, replete with synagogues, yeshivas (religious schools), many Jewish bookstores and even the **Jewish Youth Library**. Kosher food stores aplenty offer the traditional chopped liver, chicken soup, eggplant salad, and baked goods. **Taam Eden** is a dairy restaurant straight out of Tel Aviv. Seafood lovers—kosher or not—will be thrilled with Brooklyn's most widely acclaimed new seafood restaurant, **Ossie's**, located here.

Borough Park is a formidable Jewish melting pot of immigrants from Israel, Russia, and Europe, plus members of more than twenty Hasidic sects, such as the Satmar, Bobov, and Belz. The air is filled with a babel of English, Yiddish, Hebrew, Russian, and various Eastern European languages. This is no accident—Borough Park is reputed to have the highest concentration of Orthodox Jews outside of Israel. The focus here, where four or more children per family is more the norm than the exception, is on family life. Numerous hat and wig shops reflect the Orthodox requirement that Jewish men and their wives cover their heads. It seems fitting that **Gold's Horseradish** is based here, complete with a root cellar underneath the nearby subway, and that in the weeks before Passover you can watch a centuries-old tradition being reiterated at the **Shmura Matzoh Factory**.

If you want a feel for the pace of the Orthodox Jewish life-style, visit Borough Park early on a Friday afternoon. During this pre-Sabbath rush hour (several hours before sundown), scholarly looking bearded men in black coats wait in line to buy foot-long *challahs* (traditional braided egg breads). Women with multiple children in tow rush to finish last-minute food shopping. Solemnly dressed school children, the boys in yarmulkes, play on the sidewalks. From the start of the Sabbath on Friday evening until its completion on Saturday evening, this community does not drive, turn on electricity, carry or use money, or conduct business. By late Friday afternoon the streets are completely devoid of activity, save groups of men and some women walking to synagogue.

Historical Notes

In the 1880s the Litchfield family, major landowners who also owned the vast area that became Prospect Park, developed a settlement in this area and called it Blythebourne. A nearby tract was called Borough Park. As the tale goes, a local realtor tried to convince Mrs. William B. Litchfield to sell Blythebourne, warning her that real estate values would plummet in rural Brooklyn as Jews fleeing pogroms in Eastern Europe invaded the area. She refused to sell. As it turned out, there was indeed an influx of refugee Jews into Borough Park. However, land values rose and Borough Park expanded, eventually overtaking Blythebourne. Today the only trace of Blythebourne is in the name of the Borough Park post office.

Borough Park has seen at least four waves of Jewish immigrants. The first group arrived at the turn of the century, marked by the construction of the synagogue that is now home of **Congregation Anshe Lubawitz**, at 4022 12th Avenue, and to **Temple Emanu-el**, at 1364 49th Street. The second wave arrived after World War I, as new train and trolley tracks made the area more accessible to Jewish residents of Williamsburg and Manhattan's Lower East Side. Another group fled Europe before and after World War II and the Holocaust. Since the 1970s, immigrants from Russia, Hungary, Poland, Romania, and Israel have come to Borough Park.

Shopping Areas

The majority of shops line 13th Avenue between 39th and 54th streets; others are scattered throughout the area. Some new stores have a spiffy, Madison Avenue look, but a few are overstuffed with a jumble of goods. Don't worry —there is a method to the madness and you'll get plenty of help if you ask for it.

Shopper's advisory: (1) Don't even *think* of setting out for a shopping expedition to Borough Park on Friday night or Saturday. Everything shuts down for the Sabbath. Most shops close early on Friday, are closed on Saturday, and are very busy on Sunday. If you can, shop during the week. (2) To feel comfortable in this neighborhood, it helps to "go native" a bit. Both women and men are advised to avoid short shorts and other scanty clothing, in keeping with the modest dress code of Borough Park residents. (3) In the kosher tradition, restaurants serving dairy meals such as pancakes or blintzes do not serve meat, and vice versa.

Kidstuff

It would be an understatement to say that this is a neighborhood geared toward children; there are children absolutely *everywhere*. If you have little ones, bring a supply of quarters for the mechanical rides on just about every block along 13th Avenue. There are many informal, inexpensive places to eat, such as (kosher) pizzerias. **Teacher's Pet** and **G & Sons** department store sell practical, fun, and inexpensive items. Nearby is **Train World II**, which will be of interest to school-age kids. If the shopping doesn't tire the kids out, there is a playground nearby.

PARKS AND PLAYGROUNDS

Borough Park Playground. 18th Avenue, between 56th and 57th streets. ✳

It is not worth a special trip, but this urban playground, complete with climbing equipment, sand, and even tennis courts, is great for shopping-weary children.

POINTS OF CULTURAL INTEREST

Bobover Hassidic World Headquarters. 15th Avenue, near 48th Street, 853-7900.

The Bobover sect is one of the largest Hasidic groups in Borough Park. Hasidism was born around 1800 in Eastern Europe as a populist revolt against a stringently intellectual Talmudic tradition. Religious but unlearned Jews led by charismatic leaders (*rebbes*) created an alternative approach, stressing joyous prayer over scholarship and illustrative moralistic tales (*midrash*) over legalisms. Most of Borough Park's Hasidic population arrived here after World War II. Today many Hasidic sects have themselves become insular, differing from one another in ways only the initiated might appreciate. Unlike most large synagogues, this one has no fixed pews, platform (*bimah*), or tables. Instead, the abundant floor space better accommodates the crowds of men praying, singing, and dancing when the revered Bobover Rebbe holds a gathering, which in these parts is called a *tish*.

Brooklyn Public Library. 1265 43rd Street, between 12th and 13th avenues, 435-3375. Call to check hours. ✳

Central to the main shopping district on 13th Avenue, this is a good place for a respite, a read, and a run to a clean restroom.

Congregation Anshe Lubawitz. 4022 12th Avenue, at 40th Street, 436-2200.

This 1906 synagogue, originally known as Temple Beth El, was the first built in the area and became a haven for many Jews seeking to escape the overcrowding and slumlike conditions of Manhattan's Lower East Side. In 1916 the opening of the subway lines (B train) that connected Borough Park to Manhattan and Coney Island further increased the area's accessibility and created a housing boom. Today there are more than seventy-five active Orthodox congregations in Borough Park, including Russians, the most recent wave of Jewish immigrants to New York.

Gold's Horseradish. 895 McDonald Avenue, off Avenue F, 435-1910. Mon.–Fri., 9 a.m.–5 p.m.; no public tours.

Where other than Brooklyn could it be made? Three generations have been grinding out hundreds of thousands of bottles of Gold's Horseradish since it all started in Grandma Gold's kitchen in 1932. The family swears that among its other uses, their product goes great with tuna, egg salad, and chicken salad. (A free recipe book is available.) Some customers, they claim, say it has aphrodisiac qualities. Unbeknownst to most Brooklynites, Gold's claims to have the world's biggest root cellar—underneath the elevated F train near McDonald Avenue.

Jewish Youth Library. 1461 46th Street, between 14th and 15th avenues, 435-4711. Open afternoons; closed Sat. Call to check hours. ✳

Jewish books for kids make this library unique. There are preschooler volumes in English that cover a wide range of Jewish topics. Visitors can use the comfortable reading room or borrow books with a $15 annual membership. Some volumes are also available in Hebrew and Yiddish.

Shmura Matzoh Factory. 36th Street, end of 13th Avenue, 438-2006. Open in the pre-Passover season only. Call for hours. ✳

There are a handful of Orthodox handmade matzo factories in Borough Park and Williamsburg, and it's worth a visit for those interested in T·R·A·D·I·T·I·O·N. Open only in the period before Passover, these hole-in-the-wall bakeries produce the most kosher of matzos, called *schmura*. Schmura means "watched," and there is a complement of rabbis on hand to watch the clock and the workers: Jewish law stipulates that to be kosher, matzo must be unleavened and cannot touch any leavened dough, and the entire process must not exceed eighteen minutes. Each time the dozens of workers complete a round, all utensils are changed, washed, and inspected, to avoid contact between batches. Don't expect to stay long; everyone is bustling about, and the place is not set up for tourists. No bare thighs or arms are permitted in this religious environment.

NOTABLE RESTAURANTS

Two quite different restaurants in Borough Park stand out from the others:

Ossie's Table. 1314 50th Street, near 13th Avenue, 435-0635. Sun.–Thurs., 11 a.m.–3 p.m. and 5–10:30 p.m.; Sat., 8:30 p.m.–midnight. Major credit cards.

The chef here used to work at the Greene Street Cafe and Soho Kitchen & Bar in Manhattan, and one New York daily newspaper recently gave Ossie's a three-star ("excellent") rating. Unlike most kosher restaurants, Ossie's offers elegant, upscale dining. There is a wide selection of fish, all fresh. This is no surprise, given that the restaurant is owned by the same people who run the fish store next door, which has been in the neighborhood since 1966. The crowd is mixed: Hasidic, modern Orthodox, and everyone else. At $8, the extensive luncheon buffet is a steal. Dinner entrées average about $15. Homemade breads and desserts and outdoor seating in fine weather make this a welcome addition to Brooklyn's seafood dining options.

Red's Brick Oven Pizza. 3716 13th Avenue, between 37th and 38th streets, 438-8020 or 436-1818. Tues.–Thurs. and Sun., noon–10 p.m.; Fri.–Sat., noon–11 p.m. Major credit cards. ✳

You'll never settle for ordinary pizza again. Red's, situated at the end of Borough Park's main shopping street, has a seventy-year-old brick oven that turns out light, crispy, absolutely scrumptious pies ($9.50), calzone ($3.50), and rolls. The "small" broccoli roll ($3.50), for example, is loaded with cheese and fresh broccoli and is easily a meal in itself. The pizza is fantastic—crispy with fresh crushed tomato sauce and little if any oil. The food and relaxing atmosphere (complete with a stuffed shark on the wall) make this a welcome retreat. This restaurant is not kosher.

Other restaurants include the following:

Ach Tov. 4403 13th Avenue, near 44th Street, 438-8494. Mon.–Thurs. and Sun., 8 a.m.–8 p.m.; closes in midafternoon on Fri.; closed Sat. ✳

The name means "so good." Maybe that's why this small, kosher dairy eatery comes so highly recommended by locals. You'll find blintzes, potato pancakes, noodle dishes, salads, and cheese dishes for under $10.

Adelman's Glatt Deli. 4514 13th Avenue, between 45th and 46th streets, 853-5680. Mon.–Thurs. and Sun., 11 a.m.–10:30 p.m.; closes in midafternoon on Fri.; closed Sat. No credit cards. ✳

Here's the place to go for an old-fashioned corned beef (or pastrami or brisket) sandwich on rye with a good pickle. You couldn't get more authentic New York deli sandwiches, all for under $7, anywhere else. The restaurant is kosher; no dairy products are served. Don't be surprised to see the Orthodox clientele washing their hands at a small public sink before eating, and quietly mouthing a prayer after the meal; both are standard Orthodox tradition.

Cafe Shalva. 1305 53rd Street, near 13th Avenue, 851-1970. Mon.–Thurs. and Sun., 10 a.m.–6 p.m.; closes in midafternoon on Fri.; closed Sat.

For a pick-me-up while shopping, try the cappuccino and espresso at this unpretentious coffee shop. There's also a small lunch menu, and everything is kosher. Prices are low, low, low.

Shem Tov Dairy Restaurant. 1040 46th Street, between Fort Hamilton Parkway and 10th Avenue, 438-9366. Mon.–Thurs. and Sun., 8 a.m.–7 p.m.; closes in midafternoon on Fri.; closed Sat.

In keeping with the kosher tradition of separating dairy and meat dishes, this restaurant serves traditional home-style dairy and vegetarian cooking, but with an Italian twist. Try the kosher eggplant parmesan, baked ziti, and fish.

Taam Eden Kosher Dairy Restaurant. 5001 13th Avenue, near 50th Street, 972-1692. Mon.–Thurs., 7 a.m.–11 p.m.; Fri., 7 a.m.–4 p.m.; Sun., 7 a.m.–6 p.m.; closed Sat. ✴

If it is home-style Jewish cooking you want, stop here. This tiny spot, with only five booths and a dozen seats at the counter, is where you'll taste the real thing: smoked whitefish salad, gefilte fish, stuffed cabbage, pea and dumpling soup, matzo ball soup, and, of course, knishes. Inexpensive and tasty, kids will love this place. Takeout is available. The name, by the way, means "Taste of Eden."

Food for a Traditional Jewish Feast
matzo ball soup
potato, kasha, and spinach knishes
chopped liver
challah or rye bread
dill pickles
baked salmon salad
babka cake
halvah

SHOPPING

Specialty Food Shops

European American Deli. 473 McDonald Avenue, near Church Avenue, 438-6861. Daily, 8 a.m.–8 p.m.

For those who don't want to schlep all the way to Brighton Beach for Russian goodies, try this Russian-owned deli on the outskirts of Borough Park. Great eggplant salad, Russian sausages, Russian cheeses, and cakes are among the many delicious items you'll find.

Fine-Ess Kosher Ice Cream. 4906 13th Avenue, near 49th Street, 436-1909. Mon.–Thurs. and Sun., 10 a.m.–8 p.m.; closes in midafternoon on Fri.; closed Sat. ✳

Check out the tofu and nondairy ice cream, as well as standard fare. The novelty ice-cream cigars, parfait cups, and seashells are fun for a party. After an afternoon of shopping, this is a winner with the kids.

Korn's. 5004 16th Avenue, near 50th Street, 851-0268 or 633-7466. Mon.–Thurs. and Sun., 6 a.m.–9 p.m.; closes Fri. in midafternoon; closed Sat. ✳

Korn's has all of those Jewish baked goodies your bubba used to bring over, like great rye breads and huge *challahs*. For dessert try the rugalach, *babka*, and other freezable noshes. There's another store on 12th Avenue near 49th Street.

Oneg Take Home Foods. 4911 12th Avenue, between 49th and 50th streets, 438-3388. Mon.–Thurs. and Sun., 9 a.m.–7 p.m.; closes Fri. in midafternoon; closed Sat.

Got a cold, or just a yen for traditional Jewish food? Of course, bubbie, there is chicken soup and schmaltz here. But eat, eat! Try the stuffed cabbage, corned beef, pastrami, potato knishes, or one of three dozen prepared salads. The store is conveniently located across from the 50th Street station, where you can catch the B and M trains. On Thursday and Friday, orders over $15 can be delivered to other Brooklyn neighborhoods. The food is kosher.

Ossie's. 1314 50th Street, near 13th Avenue, 436-4100. Mon.–Thurs., 7 a.m.–7 p.m.; closes Fri. in midafternoon; Sun., 8 a.m.–4 p.m.; closed Sat.

Some of the excellent take-home items made here are also sold at Zabar's in Manhattan and come highly recommended: whitefish with almonds and raisins, pastrami-cured carp, and, most particularly, baked brook trout filled with spinach and garlic—all kosher. Ossie's also has a new, very popular restaurant next door (see Ossie's Table, page 62).

Strauss Bakery. 5209 13th Avenue, near 52nd Street, 851-7728. Mon.–
Thurs. and Sun., 6 a.m.–7 p.m.; closes early on Fri.; closed Sat. ✳

Yum—cream cakes! Napoleons! Roll your eyes if you've tasted heaven.
Everything here is kosher, to boot.

Tell's Bakery. 217 Church Avenue, between East 2nd and 3rd streets,
438-9069. Mon.–Fri., 6:30 a.m.–7:30 p.m.; Sun., 6:30 a.m.–5 p.m.; closed
Wed. ✳

This truly great bakery with fabulous *babka*, breads, and other Jewish goodies
is just a few blocks from the Parade Grounds at the southwestern corner of
Prospect Park. It's definitely worth a visit—bring an empty stomach.

Weiss Homemade Kosher Bakery. 5011 13th Avenue, near 50th Street, 438-
0407. Mon.–Thurs. and Sun., 6 a.m.–8 p.m.; closes Fri. in midafternoon;
closed Sat. ✳

Judging from the number of customers and what they're buying, everything
here must be tasty. The home-baked six-grain bread is particularly healthy
and delicious. This is a good place to treat the kids after shopping.

Women's Clothing and Accessories

A Touch of Class. 4921 16th Avenue, between 49th and 50th streets, 854-
6814. Mon.–Thurs., 11 a.m.–5:30 p.m.; closes Fri. in midafternoon; closed
Sat. Major credit cards.

Beautifully displayed and tastefully selected top-of-the-line women's Italian
and French suits and dresses are the ticket at A Touch of Class. Designers
like Mondi and Escada are represented, with prices starting at $400. There is
a small selection of terrific hats suitable for Soho or Madison Avenue, including some showy designs by Kokin. Started more than a decade ago by
three ambitious housewives named Bayla, Chedva, and Miri (two are Israeli),
this boutique has a verve and spunk uncharacteristic of most in this area.

B&R. 4513 13th Avenue, near 45th Street, 436-8388. Mon.–Thurs.,
10 a.m.–6 p.m.; closes Fri. in midafternoon; closed Sat. Major credit cards.

The best bargains at B&R may be the leather coats by Marvin Richards
and Winlit. Lots of women's clothes at a 30 percent discount are sold here.
The selection includes designs by Harve Bernard, Diffusion, and others. Catering to the local Orthodox clientele, most of the clothes here have long
sleeves and high necklines.

Beauty Fashion Wigs. 4608 13th Avenue, near 46th Street, 871-1366.
Mon.–Thurs., 10 a.m.–6 p.m.; closes Fri. in midafternoon; closed Sat. Major
credit cards.

If you want or need a high-quality wig, this is a good place to go. Following Orthodox tradition, just about all of the women in this neighborhood wear hats, scarves, or wigs to cover their hair when in public. This store is reputed to be one of the best of its kind in the neighborhood.

Coat Plaza. 4414 13th Avenue, between 44th and 45th streets, 972-2682. Mon.–Thurs. and Sun., 10 a.m.–6 p.m.; closes Fri. in midafternoon; closed Sat. Major credit cards.

Coat Plaza has a good selection of classic raincoats and conservative wool coats at 25 percent or more below department store prices. The inventory changes frequently, so call ahead if you're looking for a particular designer.

Gold's Trimmings & Accessories. 4710 13th Avenue, near 47th Street, 633-3009. Mon.–Thurs., 10 a.m.–7 p.m.; closes Fri. in midafternoon; Sun., 10:30 a.m.–5 p.m.; closed Sat. Major credit cards.

Hats are coming back in style, so don't be surprised at the high-fashion numbers sold here in Borough Park. This store appeals not just to the local Orthodox women for whom covering the hair is de rigueur—hat lovers come from all over to get simple $20 berets or exuberant, flashy styles costing well over $100. Gold's has belts and other accessories as well. Go downstairs for an excellent sewing and notions department.

Hindy's Maternity. 4902 New Utrecht Avenue, corner of 49th Street, 438-3840. Mon.–Thurs. and Sun., 11 a.m.–5:30 p.m.; closes Fri. in midafternoon; closed Sat. Major credit cards.

Expecting a baby? Check out both of Hindy's stores. The New Utrecht Avenue location sells it all, from bathing suits and underwear to coats. They'll also sew fancy maternity clothes in fine fabrics to order. For maternity closeouts try the second store, at 4307 13th Avenue, near 43rd Street (438-2453).

Italian Shoes Corporation. 4902 13th Avenue, near 49th Street, 851-7474. Mon.–Thurs. and Sun., 10 a.m.–7 p.m.; closes Fri. in midafternoon; closed Sat. Major credit cards.

It's unusual to find such a wide selection of high-quality Italian women's shoes in Borough Park. Many sell for just $100. The store also carries boots.

Lingerie Boutique. 4605 16th Avenue, near 46th Street, 438-3454. Mon.–Thurs. and Sun., 10 a.m.–6 p.m.; closes Fri. in midafternoon; closed Sat. Major credit cards.

Nightgowns and robes by designers like Christian Dior, Lily of France, and Carol Hochman are the draw here. In the friendly jumble you'll find some great and some not-so-great discounts. It helps to get a salesperson to point you to the real bargains.

M and H Cosmetics. 4911 13th Avenue, near 49th Street, 871-6600. Mon.–Thurs. and Sun., 10 a.m.–6:30 p.m.; closes Fri. in midafternoon; closed Sat. Major credit cards.

Enormous, modern, and very popular, the entire store resembles a cosmetics department at Macy's or Bloomingdale's. However, many prices are pure Brooklyn—meaning discounted. This is one of several cosmetics stores in the area that sell Chanel, Dior, Borghese, and other top-of-the-line cosmetics.

S and W. 4217 13th Avenue, between 42nd and 43rd streets, 438-9679. Sun.–Thurs., 10 a.m.–6 p.m.; closes early on Fri.; closed Sat. Major credit cards.

In the tradition of Loehmann's, the great Brooklyn-born discount store, this women's clothing store is a big discounter of both American and European fashions. Even the separates tend to be dressy rather than sporty, and all items have long sleeves and high necklines.

Underworld Plaza. 1421 62nd Street, near 14th Avenue, 232-6804. Mon.–Thurs. and Sun., 10 a.m.–5 p.m.; closes Fri. in midafternoon; closed Sat. Major credit cards.

What **Train World II** (page 69) is to model trains, Underworld is to those little unmentionables. This is one store to visit at least semiannually. Whether you're rejuvenating a worn collection of underwear or looking for a romantic teddy that won't break the bank, come here. The selection of name-brand negligees, bathrobes, slips, bras, panties, and so on at wholesale prices is vast. Parking is free.

Clothing, Equipment, and Supplies for Kids

Berkowitz. 5216 13th Avenue, between 52nd and 53rd streets, 436-3333. Sun.–Thurs., 10 a.m.–8 p.m.; closes early on Fri.; closed Sat. No credit cards.

This is one of several discount juvenile furniture shops on 13th Avenue that stock cribs, dressers, rocking chairs, and other items.

Boom. 5123 13th Avenue, near 52nd Street, 972-2666 (972-BOOM). Sun.–Thurs., 11 a.m.–7 p.m.; Fri., 11 a.m.–2:30 p.m.; closed Sat. Major credit cards. *

If it's fun and trendy children's shoes and clothes you want, this is the place for you. Prices are moderate to expensive, with shoes and outfits starting at about $30.

Judy's Nook. 4608 16th Street, near 46th Street, 633-4340. Mon.–Thurs. and Sun., 11 a.m.–5:30 p.m.; closes Fri. in midafternoon; closed Sat. Major credit cards. *

Shop here for a tasteful selection of upper-end children's clothing, from infant to preteen. Prices generally are discounted at least 10 percent. Still, snowsuits are in the $120-and-up range, and complete outfits for boys and girls run $50 and up. Weary customers can relax on the pastel sofa and armchairs.

Le Petit. 4619 18th Avenue, between 46th and 47th streets, 851-2921. Mon.–Thurs. and Sun., 10:30 a.m.–6:30 p.m.; closes Fri. in midafternoon; closed Sat. Major credit cards. ✳

You would have to go to the Champs Elysée to find some of these designs. The owners travel to Italy and France to select these top-of-the-line clothes for infants through juniors. For special occasions there are black velvet dresses, satin jumpsuits, and fur-collared wool coats. Little boys aren't left out—there is plenty of tailored, classic clothing for boys, plus dressy items, such as tuxedo shirts. Coats are $250 and up; dresses start at $150. Even the play clothes are elegant. Ask to be put on their mailing list for seasonal sales.

Little King and Queen. 5018 13th Avenue, between 50th and 51st streets, 438-2007. Mon.–Thurs. and Sun., 10 a.m.–7 p.m.; closes Fri. in midafternoon; closed Sat. Major credit cards. ✳

Just start with the baby carriages—MacLaren, Inglesina, Chico, Silver Cross—and you'll know you've found a huge selection of furniture and equipment for your little "royals." The prices are discounted 10 percent or more and the salespeople couldn't be nicer. Imported cribs are $190 to more than $500; carriages start at $200.

Rachel's Boutique. 4218-22 13th Avenue, between 42nd and 43rd streets, 435-6875. Mon.–Thurs. and Sun., 10 a.m.–6 p.m.; closes Fri. in midafternoon; closed Sat. Major credit cards. ✳

Rachel's has a truly huge inventory of tops and mid-tier children's clothing, all heavily discounted. The sheer volume—for instance, floor-to-ceiling racks of boys' shirts—is unusual for a children's store. Pick a size and you'll find about 150 outfits available for your toddler (we know, we counted). And that doesn't include the nighties, raincoats, jackets, suspenders, socks, and other incidentals for newborns to size 14 boys and junior girls. It gets busy on Sundays, but there's a twenty-five-cent "movie machine" to help keep restless kids entertained.

Stern's Fashions. 5501 16th Avenue, corner of 55th Street, 972-7931. Mon.–Thurs. and Sun., 10 a.m.–7 p.m.; Fri., 10 a.m.–2 p.m.; closed Sat. Major credit cards.

Stern's is straight out of an old-fashioned retail mold. Like many other children's clothing stores in Borough Park, the accent is on classic styles, durable quality, and discounted prices. Oshkosh, Healthtex, and other popular brands for infants through size 14 are crammed into racks and racks here. There is also a good collection of bathrobes, 1950s-style crinoline slips, and Carter's underwear.

Teacher's Pet. 4809 16th Avenue, between 48th and 49th streets, 436-6600. Mon.–Thurs. and Sun., 10 a.m.–7 p.m.; Fri., closes in midafternoon; closed Sat. ✳

Teacher's Pet sells inexpensive, practical arts and crafts and school supplies. Giant money-saving sizes on everything from glitter and glue to maps and toys are typical. You can phone your order in for shipment by UPS, but visiting is half the fun.

Train World II. 751 McDonald Avenue, near Ditmas Avenue, 436-7072. Mon.–Sat., 10 a.m.–6 p.m. Major credit cards. ✳

Even if you're not a train buff when you enter, you will be before leaving this store. Loaded with hundreds of trains, pieces of scenery, miniature figures, and lots of track, you'll think you've landed in Penn Station. One of the biggest train stores in New York City, Train World carries Lionel, American Flyer, and LGB among others. Prices range from under $10 to $300. This is a terrific place to bring children, but expect to go home with something on wheels.

Wonderland. 5309 13th Avenue, near 53rd Street, 435-4040. Sun.–Thurs., 10 a.m.–6 p.m.; closes early on Friday; closed Sat. Major credit cards. ✳

Like **Rachel's** (opposite) but in more modern facilities, this huge, busy, and very popular clothing store has better-quality merchandise for children at a hefty discount. Sizes range from layette to preteen.

Yeedl's. 4301 13th Avenue, corner of 43rd Street, 435-5900. Mon.–Thurs. and Sun., 11 a.m.–6 p.m.; Fri., 11 a.m.–3 p.m.; closed Sat. Major credit cards. ✳

For great prices on imported, top-drawer strollers, cribs, and other juvenile furniture, check out Yeedl's. Beware of stroller gridlock, however; this place gets busy!

Interesting Neighborhood Shops

A to Z Luggage. 4627 New Utrecht Avenue, near 47th Street, 435-6330 or 435-6331. Mon.–Thurs., 9 a.m.–6 p.m.; Fri. and Sun., 9 a.m.–5 p.m.; closed Sat. Major credit cards.

Some people won't buy luggage anywhere but this Brooklyn shop under the "el." You'll find unbelievable discounts on more than a dozen well-known brands of handbags, suitcases, garment bags, and sample cases. Orders can be placed by phone. A to Z also has half a dozen stores in Manhattan.

BH: Better Health. 3622 13th Avenue, between 52nd Street and New Utrecht Avenue, 436-4801. Mon.–Wed., 10 a.m.–6 p.m.; Thurs., 10 a.m.–8 p.m.; Sun., noon–5 p.m.; closed Fri. and Sat. Major credit cards.

Fitness buffs and even a few couch potatoes will go crazy over the top-of-the-line exercise equipment at 10 to 50 percent discounts. Brands include Trotter, Lifecycle, Bodyguard, Marcy, Precor, and Universal. The store provides free consultation on setting up a home gym and sometimes will swap equipment with you. Rowers, bikes, treadmills, stair climbers, ski machines, weights, mats, benches, and pool tables—they've got it all.

Continental Tablesettings. 4515 13th Avenue, near 45th Street, 435-1451 or 438-2522. Mon.–Thurs., 11 a.m.–6 p.m.; Fri., closes in midafternoon; closed Sat. Major credit cards.

You wouldn't travel all this way for one fork, but you'll save a bundle if you're looking for a set of new crystal, china, or silver. Top brands include Lenox, Limoges, Royal Dalton, Villery and Boch, Wedgewood, Rosenthal, and Orrefors. Some are discounted 25 percent below department store prices.

D'Rose Linens. 1315 47th Street, off 13th Avenue, 633-0863. Sun.–Thurs., 10:30 a.m.–6 p.m.; closes early on Fri.; closed Sat. Major credit cards.

After one visit to this discount shop, you'll never consider buying sheets at full retail price again. Better-quality sheets, towels, tablecloths, bedspreads, and comforters are all sold at 30 percent off department store prices. Name brands include Luxor, Springmaid, Martex, and Dan River. Got a pear-shaped or half-oval table? Want custom made curtains or bedspreads in designer fabrics? If they don't have it here, they can order it for you.

East Side China. 5002 12th Avenue, at 50th Street, 633-8672. Mon.–Thurs., 10:30 a.m.–6 p.m.; Fri., closes in midafternoon; Sun., 10 a.m.–5 p.m.; closed Sat. Major credit cards.

For over a dozen years this store has made its reputation on discounted giftware, china, and dinnerware with names such as Wedgewood, Lenox, and Mikassa. You can choose from the variety of items on display or order a specific pattern. Discounts are substantial, starting at about 25 percent.

Flohr's. 4603 13th Avenue, at 46th Street, 854-0685. Mon.–Thurs. and Sun., 10 a.m.–6 p.m.; Fri., closes in midafternoon; closed Sat. Major credit cards.

Hand in glove, Orthodox Jewish communities and bookstores go together. There are at least eight bookstores in this neighborhood—many more than in Brooklyn's gentrified brownstone communities. Although you won't be able to read most of these tomes, called *sphorim*, unless you are fluent in Hebrew or Aramaic, the sheer volume is impressive. In addition to books, Flohr's sells gift items and Judaica.

G and Sons. 4802-4810 New Utrecht Avenue, near 48th Street, 438-2604. Mon.–Thurs., 10 a.m.–9 p.m.; Fri., closes midafternoon; Sun., 10 a.m.– 4 p.m.; closed Sat. Major credit cards. ✱

If you're the nostalgic type, tight-fisted, or both, you'll *love* this old-fashioned department store with its well-worn hardwood floors, bargain-basement prices, and reputation for outstanding service. There's row upon row of kitchenware, from microwave ovens, clocks, and irons to ice-cream scoops. You'll also find flatware, luggage, socks, mittens, underwear, and an extensive toy department that includes some of the Fisher Price line. Plan to spend some time here; the store occupies the better part of a city block. Frequent "Thursday night madness" sales are a specialty—that's when selected merchandise is priced below cost.

Gadamo Imports. 4812 13th Avenue, between 48th and 49th streets, 438-4949. Sun.–Wed., 10 a.m.–7 p.m.; Thurs., 10 a.m.–9 p.m.; Fri., 10 a.m. –4 p.m.; closed Sat. Major credit cards.

For a stylish European look, this shop sells a variety of suits imported from Italy, France, and Holland in the $250 to $400 price range. Men's slacks, ties, and overcoats are also in abundance. A second store at 1414 Avenue J, between East 14th and 15th streets, carries a wider selection, including expensive silk shirts, leather jackets, and evening wear.

Grand Sterling Company. 4921 13th Avenue, near 49th Street, 854-0623. Mon.–Thurs. and Sun., 10 a.m.–7 p.m.; Fri., closes in midafternoon; Sun., 10 a.m.–6 p.m.; closed Sat. Major credit cards.

Known for being the top-of-the-line in the silver trade, Grand Sterling has a wide variety of candlesticks, frames, trays, and other items. Call ahead if you're looking for something special.

Lamp Warehouse. 1073 39th Street, corner of Fort Hamilton Parkway, 436-2207. Mon.–Tues. and Fri.–Sun., 10 a.m.–5 p.m.; Thurs., 10 a.m.–8 p.m.; closed Wed. Major credit cards.

Here's a bright idea: reduced prices on all major names in lamps. This is purported to be New York's largest discount lamp store, so it is well worth the trip if you're buying to light up an apartment or a house. If you listen to New York radio news stations, you may well know this store by its humorous ads.

London Silver Vaults. 4922 16th Avenue, between 49th and 50th streets, 436-2800. Mon.–Thurs., 9:30 a.m.–8:30 p.m.; Fri., closes in midafternoon; Sun., 10 a.m.–7 p.m.; closed Sat.

Have you always wanted silver just like grandma's? The proprietor buys his flatware from estates, polishes it, and sells it for between $100 and $250 for a five-piece setting. The store also sells candelabras, tea sets, serving trays, and an extensive collection of Judaica, ranging in price from $200 to $2,000. There is a silversmith on the premises.

Mandel. 4215 13th Avenue, between 42nd and 43d streets, 435-6695. Mon.–Thurs. and Sun., 8 a.m.–7 p.m.; Fri., closes in midafternoon; closed Sat. Major credit cards.

This forty-year-old family business sells a wide range of men's everyday and dress suits from mainstream designers at a 20 to 40 percent discount. A typical two-piece suit averages $250, including alterations. High-end suits sell for about $450. The salespeople are friendly and helpful.

Mildred's for Fine Linen. 4612 13th Avenue, near 46th Street, 435-2323. Mon.–Thurs. and Sun., 10 a.m.–6 p.m.; Fri., closes in midafternoon; closed Sat. Major credit cards.

If you want your bedroom to look like that luscious magazine picture, with just a phone call Mildred's can ship the goods to you—at up to a 25 percent discount. There are half a dozen curtain and linen shops in Borough Park, but Mildred's claim to fame is a big phone-and-mail business on duvets, sheets, bath accessories, shower curtains, and other linens. The store itself has two floors crammed with attractive name-brand items and includes an extensive bath shop.

Royalty Tableware. 1845 50th Street, between 18th and 19th avenues, 854-6689. Hours are by appointment.

You'll have to put up with the limited hours here if you want to find stainless steel and silver-plated tableware at 25 to 60 percent discounts. But at $150 for twelve place settings, it's worth the hassle.

Toeffler. 5127 New Utrecht Avenue, between 51st and 52nd Streets, 436-8989. Mon.–Thurs., 10 a.m.–7 p.m.; Sun., 10 a.m.–6 p.m.; closed Fri. and Sat. Major credit cards.

Toeffler is one of Brooklyn's largest discount decorator furniture stores. The high-fashion merchandise is from top designers—sofas, bedroom sets, dining room sets, and accessories—all at 10 to 40 percent off. Brand names include Confort, Handrinden, Comfort Design, Harold Zimmerman, and Alexrale.

Whispers 'N' Whimsies. 4919 16th Avenue, between 49th and 50th streets, 633-3174. Mon.–Thurs. and Sun., 10:30 a.m.–6 p.m.; Fri., 10:30 a.m.–2 p.m.; closed Sat. Major credit cards. ✳

The housekeeping may be a bit helter-skelter here, but don't be discouraged. Unusual toys, books, funny pencils, and well-designed backpacks, lunch boxes, and other practical gear are sold here at reasonable prices. There's even a collection of Pauline dolls downstairs.

HOTELS

Park House Hotel. 1206 48th Street, at 12th Avenue, 871-8100. Major credit cards.

One of the few hotels in Brooklyn, this small one caters to the kosher crowd. It is only one block from the nearest synagogues for visitors observant of the Sabbath. Rates start at $75 per night for a double room.

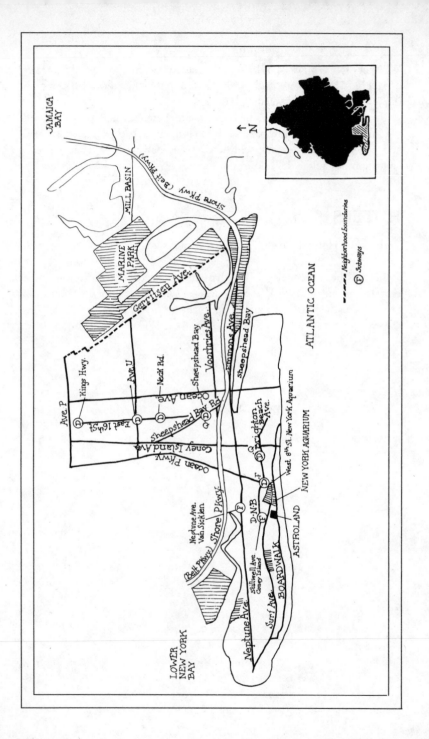

BRIGHTON BEACH, CONEY ISLAND, AND SHEEPSHEAD BAY

Snug against the Atlantic Ocean at Brooklyn's southern end, Brighton Beach, Coney Island, and Sheepshead Bay offer an unparalleled combination of fun, food, and fashion. Because you can spend a full day here, combining a walk on Brighton's boardwalk with a roller coaster ride in Coney Island and dinner in Sheepshead Bay, we've included all three neighborhoods in this single chapter.

Where they are: Along the Atlantic Ocean. From west to east: Coney Island, Brighton Beach, and then Sheepshead Bay.

How to get there:
   By *car:* Take the Belt Parkway to exit 7, head south along Ocean Parkway toward the ocean, then west on Surf Avenue (Coney Island) or east on Brighton Beach Avenue (Brighton Beach). Exits 8 and 9 drop you at either end of Sheepshead Bay's Emmons Avenue.
   By *subway:* D or Q train to Brighton Beach Avenue (Brighton Beach), or Sheepshead Bay Road (Sheepshead Bay). The D or F train to West 8th Street (Coney Island).
   Cab services: Best Way Car Service (252-6363), Avenue J Airport Service (251-3200), Five Star Livery (891-8200), Sheepshead Car Service (769-2700), Plaza Car Service (615-2000). Fares are about $13 to $15 from Brooklyn Heights, $20 to $25 from Grand Central Station.

Kidstuff

Plan to spend at least half a day with kids in this section of Brooklyn. The **New York Aquarium** at Coney Island is educational, fun, and parent-friendly. Weather permitting, more vigorous play can be found at nearby **Astroland** amusement park or the indoor ice-skating rink at **Abe Stark**.

Sheepshead Bay's **Emmons Avenue fishing pier** is entertaining for all ages, and when combined with dinner nearby, it makes for a refreshing family outing. Very young children will happily walk across the **Ocean Avenue Bridge**, a long footbridge to **Manhattan Beach**, and then back again. The huge **UA Cinema Complex** at Sheepshead Bay is always inviting. Older kids may want to blow their accumulated savings on learning to sail, or on some fishing gear and a day hanging a line off the pier. You also can take the whole family out on a fishing boat.

Of course, people of all ages enjoy playing in the sand and surf at **Coney Island, Brighton Beach**, or **Manhattan Beach Park**, and strolling or biking along the boardwalk.

BRIGHTON BEACH

Special Events: Brighton Jubilee, street fair and concert, the last Sunday in August. Call 891-0800 for information.

How it got its name: Named after England's most distinguished seaside resort, Brighton Beach was developed in the 1880s as a posh competitor with nearby Coney Island.

ABOUT THE NEIGHBORHOOD

At Brooklyn's southernmost end is a seaside neighborhood you won't want to miss. Commonly referred to as "Little Odessa," Brighton Beach is a Russian enclave in New York.

The main thoroughfare, **Brighton Beach Avenue,** is peppered with Russian delis and restaurants, Russian-run clothing shops, and Russian-language newspaper stores and shop signs. During the winter months an amazing number of both men and women do their daily errands dressed in heavy fur or leather coats. Residents of Brooklyn, surrounding suburbs, and even Manhattan trek here to "ooh" and "aah" over the delicious authentic Russian foods and wild tabletop dancing at such well-known Russian nightclubs as the **National Restaurant**, the **Odessa**, and **Kaukas**. If fifty years of the cold war (*glasnost* notwithstanding) hasn't whet your curiosity about the Soviet Union, a trip to Brighton Beach will.

To be precise, the community here (and increasingly in neighboring Manhattan Beach, Sheepshead Bay, and Midwood) is composed mainly of refuseniks and other Soviet Jewish émigrés. With an immigrant population of thirty thousand, Brighton Beach is home to the largest population of Soviet Jews in the nation.

Along Brighton Beach Avenue, shops with such names as **Stolichny Deli** are packed tightly under the elevated subway tracks. In this darkish, noisy atmosphere you can almost imagine yourself in Kiev or Moscow. But the shopping is pure New York: there are sophisticated Italian women's clothing stores, imported shoe shops, and furriers. Visitors may be surprised by the number of vegetable stands. As one local Russian summed it up: "They are hungry from Russia still. One vegetable stand here would be for the whole town there."

Food mavens should not miss three specialty stores in the area. **M&I International** is the largest of several Russian stores; the array of sausages, syrups, cheeses, and breads is boggling. Snackers will delight in nearby **Mrs. Stahl's Knishes**, in business for more than fifty years, and the new **Burekas Plus** on Coney Island Avenue.

To tourists bent on having a good time the Russian shopkeepers and waiters may seem preoccupied, even world-weary. Many are terse because they have difficulty speaking English. Still, impromptu local vignettes shed light on the long, hard journey made by many of Brighton Beach's residents: you may see a woman crossing the street give a shriek of recognition and embrace a long-lost friend, neighbor, or relative.

Historical Notes

Like the Cyclone in nearby Coney Island, Brighton Beach has had its ups and downs. In the 1880s it was an affluent seaside resort complete with casino, racetrack, and a major hotel. It remained this way for decades; in 1907 the new Brighton Beach Baths (now the Brighton Beach Bath and Racquet Club) boasted several swimming pools, a beach, and nightly entertainment by the country's top performers. By the 1930s Brighton Beach had become a densely populated year-round residential area with a large number of apartment buildings. After World War II the area went into decline along with Brooklyn's economy and an aging local population. But since the arrival of the Russian community in the 1970s and 1980s Brighton Beach is once again on the rise.

ENTERTAINMENT

Brighton Beach is known for its Russian restaurant-nightclubs. Some are also open for lunch, but entertainment is evenings only.

Kaukas. 405 Brighton Beach Avenue, near Brighton 4th Street, 891-5400. Daily, 11 a.m.–midnight. Major credit cards.

Big portions, "international" music, a dance floor, and dinner banquets loaded with appetizers and vodka make for a truly memorable evening. Come with a group or you'll feel lonely even in this intimate, 80-person restaurant. The band recently has tended toward more contemporary, popular music—including Russian-style rock and roll. A deposit is required for large parties; plan on $25 to $30 per person for the evening. Weekend reservations are recommended. Kaukas is also a good lunch spot.

National Restaurant. 273 Brighton Beach Avenue, between Brighton 2nd and 3rd streets, 646-1225. Fri. and Sat., 9 p.m.–3 a.m.; Sun., 8 p.m.–2 a.m. No credit cards.

It's nostalgic. It's exotic. It's camp. Bring your ten best friends here for an evening of food, music, and dance on Friday or Saturday night. Although there are non-Russian "tourists" here, the crowd is predominantly local Russian Jewish immigrants of all generations, dressed to the nines. Part of the excitement is that you never know what is going to happen next. When you walk in, the banquet-style tables already are set with about twenty cold appetizers, including eggplant salad, cold duckling, pickled vegetables, pâté, big plain boiled potatoes, and of course, a cold bottle of vodka. That's just for starters—wait until the hot foods arrive. The live entertainment tends toward fabulously schmaltzy renditions—go ahead and sing along, no one will mind—and the dance floor is packed. A wonderful night that starts no earlier than 8:30 and can go on until 3 a.m. costs about $45 per person. The building is huge; it used to be a large movie theater, and accommodates more than 350 people. The National is famous for being Robin Williams's haunt in *Moscow on the Hudson.* You've got to make reservations, and don't forget to bring cash.

Odessa. 1113 Brighton Beach Avenue, between Brighton 13th and 14th streets, 332-3223. Tues.–Thurs., 10 a.m.–midnight; Fri.–Sat., 9 p.m.–3 a.m.; Sun., 8 p.m.–2 a.m. Major credit cards.

Odessa has wonderful atmosphere, lively dancing, terrific food, and keeps the vodka flowing. While more "hamish" (family-style) than the National, Odessa is still a huge place; one flight above street level, it occupies the space taken up by a half-dozen shops, and seats over 300 people. The Odessa is a favorite of Russian locals who congregate here at lunchtime. Try the chicken Kiev, meatloaf, and potato salad with meat. Dinner and entertainment run about $40 per person on the weekend; during the week the Russian foods are a la carte at about $12 for dinner, sans music. This restaurant is about ten blocks away from the heart of Russian Brighton Beach Avenue.

Primorski. 282 Brighton Beach Avenue, near Brighton 3rd Street, 891-3111. Daily, 11 a.m.–midnight. No credit cards.

With capacity for about 80 people, Primorski is one of the more intimate Russian restaurants, but still is a spot for a boisterous evening reminiscent of a wild bar mitzvah, with loud music, dancing on the tables, and plenty of vodka. Entrées here are very tasty, but after countless hors d'oeuvres, some good dumplings, and a couple of shots of vodka you probably won't remember the rest of the meal. Dinner is less than $30 per person. On weekdays you can get an enormous lunch for under $6. Reservations are recommended.

PARKS AND PLAYGROUNDS

Brighton Beach and Playground. Brightwater Court, near Brighton 2nd Street. ✷
One block from Brighton Beach Avenue, here is the boardwalk, the sand, the surf, and good people-watching. If it's too cool or windy for the beach, there's a large urban playground (no grass) to keep kids happy.

POINTS OF CULTURAL INTEREST

Black Sea Bookstore. 3175 Coney Island Avenue, near Brighton Beach Avenue, 769-2878. Daily, 10:30 a.m.–6 p.m.
Two doors down from **Mrs. Stahl's Knishes** (see page 82), is this one large room, stuffed with tomes in Russian. It has a somber air: unlike American bookstores, there are no posters, promotional displays, gift items, or knick-knacks, just rows and rows of mostly hardcover volumes. If you don't read Russian, don't despair—the store carries some Russian audiotapes plus tickets to occasional cultural events, such as poetry readings in Russian.

Brooklyn Public Library. Brighton 1st Road (between Brighton 1st Place and Brighton 1st Street), near Brighton Beach Avenue, 266-0005. Call to check hours. *

Special cultural programs here are tailored to the immigrant Russian population, and you'll also find a good general selection of children's and adult reading materials. The library is located on one end of the shopping strip, just a few blocks from the boardwalk and beach.

Theater for Children. 501 Brighton Beach Avenue, at Brighton 5th Street, 934-9542. Call (the staff's English is so-so) or drop in for a schedule. *

It is hard to find out about the schedule of performances here unless you speak Russian, but it is interesting nonetheless that the Brighton Beach community supports a children's theater that features old Russian folk tales combined with magic shows, clowns, Punch and Judy shows, and a puppet salute to the American flag.

Vegetable stands. Along Brighton Beach Avenue. Daily, 8 a.m.–8 p.m.

Maybe these folks are making up for lost time—and food shortages—in the old country. Fresh produce is everywhere in Brighton Beach. It seems as if there are hundreds of Korean-owned vegetable stands in this neighborhood —sometimes two or three per block. The prices are among the lowest in Brooklyn: if kiwis are two for a dollar in your neighborhood, you'll find the same quality here at five for a dollar. People stand around the fruit stands looking, selecting, discussing—from a distance, you'd think the stores were giving the stuff away.

NOTABLE RESTAURANTS

In addition to the following eateries, most of the nightclubs listed in the entertainment section (pages 78–79) serve lunch and dinner.

Cafe Cappuccino. 290 Brighton Beach Avenue, near Brighton 3rd Street, 646-6297. Daily, 10 a.m.–9 p.m. *

Highly recommended for lunch, this small European-style café offers a range of relatively light Russian food—you won't need a three-hour nap after eating here. There are Russian-style ravioli, pickled vegetables, borscht, steamed cabbage, schnitzel, cheesecake, baba-rum pastries, and excellent coffee. The decor is understated but elegant: black tablecloths and flowers on every table. It's the custom here to share a table with other customers if the place is full, so this can be a good place to meet local Russians. Lunch costs less than $10. High chairs are available.

Zei-Mar. 1047 Brighton Beach Avenue, near Brighton 11th Street, 646-9751. Daily, 10 a.m.–9 p.m. *

The vintage decor looks as if it hasn't changed since the 1940s in this kosher-style deli, but the really important news is that they've got some of the best *lean* corned beef in Brooklyn. The pastrami, corned beef, and other meats and the excellent soups are all made on the premises. This quiet eatery is across from the ocean, and its proprietor, Arnie, couldn't be friendlier. Recommended for lunch.

Food for a Russian Feast
pickled mushrooms
lobio satsivi—string beans in walnut sauce
chicken Kiev
pilmeni—dumplings
bureka—*phyllo* dough filled with cheese
seltzer with strawberry juice

SHOPPING

Specialty Food Shops

Burekas Plus. 2550 Coney Island Avenue, 339-3100. Mon.–Thurs., 8 a.m.–6 p.m.; Fri., 8 a.m.–2:30 p.m.; closed Sat. *

Move over, knishes—here come the *burekas*. These mouthwatering phyllo dough triangles filled with cheese are probably the best in Brooklyn and certainly worth the trip, even though this location isn't near much else of interest. The frozen variety keep well and are great for an impromptu party. Run by Israelis, this new combination salad bar–bakery also sells several unusual Middle Eastern pastries, including *kadaife* and *shemarim*. The food is kosher. Delivery available.

M & I International. 249 Brighton Beach Avenue, between Brighton 2nd and 3rd streets, 615-1011 or 615-1012. Daily, 8 a.m.–10 p.m.

You'll hear more Russian than English at M&I International, the biggest and best of a half dozen local Russian food stores. You'll find an interesting array of farmer, feta, and other cheeses; smoked fish; herring; spiced meats and sausages; prepared salads; and of course, caviar, borscht, and sour cream. Prepared foods include kebabs, stuffed cabbage, chicken Kiev, and eggplant in garlic sauce. Don't miss the bakery upstairs. The local color is so compelling that it's hard to know what to look at first, the people or the food. For takeout try a potato or cheese pirogi. This is a very clean, very European store.

Mrs. Stahl's Knishes. 1001 Brighton Beach Avenue, corner of Coney Island Avenue, 648-0210. Daily, 8 a.m.–7 p.m. Major credit cards. ✳

Mrs. Stahl's has used the same recipe for these famous low-cholesterol knishes for over fifty years, but today a rainbow of more than twenty fillings are available, including spinach, cabbage, cherry-cheese, kasha, mushroom-potato, and chili. Cocktail-size knishes also are available. Long-distance shipping to knish-starved friends can be arranged: the minimum order is one dozen, shipped overnight express for $39. (*Note*: If you freeze these knishes, let them thaw out naturally at room temperature; they get soggy in the microwave oven.) There's a small space for eating on the premises, but you're better off enjoying your knishes on the boardwalk or at home.

Stolichny Deli. 239 Brighton Beach Avenue, between Brighton 2nd and 3rd streets, 332-8822. Daily, 8 a.m.–10 p.m.

Light and airy, this two-story deli has the full range of Russian delectables: sausages, cheeses, canned goods, and breads. There's a bakery upstairs.

Clothing

Bella's Corset Shop. 3086 Brighton 5th Street, near Brighton Beach Avenue, 743-1084. Mon.–Sat., 10 a.m.–7 p.m.; Sun., noon–5 p.m.

This tiny store run by Bella Suvalsky has something for everyone (including free advice)—almost nothing is on display, however, so it helps to know what you're looking for before you arrive. This is a good place for discounted camisoles, bras, and other underthings.

Classic Fur. 221 Brighton Beach Avenue, near Brighton 2nd Street, 332-5138. Daily, 10 a.m.–7 p.m.; closed Wed. Major credit cards.

Visitors usually remark on the number of fur coats worn in Brighton Beach. Here, second-generation Kiev furrier Anatoly Alter and his wife Raya have assembled a beautiful collection of mink, fox, lamb, lynx, suede, racoon, and other furs with a European flair at good prices, starting at $800 and going up to several thousand. Tailoring is done on the premises, along with mono-gramming, cleaning, and storage. Another store, **Royal Furs**, is located at 1135 Brighton Beach Avenue. Lay-away plans are available.

Elegant Shoes. 203 Brighton Beach Avenue, near Brighton 2nd Street, 646-8016. Daily, 10 a.m.–7 p.m.; closed Tues. Major credit cards.

What strikes the eye here amid a collection of fashionable women's shoes are the father-son lookalike pairs of men's and boys' imported Italian leather shoes. Prices start at about $45 for little boys' sizes and upwards of $90 for men's. There is also a large selection of ornate women's shoes and boots and some traditional little girls' shoes. The same family owns **European Shoes** at 515 Brighton Beach Avenue, which has an even larger selection of children's shoes. Two doors down, at **Gino Venucci**, you'll find more men's shoes at slightly lower prices.

Little Italy Boutique. 291 Brighton Beach Avenue, near Brighton 3rd Street, 934-9337. Weekdays, 11 a.m.–7 p.m.; Sat., 11 a.m.–6 p.m.; Sun., 11 a.m.–5 p.m. Major credit cards.

Some of the most unusual high-fashion women's clothing in Brooklyn can be found here. Most is imported from Italy and France, with prices starting at $200 for dresses and $100 for skirts. Brand names include Bianca Defende, Sonia Riekel, and various European designers.

CONEY ISLAND

Special events: Mermaid Parade (June); Air Shows (May and July); Great Irish Fair (September).

How it got its name: However ridiculous it may sound, the story goes that when the Dutch first discovered this area, it was overrun with rabbits. They called it "Rabbit Island"—in Dutch, *Konijn* (Coney) *Eiland.*

ABOUT THE NEIGHBORHOOD

Step right up. Though Coney Island is just a shadow of its former glorious self, the area still has substantial attractions, most notably the world-class **New York Aquarium** and the famous Cyclone roller coaster. But if you're seeking the "world's greatest playground," prepare for a heartbreak: the Coney Island of Steeplechase and Luna Park fame, of racetracks, huge beach pavilions, hotels and restaurants, and championship prize fights exists mostly in memory, imagination, and the movies. Sadly, along with the throngs of visitors in old-fashioned bathing suits, the Thunderbolt, the Mile Sky Chaser, and most of the other old rides are long gone.

Nostalgia aside, Coney Island still has a large, if tawdry, amusement park. The wooden Cyclone roller coaster still gives a dizzying ride that makes grown men and women act like kids. **Astroland** has an enormous selection of rides for kids, as well as cotton candy and generally good-natured mayhem. A honky-tonk stretch of video arcades, adult rides (bumper cars), and game booths rings the area. The original **Nathan's Famous Restaurant** remains open, and afficionados swear that for some mysterious reason (is it the old oven? the vibes?), the hot dogs and fries here top any elsewhere in New York City. Despite the sometimes ill-kept beach, Coney Island's wide boardwalk and ocean views still make for one of the city's most invigorating walks.

And that's not all. Families can easily spend hours in the spanking clean **New York Aquarium**; kids love the sea lion show. Two old, distinguished, and recently renovated Italian restaurants, **Gargiulo's** and **Carolina**, plus the famous, eccentric **Totonno's** pizzeria (which serves customers only as long as the dough lasts), are Coney Island mainstays. The zany annual **Mermaid Parade**, complete with a contingent of elaborately costumed members of the Coney Island Hysterical Society, is an entertaining caper that's not to be missed.

Historical Notes

Coney Island's sensational era as a seaside resort lasted for more than a hundred years. As early as the 1830s the rich and famous played here—from writer Herman Melville and poet Walt Whitman to actress Lillian Russell. When the subway gave millions of working-class New Yorkers access to Coney Island in the 1920s, the crowd changed, the entertainment cheapened, and it became the "playground of the people." On summer weekends, thousands of people of all ages, sizes, shapes, and nationalities poured through the subway turnstiles for entertainment and relief from the city's crushing heat. Among the most famous restaurants of the time was the German-owned Feltman's, whose founder reputedly conceived the notion of serving a sausage in an elongated roll, thereby inventing the hot dog.

Coney Island declined after World War II, and Steeplechase Park finally closed in 1965. Much of the bungalow housing around Coney Island was bulldozed and replaced with large public high-rises that remain today.

ENTERTAINMENT

Abe Stark Ice-Skating Rink. Surf Avenue and the boardwalk, at West 19th Street, 946-6536. Open Oct.–March; call for free-skating times. Rentals are $3.50. ✳

Part of a huge new New York City Parks and Recreation Department sports complex, this indoor ice-skating rink is right next to the Coney Island amusement park. When warm weather melts the ice at outdoor rinks, or when it rains, Abe Stark is the winter solution. The property is owned by the city, but operation of the facility is subcontracted, so double-check the hours (and maybe even the phone number) before you go. There is parking on the premises. Trivia question: Who was Abe Stark? Answer: One of Brooklyn's former borough presidents.

Astroland–Coney Island Amusement Park. Surf Avenue, at West 12th Street, 372-0275 or 265-2100. Daily, noon–midnight. ✳

Astroland may have lost the glamor that once made Coney Island the best amusement park in the world, but children will be thrilled with its huge assortment of rides as well as the cotton candy and general mayhem. Astroland gets particularly crowded on hot weekend afternoons. When you've had enough of the noise, go up to the **boardwalk** for a stroll along the Atlantic Ocean. Adults are in for a treat: the wood-framed Cyclone, considered one of the best by roller coaster afficionados and featured in Woody Allen's movie *Annie Hall*, is a screamer's delight. Plus there's the Flume, a waterborne roller coaster, and the 290-foot-high Astrotower ride. Hold on to your wallets if you happen to visit the nearby video arcades.

New York Aquarium. Surf Avenue, at 8th Street West, 265-3474 (265-FISH). Mon.–Fri., 10 a.m.–6 p.m.; Sat. and Sun., 10 a.m.–7 p.m. Admission is $4.75 for adults and $2.00 for children under twelve. Parking is $3. ✳

The New York Aquarium is the oldest public aquarium in the United States and today is an educational center for environmental conservation. Located along the boardwalk in Coney Island, it has more than twenty-one thousand living specimens, from a baby beluga whale to giant octopi. The dolphin and sea lion shows keep the kids coming back month after month, even in the middle of winter. Lots of snacks are available at an indoor cafeteria, or bring your own lunch to the beach.

Recently the aquarium doubled its exhibition area with a wonderfully designed building called "Discovery Cove." In addition to the traditional exhibits of reptiles, fish, birds, mammals, and aquatic invertebrates, this is a sophisticated display of coastal ecosystems, complete with miniature crashing waves, tide pools, and an exhibit on "People and the Sea."

Check out the seasonal programs. "Ghost Crabs and Goblin Sharks" features Halloween flashlight tours, a costume parade, and a spooky shark event. "Winter Holiday" programs feature a discovery walk along the blustery beachfront and a study of Eskimo survival methods. The Summer Family Camp explores beaches and marshes and the Fulton Fish Market and includes crafts, cooking, a boat ride, and lab workshops. You can have birthday parties here and also can get information on "Setting Up a Home Aquarium."

PARKS AND PLAYGROUNDS

Coney Island Boardwalk. Along the Atlantic Ocean, between Coney Island and Brighton Beach, 946-1350. ✳
Coney Island's massive wooden boardwalk is as much a symbol of this section of Brooklyn as the Brooklyn Bridge is an icon for Brooklyn Heights. This big, beautiful boardwalk extends all the way from Brighton Beach through Coney Island. The natural scenery is as you would expect: the crashing Atlantic, a somewhat littered broad beach—and the people-watching is good too. The old-timers and retirees stroll and converse on the myriad benches along the route, as parents push carriages and joggers and bikers speed past. In the winter, the Polar Bear Club has been known to take an icy dive here. This is a well-patrolled and safe stroll during the day, which makes it perfect for a walk after eating in either Brighton Beach or Coney Island. By order of the Parks Department it's also a "quiet zone," which means that loud radios are prohibited.

Seaside-Asser Levy Park. Next to the New York Aquarium, between Surf and Sea Breeze Avenues, 946-1364. ✳
This little twenty-two-acre park is a good place to let kids run off some steam after an afternoon at the **New York Aquarium** (see page 85), and it's also notable for summer performances in its bandshell. These shows are arranged in cooperation with BACA, the Brooklyn Arts Council (call 783-3077 to get a schedule).

NOTABLE RESTAURANTS

Carolina. 1409 Mermaid Avenue, between West 15th Street and Stillwell Avenue, 714-1294. Mon.–Sat., noon–10 p.m. Sun., 1 p.m.–10 p.m. Major credit cards.

Carolina was founded in 1928, just seven years after the boardwalk opened. In those days the Luna and Steeplechase amusement parks were flourishing and masses of working-class people of many nationalities—Italian, Jewish, Greek, Polish, German, African-American, Irish—came by subway from Manhattan every summer weekend for relief from the heat. Along with Gargiulo's, Carolina is one of the few surviving eateries from that era, which included the now-defunct Childs and Feltman's, which was then Coney Island's largest restaurant. There is lots of colorful history here and the food is good, with big portions of old-fashioned Neapolitan home cooking. The interior was renovated recently and now sports lots of mirrors, a glass wall, and seats for three hundred people. Prices are moderate (entrées range from $8 to $18), and you're just a few blocks from the ocean. Valet parking is available.

Gargiulo's. 2911 West 15th Street, between Surf and Mermaid avenues, 266-4891. Wed.–Mon., 11 a.m.–10:30 p.m.; closed Tues. Major credit cards. ✷

When people speak of dining in Brooklyn, they often mention Gargiulo's. This large, family-run Italian restaurant is so popular that regular customers come from as far as New Jersey and Long Island—just check the license plates in the restaurant's huge parking lot. Kids will love the enormous papier-mâché octopus that hangs from the ceiling. While the menu is extensive and many half-portions are available, ask your waiter for the specials. Don't be shy about asking for something you don't see on the menu or hear about—they'll prepare almost any dish you can think of. One final note: you can eat here for free if you're lucky. At the meal's end, your waiter will ask you for a number from one to ninety. He'll then produce a bucket of small chips, shake it up, and pull one from inside. If the numbers match, the meal is on the house. Reservations are necessary almost anytime.

Nathan's Famous Restaurant. Surf Avenue, near Stillwell Avenue, 946-2202. Sun.–Thurs., 8 a.m.–4 a.m.; Fri. and Sat., 8 a.m.–5 a.m. ✷

This is the original Nathan's, and the experts contend that the fries here are still better than those at the franchised Nathan's. You can just stand here munching on hot dogs, corn on the cob, and fries while imagining the days when shrieking riders enjoyed the Thunderbolt, the Mile Sky Chaser, the Loop-o-Plane, the Whip, the Flying Turns, the Chute-the-Chutes, and the Comet. Or come on the Fourth of July for the twelve-minute Annual Hot Dog Eating Contest.

Totonno's. 1524 Neptune Avenue, between West 15th and 16th Streets, 372-8606. Fri.–Sun., until they run out of dough. No credit cards. ✷

You probably wouldn't stop here in a million years unless you knew what was inside. This Brooklyn institution serves what many consider to be the best brick-oven pizza in the city. There can be a long wait, but the crowd is jovial and the owner, stooped over his pizzas and lovingly decorating each one, is an old-fashioned showman. What you've heard is true: they are open only as long as the dough lasts, which means that often they're through before 8 p.m.

SHEEPSHEAD BAY (INCLUDING MANHATTAN BEACH AND MILL BASIN)

Special events: Art shows along Emmons Avenue (May and September). Commemoration of Holocaust Memorial Mall (June).

How it got its name: Sheepshead Bay is named for the sheepshead, a once-common fish in nearby waters, now long gone due to urban pollution.

ABOUT THE NEIGHBORHOOD

The pressure of New York's urban hustle fades quickly amid piers and fishing boats, dressed-down seafood restaurants, and the lovely beach breezes of Sheepshead Bay. Maybe it's the ocean air, but the waterfront at Sheepshead Bay feels as if it belongs in Rhode Island. You can go out with a half-day fishing boat from the **Emmons Avenue piers** anytime in the morning, or come around 4 p.m. to purchase the day's catch. **VIP Yachts** operates fancy dinner cruise boats daily. There's a wonderful lobster and fish shop called **Jordan's Lobster Dock** and a completely suburban **ten-screen movie theater** in Sheepshead Bay. **Lundy's** restaurant—famous in its heydey for accommodating up to three thousand guests—is now a sad, empty shell; declared a historic landmark, it has yet to reopen. But **Pips on the Bay** is still in business. This pioneer comedy club gave the young Joan Rivers, David Brenner, and Rodney Dangerfield their early breaks. For dinner there is excellent Italian fare at **Maria's** and **Nino's** among others; Chinese cuisine at **Hunan Seafood King**, and hearty, inexpensive roast beef dinners at **Brennan & Carr.**

Inland, don't be fooled by the modest presence of some of the stores along Sheepshead Bay Road or Avenue U. Like so much of Brooklyn, the plain facades at stores like **Jamar** mask behind-the-scenes bargains on top-of-the-line merchandise. Shoppers can find elegant women's bathing suits year-round at **Seahorse**; discounted designer shoes at **E. J. Robins**; sports gear by Head, Swatch, and Vuarnet at **Downtown**, and a crazy quilt of new fashions plus bargains on high-quality consignment clothes at **Allen & Suzi**. Engage some of the shopkeepers in a conversation—they are personable, funny, and down-to-earth.

Across the inlet from Sheepshead Bay is **Manhattan Beach**, an exclusive residential area. The homes here are luxurious; many have views of the ocean or inlet. Residents now include a growing number of Russians spilled over from nearby Brighton Beach. At its eastern end, **Kingsborough Community College** occupies a stunning piece of real estate, bounded on three sides by the water. The view alone is reason enough to attend one of the free outdoor concerts held here in the summer.

East of Sheepshead Bay in the Mill Basin are a number of attractions, including **Marine Park**, the **Jamaica Bay Riding Academy**, the **Kings Plaza Shopping Mall**, and **Gateway National Park**.

Historical Notes

A bit of colorful history graces Sheepshead Bay. In the late 1800s a horse-racing track ran along Ocean Avenue between Jerome Avenue and Neck Road. During this era wealthy Manhattanites frequented the many fancy Manhattan Beach hotels and resort homes. After racetrack betting was outlawed, the racetrack tried unsuccessfully to shift from horses to cars. The Sheepshead Speedway lasted a brief four years, giving way in 1919 to residential development.

The area benefited greatly from two municipal building programs. In the 1930s the piers along Emmons Avenue were built as part of a Works Progress Administration project. In the 1950s the new Belt Parkway vastly improved access to Sheepshead Bay, which stimulated the growth of the solidly middle-class Jewish and Italian community.

Driver's advisory: have patience. You'll need it to find a parking spot in the Emmons Avenue area.

ENTERTAINMENT

Century Theater—Cineplex Odeon Kings Plaza. 5201 Kings Plaza, at Flatbush Avenue and Avenue U, 253-1110 or 253-1140. Call for show times. ✳

There are four screens here, on the upper level of the mall. You can send the kids here while you shop; ample parking space is available.

Kingsborough Community College. 2001 Oriental Boulevard, off Quentin Avenue, 368-5000. Call for a concert schedule. ✳

For a romantic oceanside Saturday evening, check out the summer concerts here at the far eastern end of Brighton Beach. Bounded on three sides by the Atlantic Ocean, this modern fifty-three-acre campus with its own private beach is one of New York City's loveliest and most secluded spots. Regional dance companies, big band orchestras, and touring groups such as the Peking Acrobats visit Kingsborough year-round, and tickets usually cost about $5. In addition to occasional juvenile shows, there is a year-round "College for Kids" program for seven- to twelve-year-olds.

Pips on the Bay. 2005 Emmons Avenue, corner of Ocean Avenue, 646-9433. Wed.–Sun., opens at 8 p.m.

Joan Rivers, David Brenner, Rodney Dangerfield, and Andy Kaufman all tried out their early comic routines at Pips. You never know what up-and-comer you may hear first at Pips, or what star may pop in to test a new bunch of jokes. If you're given to making people laugh, you may want to come here, too; talent agents have been known to haunt the place. Food is pretty basic —mozzarella sticks, burgers, chicken—but that's not the main attraction. Shows are at 10 p.m. during the week and 9:15 p.m., 11:15 p.m., and 12:45 a.m. on weekend nights. There is a $5 cover and two-drink minimum on Wednesday, Thursday, and Sunday. On Saturday expect an $8.50 cover and a two-drink minimum. Reservations are recommended.

UA Movies at Sheepshead Bay. 3907 Shore Parkway, between Knapp Street and Harkness Avenue, 615-1700. Call for show times. ✳

It seems like the suburbs here at Brooklyn's largest movie complex, a ten-screen theater easily reached from the Belt Parkway's Knapp Street exit. It's only twenty minutes from Brooklyn Heights in moderate traffic, so you may wait longer to get into the movie than to get to it. There are noontime and afternoon shows, as well as midnight shows on the weekends. The picturesque harbor and **Jordan's Lobster Dock** (see page 97) across the street both contribute to a sense that you've left the city behind.

PARKS, PLAYGROUNDS, AND BEACHES

Bill Brown Park Playground. Bedford Avenue, at East 24th Street between Avenues X and Y, 934-3695. ✳

Set among well-kept red brick row houses but at some distance from the commercial hub of Sheepshead Bay is this pleasant three-acre playground. There's another at Avenue V and East 24th Street.

Fishing Boats. Emmons Avenue, between Ocean and Bedford avenues. ✳

For a wonderfully picturesque Brooklyn activity, walk along this pier at around 4 p.m. any afternoon and watch the fishing boats unload their daily haul of bluefish, flounder, and mackerel. You can buy fresh fish at rock-bottom prices or, if you are in the mood, you can book onto any one of about a dozen party fishing boats that dock here. Both half-day bay fishing boats and full-day ocean fishing boats are available. Half-day boats, more appropriate for families and casual fishermen, leave hourly from 6 a.m.–1 p.m. for four-hour trips and cost $15 for adults, with discounts for kids under twelve. Try the *Pastime II* (252-4398); *Sea Star* (625-6857); *Dorothy B.* (646-4057); and *Apache* (339-1200). It's a good idea to chat with the captains to get full details. Find out where they will be fishing, whether they supply bait and rods, if the crew can help out, and if they provide snacks, restrooms, and, just in case, motion-sickness medication on board.

Manhattan Beach Park. Oriental Boulevard, between Ocean and Mackenzie streets, 965-1373. ✳

A favorite among families, Manhattan Beach is a forty-acre public park and beach area, complete with ball fields, surf and sand, concession stands, and room for parking. Located at the southernmost tip of Brooklyn, the beach is most easily accessible by car. After a few hours at the beach, head over to Emmons Avenue for a stroll past the fishing fleet, or inland to Sheepshead Bay Road to do a little shopping. If you're lucky, you may catch an outdoor concert at nearby **Kingsborough College** (see page 90).

Sheepshead Bay Sailing School. 377-5140. Mid-May through Oct. ✳

You can learn to handle sails and moorings and maneuver a sailboat right here in Brooklyn. Since 1966 Irving Shapiro has given private lessons to aspiring sailors ranging in age from thirteen to sixty. There are beginner, intermediate, and advanced sessions aboard his *Ensign* sloop, which leaves from one of the yacht clubs in Sheepshead Bay on Emmons Avenue. For $60 a person you can hire out a thirty-five-foot C and C sailboat for a six-hour cruise, provided that you have at least four people in your group.

The following parks are in nearby Mill Basin:

Gateway National Park. Floyd Bennett Field, below Shore Parkway, 338-3799. *

Go on an adventure stargazing or bird watching or take a self-guided nature walk at America's largest national urban park. The entire expanse of Gateway stretches over twenty-six thousand acres of coastline, marsh, and parks that include Floyd Bennett Field in Brooklyn, Jamaica Bay Wildlife Refuge in Long Island, Breezy Point in Queens, and Sandy Hook in New Jersey. The Brooklyn section, named after the aviator who flew Admiral Byrd across the North Pole in 1926, was the city's first municipal airport. Now a huge, open airfield, the old airplane hangar is an exhibition hall. The wide open spaces are perfect for biking.

Gateway Sports Center. 3200 Flatbush Avenue, across from Floyd Bennett Field, 253-6816. Daily, 9 a.m.–11 p.m. *

At Gateway you can brush up your golf skills, hit a few tennis balls, or take a swing or two at some fastballs. Open year-round, this facility has a driving range, tennis courts, and batting cages plus an eighteen-hole miniature golf facility. It isn't far from **Toys "Я" Us**, the huge **Kings Plaza** shopping mall (page 101), or **Marine Parkway Bridge** (opposite) which leads to **Jacob Riis Park Beach**.

Jamaica Bay Riding Academy. 7000 Shore Parkway, between exits 11 and 13, 531-8949. Daily, 10 a.m.–4:30 p.m. *

It isn't exactly a dude ranch, but your child can learn to ride a horse in Brooklyn. There are wonderful trails through three hundred acres of bird watching country, including three miles along the beaches of Jamaica Bay. Kids as young as four can take lessons, and teenagers can ride with a guide for nearly an hour for only $20. The under-four set gets a half-hour pony ride—with mom or dad holding the horse—for $10. The exit for the riding academy is marked by a large horse. Call for directions.

Marine Park. Between Flatbush and Gerritsen avenues, exit 11 off Shore Parkway, 965-6551 or 965-8973. *

At 798 acres, Marine Park is Brooklyn's largest outdoor recreation area, and it's worth a visit. There are about a dozen tennis courts on Fillmore Avenue and Stuart Street (call 965-8993 for permit information), playgrounds at East 38th and East 33rd streets, and a running track at East 33rd street. The Urban Park Rangers lead a "haunted" twilight walk at Halloween that some youngsters call "intense"—flashlights are provided. This walk is so popular that the line starting at the ball field has been known to run three blocks. You also can enjoy kite flying, bird watching, biking, and the usual park-related activities, as well as summertime concerts. Marine Park also is home to Brooklyn's largest golf course (call 338-7113 for information).

Marine Parkway Bridge. Southern end of Flatbush Avenue. The one-way car toll is $1.50. ✳

Most kids love bridges, and this is a pleasant one, connecting Brooklyn to the public beach at **Jacob Riis Park** and more secluded beaches off residential streets in Rockaway, Queens. Between the bridge and **Kings Plaza Shopping Center** (see page 102) you will pass a **lobster shop, Toys "Я" Us, Gateway Golf and Tennis Range, Dead Horse Inlet,** and the old **Floyd Bennett Field.** Once over the bridge, bear left and follow the signs to the public beach areas. The bridge also has a bike path.

POINTS OF CULTURAL INTEREST

Brooklyn Public Library. East 14th Street, near Avenue Z, 743-0663. Call to check hours. ✳

Close enough to Sheepshead Bay Road and Avenue U shopping, this library is a good place for a respite and a read.

Wyckoff-Bennett Residence. 1669 East 22nd Street, corner of Kings Highway.

Admire this homestead, a national historic landmark, from the outside only; it is still privately owned. Built in the Dutch style, it was used by Hessian troops during the Revolutionary War. The date of its construction is discreetly carved into one of the wooden beams: 1766.

NOTABLE RESTAURANTS

Along Emmons Avenue or within walking distance of the piers you'll find the following:

Castle Harbour. 3149 Emmons Avenue, corner of Coyle Street, 332-0046. Weekdays, 11 a.m.–9 p.m.; weekends, 1:30–10:30 p.m. Major credit cards.

Tasty continental cuisine and seafood are the main attractions at Castle Harbour, but so is the decor. Come inside and you'll be met by a grizzly bear and a lion, courtesy of the big game hunter–owner. Entrées average about $14 and include fresh fish, veal marsala, and chicken dishes. Sheepshead Bay denizens give Castle Harbour a big thumbs up.

Gran Torino. 7409 Avenue U, between 74th Street East and Royce Street, 531-8349. Daily, 6 p.m.–10 p.m.; Fri. and Sat., 6 p.m.–midnight; Sun., 4–10 p.m. Major credit cards.

This restaurant actually is in Mill Basin, but the French and Italian dishes here are so good and the chef so accommodating that it's worth mentioning. Picky customers will love Gran Torino: even if the dish they want isn't on the menu, the cook will make just about anything they request, as long as the ingredients are available.

Hunan Seafood King. 3081 Emmons Avenue, near Knapp Street, 891-9068. Daily, 12:30–11 p.m. Major credit cards.

If you like Chinese seafood dishes, chances are you'll like the food here. Hunan Seafood King takes advantage of being down by the docks and gets the freshest ingredients it can. Not only that, but the dining room is remarkably modern and spacious. If you're coming by car, take exit 9 off Shore Parkway.

Joe's Clam Bar. 2009 Emmons Avenue, at East 21st Street, 646-9373. Mon.–Thurs., 10 a.m.–10 p.m.; Fri.–Sun., 10 a.m.–midnight. Major credit cards.

If you like fresh shellfish and the ambience of a fisherman's dock, Joe's has both. It's been serving moderately priced fresh seafood for three generations and is a local favorite. Joe's is right across from the fishing boat piers.

Maria's Restaurant. 3073 Emmons Avenue, near Brown Street, 646-6665. Daily, noon–11 p.m.; closed Tues. Major credit cards. ✱

For more than fifty years Maria has won the hearts of locals. The food is fresh, the service is friendly, and it is as good a restaurant for the entire family as you're likely to find. There are many seafood specials, along with traditional veal Milanese, chicken *rollatini*, and pasta dishes. Most entrées are about $10. And since the restaurant is just a few blocks from the fishing piers, you can take a stroll before or after you eat.

Paradise. 2814 Emmons Avenue, between Nostrand and Bedford avenues, 934-2283. Fri.–Sun., 9 p.m.–3 a.m.; Sun., 7 p.m.–1 a.m. Major credit cards.

The scene at Paradise is hard to match, at least this side of the Volga. At this Russian nightclub you can plan on a late night of dancing, eating, and general fun. It is open only on weekends, when the eleven-piece band playing "international" music is the big attraction. The food is plentiful, good, and heavy; the cost is about $45 a person. As with the other Russian hot nightspots in nearby Brighton Beach, expect to stay late and find a sober driver to take you home. Reservations are required.

Randazzo's Italian Seafood Restaurant and Clam Bar. 2127 Emmons Avenue (restaurant) and 2017-23 Emmons Avenue (clam bar), between Ocean and Bedford avenues, 769-1000. Daily, noon–midnight. Major credit cards. ✳

Unpretentious, noisy, and fun, Randazzo's has been serving up a decent shrimp diablo, pasta, and fresh broiled fish for more than fifteen years. It's a relaxed, casual place with moderate prices. Randazzo's Clam Bar down the street at 2017-2023 Emmons Avenue (615-0010), specializes in fried calamari, scungilli, and baked clams and its outdoor clam bar delivers all over Brooklyn.

Scoop Du Jour Cafe. 1738 Sheepshead Bay Road, at Shore Parkway, 646-4923. ✳

Started by four women partners some ten years ago, this quiet little café is a great place to stop for coffee, sweets, ice cream, and hand-dipped chocolates. It's just a few blocks away from Emmons Avenue if you want a break from the fishing pier ambience. A sister shop, **Grace and Company Bake Shop**, is located on 3rd Avenue in Bay Ridge.

VIP Yachts Luxury Dining. 2239 Emmons Avenue, at Pier 5, 934-1014. Lunch: Mon., Wed., Fri., and Sat., 11:30 a.m.–3 p.m. Dinner: Mon.–Thurs., 7:30–10:30 p.m.; Fri., 8 p.m.–midnight; Sat., 7:30–11 p.m.; Sun., 5–9 p.m.

Brooklyn is bounded by water on three sides, so why not take a VIP cruise from Sheepshead Bay? The 120-person *Tampa*, a renovated fishing boat, and the larger 200-person *Romance*, a catamaran, offer moonlight, lunch, weekday, and weekend dinner cruises. A big Sunday buffet brunch cruise is also available. You can't beat the views of the Statue of Liberty and New York Harbor. Prices are in the $30 to $40 range. Reservations are required.

"Inland" restaurants worth checking out include the following:

Abbracciamento on the Pier. 2200 Rockaway Parkway, off exit 13 from the Belt Parkway, 251-5517. Sun.–Thurs., noon–11 p.m.; Fri.–Sat., noon–midnight. Major credit cards.

As you dine on Italian specialties and seafood, enjoy great views of Jamaica Bay. The peripherals here are a real attraction: the panorama, piano music in the evenings, outdoor balcony dining, and yes, courtesy docking for those who arrive by boat. Located near Kennedy Airport (not exactly in Sheepshead Bay!), it is off the beaten track but certainly offers an elegant way to reenter reality after jetting—or boating—home from a vacation. Dinner entrées range from $15 up. There is a champagne brunch on Sunday.

Brennan and Carr. 3432 Nostrand Avenue, at Avenue U, 769-1254. Mon.–Thurs., 10 a.m.–1 a.m., Fri.–Sat., 11 a.m.–2 a.m.; Sun., 11 a.m.–1 p.m. ✳

The aroma of roast beef positively wafts out of this unassuming red brick building. Brennan and Carr has been around for about fifty years, and this is still one of the best places in Brooklyn for roast beef. A good-size sandwich is about $3.50; a full plate that includes french fries and vegetables is under $9. You can take out or eat in the small, pleasant back room. A small parking lot is on the premises.

Fiorentino. 311 Avenue U, near McDonald Avenue, 372-1445. Daily, noon–midnight. Major credit cards. ✱

This large, noisy, busy two hundred–person restaurant got a rave review in the *New York Daily News* a few years ago, which brought so many people here that it was hard to get a table. The reason is clear: excellent Italian fare at moderate prices in a very convenient location on one of Sheepshead Bay's neighborhood shopping strips. Weekend reservations are recommended. A branch of the family that owns Fiorentino started **Carolina's Restaurant** in Coney Island (see page 86).

Michael's Restaurant. 2929 Avenue R, near Nostrand Avenue, 998-7851. Daily, noon–11 p.m. Major credit cards.

The setting couldn't be nicer at this family-owned, 150-seat restaurant. Live music, moderately priced excellent food—the menu runs seven pages— and a steady clientele have contributed to its success for twenty-five years. It is located in Marine Park between Sheepshead Bay and Midwood. Reservations are needed on weekends.

Nino's Restaurant. 1971 Coney Island Avenue, between Avenue P and Quentin Road, 336-7872. Daily, noon–11 p.m. Major credit cards.

Brooklynites who wander the borough in search of good Italian fare say that moderately priced Nino's ranks high for tasty northern and southern cuisine. Pasta dishes run $8 to $10, and seafood entrées are a few dollars more. Reservations are recommended on weekends, as it can get busy.

Pizzarini Natural. 2812 Ocean Avenue, near Avenue X, 648-4248. Daily, 11 a.m.–11 p.m. ✱

Health-conscious types will love the eat-in–take-out menu here: whole wheat batter-dipped zucchini, stir-fried vegetables, lots of salads, and interesting stuffings for pita bread sandwiches. But not all is straight from the garden: the menu also includes such old favorites as chicken florentine, beef and broccoli, and shrimp marinara. Good quality, a broad range of entrées under $9, and a commitment to fresh ingredients make this a good choice. It is close to Sheepshead Bay shopping.

Roll 'N' Roaster. 2901 Avenue U, at Nostrand Avenue, 769-5831. Daily, 11 a.m.–1 a.m. ✱

The owners call this "a grownup fast-food restaurant" serving roast beef, burgers and fries. In business for more than twenty years, Roll 'N' Roaster is a little more expensive than fast-food chains, but it sells good food in a very clean environment.

Senior's Restaurant. 3752 Nostrand Avenue, near Avenue Y, 743-5700. Wed.–Mon., 11 a.m.–11 p.m.; closed Tues. Major credit cards. ✷

Super casual and good for kids, you can get away with a $15-per-person dinner of wholesome Jewish-style food: chicken and two vegetables, for instance. The service isn't great and the lines can be long, but it's a fine place to go if you don't feel like cooking at home. Senior's has no relationship to **Junior's**, the famous downtown Brooklyn restaurant (see page 117).

SHOPPING

Specialty Food Shops

Continental Pastry Shop. 1715 Sheepshead Bay Road, between Shore Parkway and Voorhies Avenue, 934-6596. Daily, 8 a.m.–6:30 p.m. ✷

There are a few small tables here where you can enjoy cappuccino and espresso. Try the strudel, cream cakes, butter cookies, or ricotta-filled pastries for a pick-me-up after shopping.

G & S Pork Store. 2611 Avenue U, between East 26th and East 27th streets, 646-9111. Mon.–Sat., 8 a.m.–7 p.m.; Sun., 8 a.m.–4 p.m.

Did you know that a six-foot-long hero feeds twenty-five people? It will if you buy it here, for about $12 per foot. Or, try the cooked specials, sausages, fresh mozzarella, and other cheeses at this Italian specialty store.

Jordan's Lobster Dock. 3165 Harkness Avenue, off Belt Parkway, 934-6300. Sun.–Thurs., 9 a.m.–6 p.m.; Fri. and Sat., 9 a.m.–7 p.m. Major credit cards. ✷

You may feel as if you're in Seattle or Cape Cod at this appealing shop that overlooks a harbor full of cabin cruisers. This is no average fish store—you can actually walk out with a complete meal. Jordan's sells delicious take-out Manhattan and New England clam chowder; lobsters steamed to order while you wait; fresh cooked shrimp; and a full clam bar from which to select your evening appetizers. There's also plenty of fresh raw fish, baskets of clams, and frozen shrimp, octopus, Alaskan king crab claws, and squid, along with plenty of condiments. Kids will enjoy watching the staff clean and chop the fresh fish and catch live lobsters from a three-tiered holding pen. A little out of the way, Jordan's is behind the cinema complex known as **UA Movies at Sheepshead Bay** (see page 90). You'll know it by the huge statue of a fisherman in foul weather gear out front.

Pita Bakery. 2610 Avenue U, between East 26th and East 27th streets, 934-4717. Mon.–Fri., 6 a.m.–1 p.m.

You have to be an early bird to get these unusual pita breads fresh from the oven. They are made in flavors, such as garlic, thyme, onion-garlic, and sesame. If you can't get to this wholesale bakery between 7 and 8 a.m., you'll find the flavored pitas in Middle Eastern grocery stores along Kings Highway between East 2nd and East 5th streets.

Weisen's Bake Shop. 1510 Sheepshead Bay Road, between East 15th and East 16th streets, 646-9241. Wed.–Mon., 5:30 a.m.–8:30 p.m.; closed Tues. ✳

An old-fashioned atmosphere and luscious breads, cookies, pies, and pastries make this a tasty place to stock up on calories. There are a few small tables and chairs, so you can have a cup of coffee and munch your treat on the spot.

Interesting Neighborhood Shops

Ace Leather Products. 2211 Avenue U, between East 22nd and East 23rd streets, 891-9713 (1-800-DIAL-ACE). Mon.–Sat., 10 a.m.–6 p.m.; Thurs., 10 a.m.–8 p.m. Major credit cards.

You'd drive right by this place if you didn't know what was inside: a fantastic selection of name-brand luggage and accessories, from leather handbags and wallets to portable shavers and alarm clocks, all at least 25 percent below retail prices. With merchandise no different from what sells on Madison Avenue, this is a perfect place to shop for gifts. The store also publishes an extensive catalog.

Allen & Suzi. 1713 Sheepshead Bay Road, between Shore Parkway and Voorhies Avenue, 332-7003. Mon.–Fri., 11 a.m.–7 p.m.; Sat., 10 a.m.–6 p.m.; Sun., noon–5 p.m. Major credit cards.

This women's clothing shop has stylishly eclectic merchandise and clientele. Half the items are new, and half are interesting consignment items. There's plenty of black Lycra and up-to-the-minute fashions here, including some fun and outrageously sexy pieces. You'll also find a small selection of heavily discounted off-season designer evening wear. Toward the back of the store are racks of high-quality consignment clothing, including 1950s and 1960s styles, and last year's cocktail dresses and fur coats. The much-publicized Allen & Suzi store on Columbus Avenue and 80th Street in Manhattan is a spin-off of the Brooklyn store.

Designer Shoes Boutique. 1414 Avenue Z, near Sheepshead Bay Road, 743-1008. Mon.–Sat., 10:30 a.m.–7 p.m.; Sun., noon–5 p.m. Major credit cards.

Slightly off the main shopping drag, this men's shoe store has a nice selection of heavily discounted imported and American shoes. Brand names include Bally, Boston, Brutine, Cardin, Zodiac, and Keds.

Downtown. 2502 Avenue U, corner of East 25th Street, 934-8280. Mon.–Sat., 11 a.m.–6 p.m.; Thurs., 11 a.m.–8 p.m.; Sun., 11 a.m.–5 p.m. Major credit cards. ✱

You'd expect a certain upbeat style in a shop that sports a sign reading OUTFITTERS FOR THE URBAN WILDERNESS. Indeed, Downtown carries a huge line of better sportswear for the young and/or trim set at lower prices than you'd find in major department stores. Familiar brands include Head, Swatch, Obermeyer, Champion, Vuarnet, and more. The ambience created by the family that has run the store for two generations is fun and friendly.

E. J. Robins. 1711 Sheepshead Bay Road, between Shore Parkway and Voorhies Avenue, 646-7500. Mon.–Wed. and Fri.–Sat., 11 a.m.–7 p.m.; Thurs., 11 a.m.–8 p.m.; Sun., noon–5 p.m.

Why fight the crowds at a big department store when you can get the same high-fashion designer shoes (Charles Jourdan, among others) for less money and less hassle? A visit here is worthwhile, especially during seasonal sales.

Field Brothers. 1665 Sheepshead Bay Road, between Emmons and Voorhies avenues, 615-3030. Mon.–Wed. and Fri.–Sat. 11 a.m.–6:45 p.m.; Thurs., 11 a.m.–8:30 p.m.; Sun., noon–5 p.m. Major credit cards.

This men's department store is part of a national chain now, but it started out as a local store on Kings Highway. The ambience is reminiscent of the men's department in an old department store, like the now-defunct Altman's: carpeted, calm, and classic. Field Brothers sells moderate to better brand-name suits, including Dior, Mani, Valentino, Louis Roth, and LeBaron, plus sportcoats, slacks, and accessories. Alterations are free.

Harvey's Sporting Goods. 3179 Emmons Avenue, corner of Bragg Street., 743-0054. Mon.–Tues. and Thurs.–Fri., 11 a.m.–8:30 p.m.; Wed. and Sat., 11 a.m.–6 p.m.; closed Sun. Major credit cards. ✱

The triangular doorway may remind you of a ski chalet. This is the place for skiing, tennis, and scuba diving gear. Harvey's specializes in the sports its proprietor and workers know best. The diving gear is top notch, with plenty to choose from. The high-quality ski clothing, which includes such brands as CB Sports, is often discounted.

Jamar. 1714 Sheepshead Bay Road, between Shore Parkway and Voorhies Avenue, 615-2222. Mon.–Sat., 11 a.m.–5:30 p.m.; Thurs., 11 a.m.–7:30 p.m.; closed Sun. Major credit cards.

Specializing in fine jewelry and giftware with brand names such as Movado, Lenox, and Waterford, this little store sells many of the better-quality items you'd expect to find only in larger Manhattan department stores. Some lines are discounted from 10 to 40 percent. The friendly sales staff will work with you on special orders.

Jazz, Jazzman, and Jazzbaby. 1732 and 1736 Sheepshead Bay Road, between Shore Parkway and Voorhies Avenue, 332-1100. Mon.–Sat., 10 a.m.–6 p.m.; Sun., noon–5 p.m. Major credit cards. ✷

Jazz operates three separate shops in two locations along Sheepshead Bay Road—one for women, one for men, one for kids. The youthful styles are selected to appeal to what locals call "sharp" dressers; conservative dressers may find some items flashy. Jazz (332-1100), the women's shop, has American and French designer sportswear. Sweaters are in the $100 range, shirt-and-skirt or -pant sets in the $140 range. Jazzman (332-4220), the men's store down the street, features such brands as Shanghai, Mexx, and White on White; shirts range from $50, and sweaters and slacks go from $40 to $100. The new Jazzbaby shop (934-9100) has better-quality American and imported clothing for infants through kids ten years old, with outfits averaging $70.

Joseph's Tape and Record World. 2727 Coney Island Avenue, between Avenue X and Avenue Y, 648-4639. Mon.–Sat., 11 a.m.–6 p.m.; closed Sun. Major credit cards.

Having trouble finding that favorite oldie? Come here. There are thousands of records from the fifties and sixties on display, and more in the warehouse. Musicians from California to London write or trek here seeking original LPs or 45s of classic jazz, rock and roll, and big band numbers. There is also a good selection of contemporary rock, jazz, vocalists, and classical recordings on compact disc and cassette tape. Located near the end of Coney Island Avenue, it is close to both Sheepshead Bay and Brighton Beach shopping areas.

Kabat Variety. 1639 Sheepshead Bay Road, between Jerome and Voorhies avenues, 332-8390, Mon.–Sat., 9 a.m.–7 p.m.; Sun., 10:30 a.m.–4 p.m. ✷

The wonderful old-fashioned sign out front still says GRAND VARIETY, although the store is now called Kabat. In the spirit of the old neighborhood, there's a five-and-dime appeal to this place. When you can't find those little things you need around the house (buttons, plastic tablecloths, bulletin boards, pool thongs) and the boutiques in your neighborhood don't carry them, you'll probably find them here.

Learning Wheel. 1514 Avenue Z, between East 15th and East 16th streets, 934-5540. Mon.–Fri., 11 a.m.–6 p.m.; Sat., 11 a.m.–5:30 p.m.; closed Sun. Major credit cards. ✳

You could call this the toy equivalent to a health food store—a large store dedicated to educational supplies. The target market is schoolteachers, but kids and parents will find plenty of games, art supplies, books, flash cards, workbooks, math and language games, puzzles, stickers, posters, and other gizmos here. The shop is a few blocks from Sheepshead Bay Road, but it's within walking distance. Ask to see the mail-order catalog. Phone orders are accepted.

Lester's. 2411 Coney Island Avenue, near Avenue U, 336-3560. Fri.–Mon. and Wed., 10 a.m.–6 p.m.; Tues. and Thurs., 10 a.m.–9 p.m. Major credit cards. ✳

Lester's is a famous discount family clothing empire. Started in 1940, the seven separate stores feature trendy styles for girls, boys, and preteen juniors. Other shops feature activewear; men's clothing and shoes; women's and kids' shoes; and clothing for infants and toddlers. This is a great place to divide and conquer—each family member to his or her own shop. Prices on name brands are about 20 percent below department store prices.

MB Discount Furniture. 2311 Avenue U, between East 23rd and 24th streets, 332-1500. Mon., Tues., Thurs., and Fri., 10 a.m.–9 p.m.; Wed. and Sat., 10 a.m.–6 p.m.; closed Sun. Major credit cards. ✳

The huge showroom here is packed with lovely, high-quality American and imported gear for the youngest generation: cribs, high chairs, and rocking chairs. The layette selection is equally attractive. Sales staff are service-oriented and friendly, and prices are heavily discounted. They'll help you design the color scheme and theme of your child's room for free. Delivery is available for a modest fee.

PJS Cosmetics. 2516 Avenue U, between East 25th and 26th streets, 646-1151. Mon.–Sat., 9 a.m.–6 p.m.; Thurs.–Fri., 9 a.m.–7 p.m.; closed Sun. Major credit cards.

Better brands of cosmetics and perfumes are sold at a discount here, from Borghese, Orlane, and Elizabeth Arden skin products to Chanel, Guerlain, and Christian Dior perfumes. There's also a good selection of jewelry and other accessories. A $25 makeover is free if your purchases total more than $50.

Sam Ash. 1669 East 13th Street, between Kings Highway and Avenue P, 645-3886. Tues., Wed., Fri., and Sat., 10 a.m.–6 p.m.; Mon. and Thurs., 10 a.m.–9 p.m.; Sun., noon–5 p.m. Major credit cards.

This Brooklyn-born institution has been "serving Brooklyn since 1924" and is famous nationwide among musicians as a discounter of top-quality musical instruments. Today there are plenty of electric guitars, synthesizers, and high-tech equipment to choose from, as well as more traditional instruments.

Seahorse. 1716 Sheepshead Bay Road, between Shore Parkway and Voorhies Avenue, 646-9133. Mon.–Wed., Fri., and Sat., 10 a.m.–7 p.m.; Thurs., 10 a.m.–8 p.m. Major credit cards. ✷

You won't find a more sophisticated and attractive collection of swimwear for the entire family north of Rio. Husband-and-wife team Marcel and Nancy Goldfarb have assembled an exciting range of imported Israeli and Italian swimwear for women, men, boys, and girls that includes such brand names as Gottex, Diva, Gideon Oberon, and Liza Bruce. They also sell beach shoes, bags, and other paraphernalia. Women's suits start at $40; top-of-the-line Le Perla suits cost about $200.

Tantrum's Kids' Shop. 2616 Avenue U, near East 26th Street, 615-0594. Mon.–Sat., 10 a.m.–6 p.m.; Sun., 11 a.m.–5 p.m. Major credit cards. ✷

Unusual, stylish clothes for boys and girls up to size 16 include three-piece outfits and sophisticated print and adorable off-the-shoulder party dresses. Name brands include Monkeywear and Arachine. Outfits average about $50.

In nearby Mill Basin you'll find the following:

Kings Plaza Shopping Center. Corner of Flatbush Avenue and Avenue U, 253-6842. Mon.–Sat., 10 a.m.–9:30 p.m.; Sun, noon–5 p.m. Parking is $1. ✷.

Anchored by Macy's at one end and Alexander's at the other, this mall has more than 135 different retailers under one roof. Clothing and shoes make up about one-quarter of all the merchandise sold here, but food, sporting goods, and jewelry are also heavily represented. Besides national chains (the Gap, Benetton, Hoffritz, and Radio Shack, to name a few), many smaller outfits (Smitty's, Undercover Agent), and regional shops (such as Bowery Lighting and Kaufman Carpets) have outlets here. Little kids can ride the indoor carousel on the lower level, and older kids can wander at will or watch one of four movies at the mall's RKO Century Theater while the adults shop (or maybe it's the other way around). Within walking distance on Flatbush

Avenue are other major chains, such as The Wiz, Lerner's and Seaman's. In the summer, weekly indoor concerts are sponsored by BACA (see page 108).

Toys "Я" Us. 2875 Flatbush Avenue, between Belt Parkway and Kings Plaza Shopping Center, across from Marine Park Golf Course, 258-2061. Mon.– Sat., 9:30 a.m.–9:30 p.m.; Sun., 10 a.m.—6 p.m. Major credit cards. ✷

Brooklyn has two Toys "Я" Us stores. Like its Bensonhurst counterpart, this Mill Basin branch of the national chain has just about anything a kid could want—at low, discounted prices. As at all Toys "Я" Us stores, disposable diapers and baby food are about as cheap as you'll ever find them.

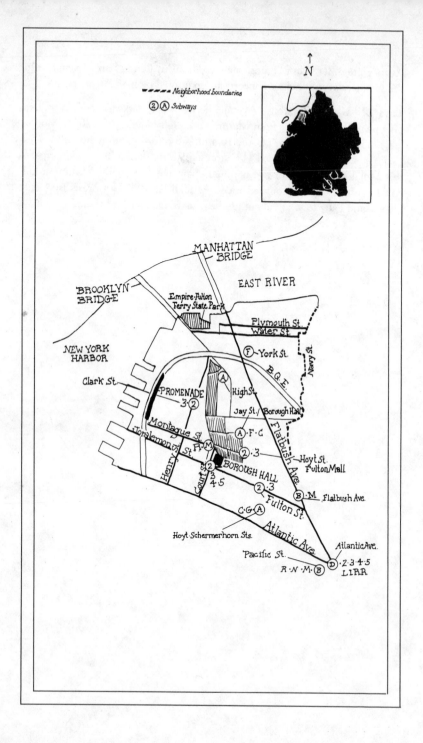

BROOKLYN HEIGHTS AND ENVIRONS

BROOKLYN HEIGHTS

Where it is: Bounded by Atlantic Avenue to the south, Cadman Plaza to the east, and the East River on the north and west.

What's nearby: Carroll Gardens, Cobble Hill, and Fort Greene.

How to get there:
By *car:* Take the first exit off the Brooklyn Bridge and proceed to Court Street.
By *subway:* Take the 2 or 3 train to Clark Street; 4 or 5 train to Borough Hall; M or R train to Court Street; or A, C, or F train to Jay Street.
Cab services: Promenade (858-6666), Atlantic (797-5666), or Janice (797-5773). Cost is about $12 from Grand Central Station, $15 from Sheepshead Bay.

Special events: Art show twice yearly; summer concerts on the Promenade. Brownstone tour through the interiors of restored private landmark homes (May).

How it got its name: Dubbed "the Heights" because of the knoll (now the Promenade) that overlooks New York Harbor. "Brooklyn," of course, is a corruption of "Breukelen," the eighteenth-century Dutch township.

What's Included in This Chapter

This chapter includes four areas: Brooklyn Heights, Atlantic Avenue, the area between the Manhattan and Brooklyn Bridges known as DUMBO, and a few highlights of downtown Brooklyn along Flatbush Avenue and in the Fulton Mall.

As delightful as Brooklyn's little neighborhoods are, the division of the borough into so many of them can be confusing for the tourist. Because we couldn't cover each and every neighborhood, readers will find bits of downtown Brooklyn and Cobble Hill listed under "Brooklyn Heights." Boerum Hill does not appear at all, but some of the shops in that neighborhood are listed under "Atlantic Avenue." We hope this caveat will quell the outrage this may produce among any neighborhood purists.

ABOUT THE NEIGHBORHOOD

Given its proximity to Manhattan, the Heights is the one Brooklyn neighborhood that most Manhattanites have heard of. (After all, the Manhattan skyline is reassuringly visible from here.) Tourists weary of the bustle of midtown Manhattan marvel at the almost European nineteenth-century charm of Brooklyn Heights. Locals describe their small (by Brooklyn standards) neighborhood of thirty thousand in similar terms: urbane in its sophistication, yet provincial in its neighborliness.

Whether shopping on the civilized "high" streets, soaking up the architectural treasures of well-kept brownstones and churches, or gazing at the enchanting Manhattan skyline at twilight from the **Promenade**, you will find that Brooklyn Heights has something to offer even the most itinerant visitor. Amid streets with names like Cranberry, Pineapple, and Orange, you can glimpse a backyard garden blooming in spring or sidewalks awash in the fallen leaves of autumn.

If you're seeking action, there is plenty here. The **St. Ann Center for Restoration and the Arts** offers an eclectic program including opera, jazz, and experimental theater; its sixty famous restored stained glass windows, the first made in the United States, are rare treasures. **BACA Downtown** is a showcase for avant-garde performance art. Exhibits at **Brooklyn's History Museum** and lunchtime tours of **Borough Hall** shed light on interesting bits of Brooklyn-abilia. And the **New York Transit Museum** is a must-see for kids.

Montague Street, a small four-block street that runs west toward the **Promenade** has restaurants, outdoor cafés, shops, and wonderful children's stores. Wandering the neighboring streets is a treat. On peaceful **Willow Street** are several Federal-style homes of architectural note (see particularly numbers 155, 157, and 159). **Grace Court Alley**, once used as a stable alley for fancy homes on Remsen Street, is a charming mews. **Pierrepont Street** is graced with some of New York City's most beautiful residences (numbers 2, 3, and 82), and Garden Place, Sidney Place, and Hunts Lane are pleasant detours from Joralemon Street. (For more tips on walking tours, contact the **Brooklyn Historical Society** or the **Fund for the Borough of Brooklyn**, listed below, to obtain a brochure, *Downtown Brooklyn Walking Tours*.)

Historical Notes

History has been kind to Brooklyn Heights. An aristocratic urban center in the nineteenth century, it deteriorated after the 1930s until a vigorous preservation movement during the 1960s led to the designation of some thirty blocks as New York's first historic district. The renaissance started by preservationists was completed by an influx of Wall Street lawyers and bankers during the late 1970s and 1980s. But for many lean years Brooklyn Heights was a bohemian haven. The young artists and writers who lived amid its slightly seedy, decaying elegance and subsequently became famous include Hart Crane, W. H. Auden, Walker Evans, John Dos Passos, Richard Wright, Thomas Wolfe, Arthur Miller, Norman Rosten, Alfred Kazin, Truman Capote, and Norman Mailer.

First settled by the Dutch, Brooklyn Heights dates to the mid-1800s. It was the civic and commercial heart of the then-independent city of Brooklyn. Secluded from Manhattan by lack of transportation other than the Fulton Ferry or private boat, Brooklyn Heights was developed by wealthy Protestant bankers, industrialists, and shipping magnates whose piers and ships were nearby. The Heights was the home of the activist nineteenth-century **Plymouth Church**, where Charles Dickens spoke and abolitionist Henry Ward Beecher preached; Walt Whitman, editor of the *Brooklyn Eagle*, first published *Leaves of Grass* here.

Many of Brooklyn's unique cultural institutions got their start here. The **Brooklyn Historical Society** was founded in the Heights under a different name in the 1860s, as were the Brooklyn Philharmonic and the original **Brooklyn Academy of Music**, first housed on Montague Street. **Packer Collegiate Institute**, housed in a fabulous Gothic building designed by Minard

Lafever, and Borough Hall, which in the mid-nineteenth century was an elegant rival to Manhattan's City Hall across the river, were both built in this era. Among the prominent citizens who grew up here was Seth Low, who became mayor of Brooklyn, president of Columbia University, and finally mayor of New York City.

The opening of the Brooklyn Bridge in 1883 destroyed the exclusivity of this remarkable community. The elite retreated to fashionable Clinton Hill, Park Slope, or Manhattan's then-developing "Gold Coast" on upper Fifth Avenue. Brooklyn Heights lost its status as an independent municipal civic center in 1898 when New York City incorporated the city of Brooklyn. Fortunately, Brooklyn Heights's early, aristocratic architecture has been preserved for later generations.

Kidstuff

Parents with kids in tow have a wide variety of choices in the Brooklyn Heights–Atlantic Avenue–Waterfront area. You can play along the **Promenade** or watch pita bread being made at the **Damascus Bakery** factory. The key is transportation, as many of these attractions are just far enough from each other to tire out small legs.

Speaking of transportation, kids can get their fill of all forms of locomotion. Combine a walk over the **Brooklyn Bridge** with a visit to the **New York City Transit Museum** or explore the **Atlantic Avenue Tunnel**. A trip to the piers to watch whatever huge ship is in port is always entertaining. There are plenty of shops catering to kids here, including **Cousin Arthur's**, Brooklyn's only literary hangout for the preteen set.

The littlest ones will find plenty to do just running up and down the many multi-stepped stoops. Try Hicks Street and the adjacent Garden Place mews just two blocks from Joralemon Street. As is the case in much of Brooklyn, the local firefighters are very friendly and open to showing curious children around their trucks.

ENTERTAINMENT

BACA Downtown. 111 Willoughby Street, Bridge and Duffield streets, 596-2222. Call for exhibit hours.

Both theater and visual arts are located at BACA Downtown, one of many projects run by the Brooklyn Arts Council, known as BACA Theater. Recognized by both *The New York Times* and the *Village Voice* as one of the leading innovative nonprofit exhibition and performance spaces in New York City,

d because it is in downtown Brooklyn—has an
lace where you can expect the unexpected.
ase for avant-garde music, dance, theater, and
Fringe Theater Series stages five to six plays
e to four weeks. Other programs include the
owcases new performance artists, and the New
lirectors. Performers and audiences alike are
sophisticated. The free-wheeling programs
r example, the chair show, the shoe show,
ice art featuring one person and forty puppet

wo visual arts galleries represent a range of
, photography, and installation works. The
uesday through Saturday, with weekend performances on
Friday and Saturday evenings.

Note: BACA Downtown's address may change in 1991.

Brooklyn Heights Cinema. 70 Henry Street, corner of Orange Street, 596-7070 or 596-7124. Call for times.

Cozy, old, and informal, this double-screen cinema is a local favorite. It is very near to **Su-Su's Yum Yum** Chinese restaurant (see page 118) and **Henry's End** restaurant (page 117) and within walking distance of Montague Street restaurants as well.

Brooklyn Heights Players. 26 Willow Place, between State and Joralemon streets, 237-2752. Call for a schedule. ✳

This resident theater company has produced both adult and children's musicals and dramas for more than fifteen years. Director's Workshops sometimes yield surprisingly original works, and the price of admission is $5 or less for children.

Diane Jacobowitz Dance Company. Triangle Theater—Long Island College, at DeKalb and Flatbush avenues, 622-1810. Call for a schedule and prices.

Several dozen performances are given each year by this modern dance company in residence, a multiracial group with a social conscience, who perform for disadvantaged groups as well as for the general public. There are open rehearsals, lectures, and demonstrations.

Fund for the Borough of Brooklyn. 16 Court Street, at Montague Street, 855-7882.

Need more tips about Brooklyn? The Fund for the Borough of Brooklyn publishes informative material, including "Brooklyn on Tour" (a map), *Down-*

town Brooklyn Beat (a newsletter), the Downtown Brooklyn Handbook, Downtown Brooklyn Walking Tours, The Brooklyn Fact and Trivia Book, plus books about neighborhoods, shopping, and things to do with kids. Get them by mail for a small fee from the fund, or for free if you pick them up at the Borough President's Office, 209 Joralemon Street. The fund organizes the Welcome Back to Brooklyn Festival in June and the Celebrate Brooklyn concerts in Prospect Park, and manages the **Rotunda Gallery** (see page 115).

The St. Ann Center for Restoration and the Arts. 157 Montague Street, corner of Clinton Street, 834-8794. Call for a schedule. *

The Arts at St. Ann's program, established in 1979, sponsors eclectic and professional programs from Bach cantatas to Marianne Faithfull. Shows include opera, jazz, blues, dance, and theater. Along with the **Brooklyn Academy of Music (BAM)**, St. Ann's has a reputation for showing some experimental new works, along with those of established artists.

Shadow Box Theater. YWCA–Memorial Hall, 30 3rd Avenue, between Atlantic Avenue and State Street, 875-1190. Call (212) 724-0677 for a schedule. Tickets are about $3.

With its original scripts and contemporary themes, this children's puppet repertory company has been a staple for New York City schools for over twenty years. In 1990 Shadow Box found a permanent home for its October–June season here at the YWCA's Memorial Hall. Expect to see a range of small and large puppets, actors, and shadow puppets in shows that convey a message, often about social values. Titles have included such shows as "Sing Out for Peace," "Uno, Dos, Tres—One, Two, Three," and "Little Is Big" (a show about nonviolence). The theater is not far from the Heights, Carroll Gardens, and the shops on Atlantic Avenue.

TKTS—Brooklyn Information Booth. Borough Hall Park, near Court and Montague streets. Mon.–Fri., 11 a.m.–5 p.m.; Sat., 11 a.m.–3:30 p.m. On Mon., open for information only. No credit cards.

The TKTS booth sells half-price, day-of-performance tickets to both on- and off-Broadway shows as well as Brooklyn concert tickets, including those for the Brooklyn Academy of Music. Get there early, before they sell out. Maps, Brooklyn information packets, and listings of free summer concerts are also available.

PARKS AND PLAYGROUNDS

Brooklyn Heights Promenade. Along the East River; access at the end of Montague and Orange Streets, and streets in between. *

Take a stroll here for what may possibly be the most spectacular view of downtown Manhattan to be had with your feet still on the ground. Also visible are the Statue of Liberty, the Brooklyn Bridge, and a constant flow of tugs, barges, and other harbor traffic. There are free outdoor concerts on summer evenings, and twice a year **BACA** (see page 108) sponsors a multimedia art show. But even if nothing's going on, you can sit or walk in peace. End to end, the Promenade is less than half a mile.

Pierrepont Playground. Columbia Place, at the end of Montague Street. ✳

Where else can a two-year-old play on a slide with a million-dollar view? This large, well-kept, and safe playground is a classic, with climbing equipment and lots of sand for toddlers and older kids. A popular place for parents, babysitters, and grandparents, it is also one of the borough's half dozen "quiet zones," where radio playing is prohibited.

POINTS OF CULTURAL INTEREST

Abraham & Straus. 420 Fulton Street, corner of Hoyt Street, 875-7200. Sun., noon–5 p.m.; Mon.–Sat., 9:45 a.m.–6 p.m.; open late on Thurs. Major credit cards. ✳

The history of this 125-year-old chain goes back in Brooklyn lore to a young Bavarian immigrant, Abraham Abraham, who turned a small dry goods shop into an innovative new concept in retailing: the one-stop department store. Abraham chose this 1870s cast iron building for his new store after correctly figuring that the area would flourish along with the opening of the new Brooklyn Bridge. A & S was fitted with stunning amenities and luxuries, such as lounging parlors for female shoppers, and a mineral spa. Renovated and enlarged in the 1920s, the decorative Art Deco building, complete with paned glass, twenty-foot ceilings, and brass-and-glass elevators was once the centerpiece of downtown Brooklyn shopping and continues to attract shoppers from all over.

Borough Hall. 209 Joralemon Street, between Adams and Court streets, 802-3700. Free tours are on Wed., 12:30–1:30 p.m. and 5:30–6:30 p.m., 855-7882. ✳

In the summertime you can enjoy this lovely place by simply bringing a bag lunch to the grand marble steps. But for civics, history, or architecture buffs, a tour of the recently restored 1848 Borough Hall, one of New York's most fabulous Greek Revival landmark buildings, is a must. Built in the era when Brooklyn was a city separate from Manhattan (they merged in 1898), it is larger than City Hall and considerably more sumptuous. High points include a hammered brass cupola restored by the same French craftsmen who restored the Statue of Liberty; a spectacular courtroom, grand rotunda, and portico; and a gorgeous marble exterior from which a century of grime was recently removed. Today it is the office of Brooklyn's borough president. Guided tours are available; groups can make reservations.

Brooklyn Heights Association Landmark House and Garden Tour. 858-9193. House tours run periodically throughout the year and cost about $25 each. Call for a schedule.

Maybe you're a landmarks buff, or you're just interested in ideas for restoring your own apartment or home. Either way, join the many veterans of Brooklyn Heights house tours as they visit private homes and landscaped gardens in historic sections of the Heights.

Brooklyn's History Museum and Brooklyn Historical Society. 128 Pierrepont Street, between Clinton and Henry streets, 624-0890. Museum: Tues.–Sun., noon–5 p.m. Library: Tues.–Sat., 10 a.m.–4:45 p.m. Nonmembers $2.50; children under twelve, $1. ✳

Take a tour here and you'll know more about Brooklyn than Ralph Kramden himself. This little-known gem of an institution houses the country's largest single collection of Brooklyn history in an elegant 1880 landmark building. Peek into the fabulous wood-paneled two-story library, then plan to spend awhile at the new four thousand-square-foot Brooklyn's History Museum. Imaginative displays include a model of the Brooklyn Bridge, a huge zinc eagle from the *Brooklyn Daily Eagle* building, scaffolding reminiscent of Coney Island, a mock-up newsstand featuring ethnic papers in many languages, and much more. The themes of the show are such primal Brooklyn symbols as the Brooklyn Bridge, Coney Island, and the Dodgers. There's plenty here for the academic history buff as well. The Brooklyn Historical Society also organizes fascinating weekend walking tours, daily educational programs analyzing folk arts and borough history, and summer storytelling sessions for kids.

Long Island University. University Plaza–Flatbush Avenue, between Willoughby and DeKalb avenues, 403-1015.

Just a few blocks down Flatbush Avenue from the Manhattan Bridge, LIU maintains one of the few remaining grand theaters from Brooklyn's past. Metcalf Hall, at the corner of Flatbush and DeKalb, was once the Brooklyn Paramount. In 1933 part of the original *King Kong* movie was filmed here. The theater's 1930s vintage Wurlitzer organ, one of New York City's largest, is still used.

LIU's twenty-two-acre downtown Brooklyn campus is distinguished by a large, brightly colored sculpture on the front lawn. More than forty nationalities are represented in the student body, including a growing number of mainland Chinese and Koreans. The English and philosophy departments occasionally open their lectures to the public; to get on the mailing list, write: Long Island University, Office of Public Relations, Brooklyn, NY 11201.

MetroTech Center. A sixteen-acre site bounded by Flatbush Avenue, Willoughby Street, Jay Street, and Tech Place.

If downtown Brooklyn seems abuzz with construction, the MetroTech Center is one reason why. The earliest signs of the renaissance that will forever change Brooklyn's downtown are the buildings of MetroTech, a nine-block academic and business center with a technological focus. Four million square feet of office space and research and other facilities are under construction, along with three acres of planned open space and parks. The first tenants will include Brooklyn Union Gas, Chase Manhattan, and SIAC, which operates the computers of the New York and American stock exchanges, and Polytechnic's New York State Center for Advanced Technology in Telecommunications.

New York City Transit Museum. Schermerhorn Street, corner of Boerum Place, 330-3060. Call for hours. $1 admission. ✳

Kids will love pretending they are passengers in this subway museum, authentically located underground. Some of the beautifully restored old subway cars are open for visitors to walk through. The museum is home to a complete history of New York's transit system, the second largest in the world. It features fully restored cars of every major type plus models of trolleys, fare collection boxes, memorabilia, and a scale model of the entire New York system. Visitors can either take a turn at the wheel of a Metropolitan Transit Authority bus or watch movies. Small groups can visit a working subway tower. In the summertime there are occasional multimedia art exhibits.

Packer Collegiate Institute. 170 Joralemon Street, between Court and Clinton streets, 875-1644. Tours are by appointment.

It looks like an urban castle, with pinnacles, Gothic arches, and a tower. But look again, because Packer is one of Brooklyn's leading private schools. Originally a school for young ladies, the lovely building dates from 1854 and was designed by Minard Lafever; inside are original Tiffany windows.

Polytechnic University—Center for Advanced Technology in Telecommunications. 333 Jay Street near Flatbush Avenue, 260–3100. Many Brooklynites aren't even aware that in their midst is one of New York State's most promising high-tech institutes. Polytechnic was the leader in spurring the development of MetroTech, a combined academic and commercial park that is expected to create 16,000 jobs in the early 1990s. With its expertise in telecommunications and computer technology, Polytechnic is forging research relationships with some of the nation's most technologically advanced Fortune 500 companies.

Watchtower. 25 Columbia Heights, 625-3600.

The Watchtower and its Jehovah's Witness followers have large real estate holdings in Brooklyn Heights, although many residents prefer to turn a blind eye. Their properties include the prominent Watchtower building, visible from the bridge, at least one prime site on Montague Street, and various residences.

Churches

There are a number of noteworthy churches in Brooklyn Heights. Don't miss the following, all of which have Tiffany-made stained glass windows. For a more in-depth appreciation of local churches, a tour is recommended (see page 112).

First Presbyterian Church. 124 Henry Street, corner of Clark Street, 624-3770. Tours are by appointment.

Dating from 1846, the First Presbyterian Church is an early example of the many cultural, educational, and religious institutions built by the affluent mercantilists who first established Brooklyn Heights. It is located in an area settled because of its proximity to the Fulton Ferry. Starting in 1814 the ferry provided fast boats from Fulton Street in Brooklyn to Fulton Street in Manhattan. First Presbyterian, which has six Tiffany windows, is across the street from the German Evangelical Lutheran Zion Church, built in 1840.

Grace Church. 254 Hicks Street, corner of Grace Court, 624-1850. Tours are by appointment.

Detour a few short blocks from commercial Montague Street and you'll stumble upon this lovely 1847 church. It was designed by the prolific architect Richard Upjohn and boasts several Tiffany windows. Even in the late twentieth century, tradition is carried on by a formidable Boy's and Men's Choir. If you visit, check out Grace Court Alley nearby—it was a true mews built for the mansions on Remsen and Joralemon streets.

Plymouth Church of the Pilgrims. 75 Hicks Street, corner of Orange Street, 624-4743.

Few national historic landmarks are known for their association with progressive social causes. This one, dating back to the mid-nineteenth century, is called the "Grand Central Terminal of the Underground Railroad" and it was used by American slaves seeking asylum in the North and Canada. Suffragist and abolitionist Henry Ward Beecher was pastor here for some forty years. Others who spoke here include Mark Twain, Clara Barton, Booker T. Washington, and Martin Luther King, Jr. Don't miss the Tiffany windows or the sculpture of Beecher in the internal courtyard.

St. Ann's and the Holy Trinity Church. 157 Montague Street, corner of Clinton Street, 875-6960.

St. Ann's and the Holy Trinity Episcopal Church is a national historic landmark, noted for having sixty of the first stained glass windows made in the United States (by William and John Bolton). As part of the ongoing restoration of the church, there is an on-site facility for stained glass and sandstone preservation. The church is open from noon to 2 p.m. on weekdays, when you can view the windows and restoration project. It is also the home of **The St. Ann Center for Restoration and the Arts** (page 110).

Art Galleries and Exhibition Spaces

Curated exhibitions at **BACA's** two visual arts galleries represent a range of contemporary sculpture, painting, photography, and installation works. The galleries are open Tuesday through Saturday, with weekend performances on Friday and Saturday evenings.

Columbus Park. Cadman Plaza, at Montague Street, 965-8900. ✳

Innovative sculpture exhibits organized by the nearby **Rotunda Gallery** (see below) and Manhattan-based Public Art Fund grace this small public park in front of the State Supreme Court Building. During April and May artists-in-residence work in the park itself. Lovely benches make it an inviting place for a respite in any season. Twice a week the **Greenmarket stalls** are set up just a stone's throw away (see page 119).

Rotunda Gallery. 1 Pierrepont Plaza, corner of Pierrepont and Court streets, 875-4031. Call for a schedule.

Works by established and emerging Brooklyn artists—many of whom have escaped Manhattan's sky-high rents—are shown at this nonprofit art and video gallery in six annual exhibits. Previously located inside the Brooklyn War Memorial, the gallery is scheduled to move in early 1991 to this new space near the shops and restaurants of Montague Street. It is also within walking distance of **BACA Downtown** and both of **AMMO's** exhibition spaces (see pages 108 and 136).

Libraries

Brooklyn Public Library and **Brooklyn Business Library.** 280 Cadman Plaza West, near Tillary Street, 780-7788. Call to check hours. ✳

A welcome oasis of quiet can be found in the second-floor children's room at the Brooklyn Public Library's Brooklyn Heights Branch. Often underutilized, this is a great place to curl up with a bookish youngster. For adults with the afternoon off, the library occasionally offers movies.

The Brooklyn Heights library also houses the largest collection of business information in the entire New York City public library system. It includes a vast assortment of business periodicals; information on stocks, bonds, and personal investing topics; phone books for U.S. and foreign cities; and other reference material, along with knowledgeable and helpful librarians. For direct access to the business library call 780-7800.

Listed elsewhere in this chapter you will find the following points of cultural interest: the **Anchorage** (page 135); **Bargemusic** (page 136); the **Brooklyn Bridge** (page 134); the **Brooklyn Historic Railway** (page 124); and the **New Waterfront Museum** (page 136).

NOTABLE RESTAURANTS

Clark Street Station. 78 Clark Street, near Henry Street, 797-2096. Sun.–Thurs., 11 a.m.–1 p.m.; Fri.–Sat., 11 a.m.–midnight. Major credit cards.

An active local bar, this is one of several Brooklyn restaurants featuring live music. You'll hear jazz, blues, or classical guitar on weekend evenings and sometimes during Sunday brunch. The country-style fare includes corn bread, pork chops, potato skins, and other American favorites. Dinners average $15 per person, but you can get away for less. It's within walking distance of the **Brooklyn Heights Cinema** (see page 109).

Foffe's. 155 Montague Street, between Henry and Clinton streets, 625-2558. Mon.–Fri., noon–10 p.m.; Sat., 4–10 p.m. Major credit cards.

You never know what politico you'll run into when you go downstairs to Foffe's for lunch or dinner. Meade Esposito used the kitchen to cook his favorite pasta dish and Brooklyn Borough President Howard Golden is reputed to be a frequent customer. This "old Brooklyn" hangout has the feel of a place that has been doing the same thing, well, for centuries. There is a lively bar with hors d'oeuvres and reliable Italian cuisine. But the atmosphere is the reason most people go. Specialties include homemade pastas, steaks, and chicken dishes. Dinner averages about $25 per person.

Gage & Tollner. 372 Fulton Street, between Boerum and Smith streets, 875-5181. Mon.–Fri., lunch, 11:30 a.m.–3 p.m., and dinner, 5–10 p.m.; Sat., dinner only, 4–11 p.m.; Sun., lunch, noon–4 p.m., and dinner, 5–9 p.m. Major credit cards.

In spite of its tawdry location in downtown Brooklyn's Fulton Mall, a visit to this popular historic eatery is a must. Established in 1879 when Brooklyn was a bustling port, the building is now a historic landmark inside and out. Gage & Tollner is famous for great seafood and turn-of-the-century ambience, with mahogany tables, gas lighting, old-fashioned mirrors, and old-time waiters. Everything has been restored and upgraded since Gage's acquisition by Manhattan restauranteur Peter Aschkenasy. Prices run about $30 per person for dinner. Try the rum drink called the "Brooklyn." Reservations for lunch are required.

Heights Cottage. 118 Montague Street, between Hicks and Henry streets, 237-0997. Mon.–Fri., 8 a.m.–8 p.m.; Sat.–Sun., 10 a.m.–8 p.m. No credit cards. ✳

Homemade soups and huge sandwiches make this relative newcomer to the Heights a popular lunch spot. The atmosphere is clean and collegiate, with stacks of magazines available for readers, and treats such as aesthetic noshes of chocolate Empire State Buildings. The food is fresh and inexpensive.

Henry's End. 44 Henry Street, between Cranberry and Middagh streets, 834-1776. Mon.–Thurs., 6–11 p.m.; Fri. and Sat., 6 p.m.–midnight; Sun., 5–10 p.m. Major credit cards.

Always busy, always noisy, always crowded, Henry's End is one of the finest restaurants in the Heights. The food is excellent—particularly the game and seafood dishes. Light eaters can order half-portions. There is an extensive wine-tasting menu and several dozen varieties of beer. Dinner runs about $25 per person, without drinks.

Junior's. 386 Flatbush Avenue, corner of DeKalb Avenue, 852-5257. Sun.–Thurs., 6:30 a.m.–1:30 a.m.; Fri and Sat., 6:30 a.m.–3 a.m. Major credit cards. ✳

Drive south on Flatbush Avenue from the **Manhattan Bridge** and you can't miss Junior's. A big, brightly lit place sporting a very nice sidewalk café, Junior's has a huge menu of deli items, plus salads and fish. They've been in this downtown Brooklyn location since 1929 and their clientele is loyal. Customers include office workers from nearby **MetroTech**, tourists, cabbies, and college students from **Pratt Institute** and **Long Island University** across the street (see pages 113, 180, and 112, respectively). Junior's is open late, so regulars include performers and artsy types from **BAM** (page 178) and **BACA Downtown** (page 108) who show up after a performance for blintzes, hamburgers, pastrami, good pickles, and big ice-cream sundaes. The ambience is clean, urban, and bright. Entrées run $10 to $15, and strawberry cheesecakes to take home are $13 to $18. There is also a children's menu.

Las Tres Palmas. 124 Court Street, near Atlantic Avenue, 596-2740. Mon.–Sat., 10 a.m.–10 p.m.; closed Sun. Major credit cards.

People have been giving Las Tres Palmas rave reviews for years. The menu offers well-spiced, well-cooked Cuban- and Puerto Rican–style cuisine. Come when you are hungry or feeling broke: the portions are huge and the prices low. Most entrées are under $9 and come with rice and beans or plantains and salad.

Leaf 'N' Bean. 136 Montague Street, between Hicks and Henry streets, 855-7978. Café: Mon.–Sat., 10 a.m.–4 p.m.; Sat and Sun., 10 a.m.–5 p.m.; Shop: Mon.–Sat., 10 a.m.–7 p.m. Major credit cards.

Is it a store or a café? Both! The store sells dozens of varieties of coffee beans plus attractive modern kitchenware, from cappuccino makers to oven mitts. The café tucked away behind the shop is open for breakfast and lunch. Locals commend the pâtés, mousse, salads, and daily specials.

Peter Hilary's Bar & Grill. 174 Montague Street, between Court and Clinton streets, 875-7900. Daily, noon–midnight. Major credit cards.

There are two "scenes" at this young restaurant. From Tuesday through Friday the upstairs dining room is open and features live piano and blues. On weekends only the downstairs bar area is open, without entertainment. Appetizers start at about $5, and while there are burgers and chili, you can also find entrées, such as steaks or smoked salmon, that start at around $15. If you're a brunch eater, on Sundays there's often chamber music to munch by.

Queen. 84 Court Street, near Livingston Street, 624-9621. Mon.–Thurs., 11:30 a.m.–1 a.m.; Fri., 11:30 a.m.–2 a.m.; Sat., 2 p.m.–2 a.m.; Sun., 2 p.m.–1 a.m. No credit cards.

When the lawyers pour out of the nearby Brooklyn courts, they head for Queen, an excellent white-tablecloth Italian restaurant with an early twentieth-century ambience. You can't go wrong here; the waiters are veterans who will gladly guide you. Prices are moderate, and the food is excellent. Try the fettuccine with pesto or the veal scallopini.

Slades. 107 Montague Street, between Hicks and Henry streets, 858-1200. Daily, 11:30 a.m.–1 a.m. Major credit cards.

It may or may not be a compliment, but *yuppie* is the word that comes to mind here: a nice bar, young clientele, a good Sunday brunch. The food is not memorable, but outdoor seating makes for fun people-watching in warm weather.

Su-Su's Yum Yum. 60 Henry Street, near Cranberry Street, 522-4531. Mon.–Fri., 11:30 a.m.–10:30 p.m.; Sat. and Sun., 11:30 a.m.–11:30 p.m. Major credit cards. ✷

There are two good things about Su-Su's aside from its extraordinary name. First is the excellent Chinese fare, which is some of the best in the borough. Second is the fact that they deliver as far away as Park Slope. The restaurant scores low marks on ambience but high on palate and pocketbook. Su-Su's also operates a sixteen-person shuttle bus to transport customers to and from the restaurant. If you are in the area, there's a two-person minimum for the shuttle; if you're going to Wall Street, you need six; and if you're going to the Upper East Side in Manhattan or out to Bay Ridge, you need a party of fifteen to get a free ride.

Tanpopo. 36 Joralemon Street, near Columbia Place, 596-2968. Tues.–Fri., lunch, 12:30–2:30 p.m., and dinner, 5:30–10:30 p.m.; Sat. and Sun., dinner only, 5:30–10:30 p.m.; closed Mon. Major credit cards. ✳

Good, authentic Japanese food and an unhurried, quiet atmosphere make this setting conducive to conversation. Family owned and run, this restaurant is particularly suitable for children. Dinner costs about $12 per person.

Teresa's Restaurant. 80 Montague Street, corner of Hicks Street, 797-3996. Daily, 7 a.m.–11 p.m. No credit cards. ✳

Just look for the lines outside at dinnertime. This new Polish-style eatery is so good and so inexpensive that you would think they were giving food away. Try the banana pancakes, apple fritters, or chicken liver omelets for breakfast, and the goulash, kielbasa, and other meats for dinner. Specialties include *babka*, pirogi, blintzes, two kinds of borscht, and pickle soup. Teresa's is clean, airy, and freshly renovated.

Listed elsewhere in this chapter you will find descriptions of more restaurants, including the following: The **Moroccan Star** (page 125); The **River Cafe** (page 137); and **Parker's Lighthouse** (page 137).

SHOPPING

Specialty Food Shops

Greenmarket. Cadman Plaza, near Court and Remsen streets. Tues. and Sat., 8 a.m.–6 p.m. ✳

On Tuesday and Saturday you can find a refreshing contrast to the urban bustle of Brooklyn Heights as well as something good to eat at these outdoor stalls which sell farm-fresh fruit and vegetables, fresh fish, and assorted baked goods. There are plenty of flowers and plants on sale as well. Smaller and less crowded than many Manhattan greenmarkets, the ambience is relaxing here.

There's another Greenmarket at Albee Square at Fulton Street and DeKalb Avenue on Wednesday.

Lassen & Hennings Deli. 114 Montague Street, between Henry and Hicks streets, 875-6272. Mon.–Sat., 7:30 a.m.–11 p.m.; Sun., 7:30 a.m.–10 p.m. No credit cards.

Get here early to avoid the lunchtime lines, because this deli serves wonderful homemade soups, sandwiches, breads, cheeses, and other hearty delectables. This is a perfect spot to get provisions for a picnic on the **Promenade** (see page 110).

Only the Best. 198 Henry Street, corner of Montague Street, 858-0028. Mon.–Fri., 11:30 a.m.–8:30 p.m.

The name says it all at this dinnertime takeout. The owner, an Oklahoman who gave up singing opera to become a caterer, turns out an assortment of delicacies that include savory pies, crab cakes, mustard-dill potato salad, and fresh loaves of bread.

Perelandra Natural Food Center. 175 Remsen Street, between Clinton and Court streets, 855-6068.

Named after the utopia described in C. S. Lewis's book by the same name, Perelandra is a big, clean, California-style health food supermarket. Along with the various healthy foodstuffs, fresh produce, and breads, the store has a small juice bar that serves protein shakes and daily specials.

Sinclair's Babka. 184 Henry Street, between Montague and Pierrepont streets, 625-9831. Mon.–Sat., 8 a.m.–9 p.m.; Sun., 8 a.m.–7 p.m. No credit cards.

If sinfully delicious *babka*, coffee rings, danish, and a good selection of cakes are your downfall, then this is the place to succumb. While there's no place to sit and munch, you can get coffee to go along with your pastries. This ancient bakery is one of several by the same name in Brooklyn and is well known not only for the *babka* but also for its pumpkin pies.

Two for the Pot. 200 Clinton Street, corner of Atlantic Avenue, 855-8173. Tues.–Fri., noon–7 p.m.; Sat., 10 a.m.–6 p.m.; Sun., 1–5 p.m.; always closed Mon., closed Sun. in the summer. No credit cards.

Savor the aroma of freshly roasted coffees here. While you're buying, check out the assortment of coffee makers, herbs, spices, and barbecue equipment, including Weber grills, flavored wood chips, and an honest-to-goodness Louisiana-style meat smoker. The personable owner, a former cartoonist, is ready with suggestions and information.

Interesting Neighborhood Shops

Brooklyn Babes. 103 Montague Street, between Hicks and Henry streets, 237-0143. Mon.–Fri., 10 a.m.–7 p.m.; Sat., 10 a.m.–6 p.m.; Sun., noon–5 p.m. Major credit cards. ✳
   Here's a good source for functional clothing for children five and under. The selection includes many imported items, 100-percent cotton pajamas and a rack of kiddie gadgets only an experienced parent can appreciate: refrigerator locks, pacifier retainers, and sassy seats. Prices are reasonable and the staff is helpful.

Brooklyn Women's Exchange. 55 Pierrepont Street, near Hicks Street, 624-3435. Tues.–Sat., 10 a.m.–4:30 p.m. Closed during the summer. Major credit cards. ✳
   For a special gift that will look like you made it yourself, try the BWE selection of charming quilts, sweaters, mittens, hats, stuffed animals, and children's clothes. Almost everything is made by the elderly or disabled. A special section features gourmet foods.

Cousin Arthur's Books for Children. 82 Montague Street, corner of Hicks Street, 643-1232. Mon.–Sat., 9:30 a.m.–6 p.m.; Sun., noon–5 p.m. Major credit cards. ✳
   Brooklyn's best bookstore for children, this excellent shop has a wide selection of literature for small fry through early teens. Owners Bob and Barbara Tramonte, a poet-publisher husband-and-wife team, offer ample advice and free cookies. Phone orders are accepted. Special events include reading hours on Sunday and midweek toddler story hours.

Etcetera/By Hand. 304 Henry Street, corner of Atlantic Avenue, 625-0499. Wed.–Sat., 11 a.m.–5 p.m.; Sun., 11 a.m.–5 p.m.; open late Thurs. and Fri. Major credit cards.
   A good place for gifts, this cozy, moderately priced store appeals to many sides of a woman's life—there are lovely shawls, jewelry, and accessories alongside cotton rugs, picture frames, and handmade baby booties. The store also carries casual skirts, dresses, and blouses plus a line of popular children's outfits by Animal Farm, discounted 25 percent.

Innovative Audio. 77 Clinton Street, between Montague and Remsen streets, 596-0888. Mon.–Fri., 10:30 a.m.–7 p.m.; Sat., 10:30 a.m.–6 p.m.; Sun., noon–5 p.m.; open late Thurs. Major credit cards.
   While many music lovers make do with mass-market stereo equipment, those who are afficionados travel great distances to come to Innovative. You'll

need a good ear, but not necessarily a good-size bankroll, to distinguish what makes this shop well known throughout New York City. The calm, informative salespeople will help you understand the differences between brands, from Nakamichi to Krell, to Spectral, to the Scottish Linn. When the people at Innovative say they carry the top of the line in audio equipment and are dedicated to customer service, they mean it.

Moby Dick Toys. 115 Montague Street, between Hicks and Henry streets, 935-9108. Mon.–Sat., 10 a.m.–6 p.m.; Sun., noon–5 p.m. Major credit cards. ✳

Only three blocks from the Promenade, this cheerful shop is chock-full of delightful toys for kids up to eight years old: blocks, books, games, and crafts plus a large selection of items under $5. Phone your order in and Moby Dick will ship it by UPS.

Seaport Flowers. 214 Hicks Street, near Montague Street, 858-6443. Tues.– Sat., 11 a.m.–7:30 p.m.; Sun., noon–5 p.m.; closed Mon. Major credit cards.

Don't let the name fool you—Seaport Flowers's current location definitely is landlocked. No ordinary florist, owner Jane Roe left a successful business in Greenwich Village for the tranquility of Brooklyn. Her arrangements are often in demand for some of the Heights' most elegant drawing rooms. Check out the extensive selection of dried flowers as well.

Takes Two to Tango. 145 Montague Street, between Clinton and Henry streets, 625-7518. Mon.–Fri., 10:30 a.m.–7 p.m.; Sat., 10:30 a.m.–6 p.m.; closed Sun. Major credit cards.

One of the classiest boutiques in Brooklyn, Tango has a full line of women's clothing, including an excellent selection of fine shoes, dressy work clothes, casual wear, lingerie, and handbags. You'll find such brands as Anne Klein, Adrienne Vittadini, Tahari, and Calvin Klein here at department store prices—but without the crowds.

Zig Zag. 121 Montague Street, corner of Henry Street, 596-1841. Mon.–Fri., 11 a.m.–7 p.m.; Sat., 10 a.m.–6 p.m. Major credit cards.

Don't be put off by Zig Zag's second-floor location. This is the kind of clothing store that budget-conscious women would love to have around the corner. Moderately priced work and play separates can be mixed and matched. Advice on how to make the most of your wardrobe is available from the helpful (but not pushy) midwestern proprietor. Brands include Leon Max, Jones New York, and a host of new designers.

ATLANTIC AVENUE

Where it is: Along Atlantic Avenue, from the East River to Flatbush Avenue.

How to get there:
By car: Take the first exit off the Brooklyn Bridge and proceed to Court Street. Follow Court Street to Atlantic Avenue.
By subway: 2, 3, 4, or 5 train to Borough Hall; or M or R train to Court Street.
Cab service: Promenade (858-6666), Atlantic (797-5666), or Janice (797-5773). Cost is about $12 from Grand Central Station, $15 from Sheepshead Bay.

Special events: Atlantic Antic street fair (September).

How it got its name: At the foot of Atlantic Avenue are the piers from which thousands of ships along Brooklyn's thriving waterfront sailed across the Atlantic Ocean.

ABOUT THE NEIGHBORHOOD

Atlantic Avenue is famous for its Middle Eastern restaurants and shops, antique stores, and offbeat retail establishments. Although it's just six blocks from the heart of Brooklyn Heights, it is worlds away in atmosphere. Here you will find **Vesture**, a Soho-style Korean hat designer, an ale house offering the largest selection of beer in Brooklyn, exotic foods to match almost anyone's tastes, and one of the largest concentrations of antique shops to be found anywhere in New York City.

This Middle Eastern enclave is a colorful remnant of the days when Brooklyn's waterfront was a bustling international seaport. Today you can visit some of New York's best-known Middle Eastern shops in one block, between Court and Clinton streets. Here you will find no fewer than four restaurants, four grocers, and three bakeries that specialize in traditional Lebanese and Syrian foods. Several outstanding establishments, including **Sahadi Importing Company, Damascus Bakery,** and **Oriental Pastry and Grocery**, are two- and three-generation family businesses.

Since it is just about impossible to wander down Atlantic Avenue without wanting to try everything, following is a recommended menu.

> **Food for a Middle Eastern Feast**
> *hummus* and *baba ganoush* spreads
> pita bread
> *tabouli* (grain and vegetable salad)
> stuffed grape leaves
> feta cheese (there are many varieties—ask for a taste)
> spicy black and green olives
> pistachio nuts
> baklava, "birds nest," or Turkish delight for dessert
> mint tea

Once you've completed your gastronomic tour, head east down Atlantic Avenue. Though they may never admit it, some of Manhattan's most discriminating antique dealers regularly peruse the wares in the antique shops scattered between Court Street and Flatbush Avenue. The biggest concentration is on the three-block strip between Bond and Smith streets. You'll find lots of oak furniture and Victoriana, and in some shops there's room for bargaining. Among the top-tier stores (these are not likely to bargain) are **Hall & Winter**, for serious collectors, the **Upholstered Room**, which carries high-quality Victoriana, and **Time Traders Antiques**, which redefines antiquing by putting reasonable prices on about twenty thousand square feet of merchandise. At **Prophecies** you'll find a messy but interesting array of architectural, subway, and church salvage items, plus remnants of the old Coney Island amusement park. The wonderful reproduction Shaker furniture at **Scott Jordan** and tasteful stained glass at **Karl Lighting** are also worth a look.

POINTS OF CULTURAL INTEREST

Brooklyn Historic Railway Association. Atlantic Avenue Subway Tunnel utility hole, intersection of Court Street and Atlantic Avenue, 941-3160. Reserved tours usually are conducted on Sat. Cost is $10 for adults, $5 for kids.

Built in 1861 and then abandoned and sealed up in 1884, the **Atlantic Avenue Tunnel** was the world's first subway tunnel. Rediscovered in 1980, it is now listed in the National Register of Historic Places. Robert Diamond, who discovered the tunnel, conducts tours—you enter through a utility hole—for groups of ten or more. Call to make reservations. If you don't have a large enough group, they'll put you on a list and call you when enough people have signed up. This is a must-see for all ages.

State Street houses, 291–299 and 290–324 State Street, near Smith Street.

Tucked away just one block from the bustle of Atlantic Avenue's antique stores is this lovely stretch of twenty-three neatly kept historic row houses. Built in the period from 1840 to 1870, they reflect the evolving architectural styles of that era, from early Greek Revival to Italiante ornamentation. Today they are private homes, but it is interesting just to walk by.

NOTABLE RESTAURANTS

Middle Eastern

Adnan Restaurant. 129 Atlantic Avenue, between Henry and Clinton streets, 625-2115. Daily, 11:30 a.m.–11 p.m. Major credit cards. ✳

Although the days are long gone when sailors from ports all over the world docked in Brooklyn, Adnan continues to serve its loyal customers large, satisfying portions of traditional Middle Eastern food. The modest dining room is lit by reproduction Tiffany lamps and is equally suitable for families with small children and for an intimate date. With the large portions of chicken kebabs with rice; lamb stewed with squash, green peppers, and onion; and such traditional appetizer favorites as *hummus, baba ganoush,* and *tabouli,* you can get away for under $14 per person for dinner. Bring your own alcoholic beverages.

Bourock Restaurant. 172 Atlantic Avenue, between Clinton and Court streets, 624-9614. Daily, noon–midnight. Major credit cards. ✳

It's not exactly *Arabian Nights* revisited, but the main attraction here is belly dancing on weekends. The food is standard Lebanese: *hummus,* fava bean salad, called *"fool,"* various chicken and lamb dishes, such as *mahloubi* and *musakhan,* and many entrées under $10. Weekend reservations are recommended.

Moroccan Star. 205 Atlantic Avenue, corner of Court Street, 643-0800. Daily, noon–11 p.m. Major credit cards. ✳

The secret to the wonderful meals here is chef Ahmed, previously of the Four Seasons and Luchow's. This is outstanding traditional Middle Eastern fare—in particular the stew of lamb or chicken with vegetables, prunes, and dried almonds. Prices are low and quantities are large, so come hungry.

Tripoli. 154 Atlantic Avenue, corner of Clinton Street, 596-5800. Daily, 11 a.m.–11 p.m. Major credit cards. ✳

There's a ship sailing out of the Tripoli's huge windows. The restaurant's interior includes walls painted in a wonderful ocean motif, replete with lazy clouds, birds, and views of a rocky coastline, along with heavy wooden seating and low lighting. Tripoli is probably the most elegant of Atlantic Avenue's Middle Eastern restaurants. If you've never had couscous, try it here. The kitchen will prepare it with meat, chicken, or just vegetables. There's live music on weekends, and prices are moderate.

Other Restaurants

B. J. Carey Provisions. 444 Atlantic Avenue, between Nevins and Bond streets, 935-1220. Tues.–Sun., 9 a.m.–8 p.m. Major credit cards.

After a hard day of bargaining down prices on antiques, you'll appreciate a restaurant as pretty and decorative as B.J.'s on Atlantic Avenue. One step in and you've entered a more genteel world. It is delightful for breakfast and lunch and rarely too crowded to enjoy. Dinner is served early (they close at 8 p.m.). Entrées may include boneless chicken with wild rice; sausage and scallions, and English steak-and-kidney pie. The mood is European and the prices are moderate. Fresh salads, homemade soups, baked goods, and coffees round out the menu. If you've just bought an antique cupboard and have nothing to put in it, the teas, jams, jellies, and other goods on display also are for sale.

Boerum Hill Cafe. 148 Hoyt Street, corner of Bergen Street, 875-9391. Wed.–Sat., 5–11 p.m.; Sun., 5–10 p.m. Checks accepted.

The unusually evocative Victorian setting takes you back to the era when this café first opened as a bar in 1860. The restaurant is located two blocks from Atlantic Avenue in a small landmark building at the corner of two worlds (literally—public housing projects are one block in one direction and expensive brownstones are one block in the other). The dark interior, long bar, pressed-tin ceilings, antique decorations, and period furniture create an intimate atmosphere. Menu items range from shrimp with leeks and curry to various pastas, with entrée prices averaging about $15. This little restaurant is a lovely setting for an intimate party.

Camille's. 311 Henry Street, near Atlantic Avenue, 624-9751. Mon.–Thurs., 8 a.m.–4 p.m.; Fri.–Sun., 8 a.m.–10 p.m. No credit cards.

For more than a decade this tiny café has offered moderately priced fare combined with a wonderful, old-fashioned ambience: pressed-tin walls and ceiling and lots of antique fixtures. Menu items include tuna sandwiches; pasta salads (chicken, pesto, broccoli, and so on) for about $7; and mushroom and red onion pie with salad for $6. It's at the far end of Atlantic Avenue, tucked away on a side street, and is popular with long-time locals.

La Mancha. 121 Atlantic Avenue, near Henry Street, 625-8539. Tues.–Fri., 11 a.m.–11 p.m.; Sat., 4–11:30 p.m. Major credit cards.

A warm atmosphere belies an unimposing facade at this Spanish restaurant, with its stucco and tiled walls, soft Spanish music, and authentic, moderately priced cuisine. Traditional sauces include green sauce, hot sauce, and garlic sauce. A pitcher of sangria is a must. Sunday *tapas* buffet, which begins at 3 p.m., is a local favorite.

Moustache. 405 Atlantic Avenue, between Bond and Nevins streets, 852-5555. Wed.–Mon., 11 a.m.–11 p.m.; closed Tues. No credit cards. ✳

The New York Times praised the freshness and flavor of the inventive foods at this informal little spot, which like **B. J. Carey** (opposite), is one inviting place to stop for a bite among the antique stores along Atlantic Avenue. Try the "mideastern pitza" (homemade pita with homemade sausage, or spread with a paste of sesame seeds, olive oil, and spices) for something new, delicious *hummus* or *tabouli* for something familiar. Recommended for lunch or an early dinner.

Peter's Ice Cream Cafe. 148 Atlantic Avenue, between Clinton and Henry streets, 852-3835. Sun.–Thurs., noon–11 p.m.; Fri. and Sat., noon–midnight. No credit cards. ✳

Forget those foreign premium ice creams—this is the real McCoy, a home-made ice-cream shop. Peter's scoops up traditional favorite flavors plus an unbelievable "Chocolate Decadence." Better restaurants, such as **Gage & Tollner** (see page 116), also serve Peter's ice cream. Call ahead to see when the ice cream is being made; kids will love to watch.

Peter's Waterfront Ale House. 136 Atlantic Avenue, between Clinton and Henry streets, 522-3794. Tues.–Sun., noon–3 a.m.; closed Mon. Major credit cards. ✳

Neighborhood stand-up comedy for brownstoners has arrived! Comedy is on Tuesday only, but this place is packed almost every night. Vegetable dumplings and Italian sausage dinners cost less than $10. The bar claims to carry Brooklyn's largest selection of beer on tap and features a different beer each week. Families come early with their kids for the informal atmosphere and good, inexpensive food.

SHOPPING

Specialty Food Shops

Damascus Bakery. 195 Atlantic Avenue, between Clinton and Court streets, 855-1456. Mon–Sat., 8 a.m.–5 p.m. No credit cards. ✳

If you live in New York, you've probably seen packages of Damascus pita bread in your local supermarket. Inside this small shop is a vast selection of freshly baked plain, whole wheat, sesame, garlic, onion, and even oat bran pitas. The business was started in 1933 by grandpa Hassan Halaby, who hailed from Damascus.

El Asmar. 197 Atlantic Avenue, between Clinton and Court streets, 855-2455. Daily, 8:30 a.m.–9 p.m. No credit cards. ✳

The late-night grocery of Atlantic Avenue, this father-and-son operation sells a panoply of Middle Eastern specialties that includes more than seven varieties of feta cheese, fifty different spices, dozens of beans, dried fruits, pickled vegetables, olives, *hummus* and *baba ganoush*, plus such desserts as *baklava* and Turkish delight. Wild rice costs less than $6 a pound.

Oriental Pastry and Grocery. 170 Atlantic Avenue, between Clinton and Court streets, 875-7687. Daily, 10 a.m.–8:30 p.m. No credit cards. ✳

The Syrians have been perfecting the sweet ancient taste of pistachio, honey, and dough for more than a thousand years, and here you'll benefit from all of that experience. Try the *burma* (shredded dough filled with honey and nuts) or the Turkish delight. For something more substantial there is take-out *hummus, lebany* yogurt, and falafel mix, along with dozens of spices and other accoutrements of Middle Eastern cooking.

Sahadi Importing Company 187–189 Atlantic Avenue, between Clinton and Court streets, 624-4550. Mon.–Sat., 9 a.m.–7 p.m.; closed Sun. No credit cards.

Part gourmet food store, part exotic deli, this is the largest and best stocked of the Middle Eastern food emporiums in New York City. There is an admirable selection of freshly prepared take-home foods, including soups, *tabouli,* stuffed vine leaves, *imjadara* (made of rice and lentils), apricot-currant chicken, *hummus,* curries, and couscous. Standard fare includes dried fruits, grains, beans, many kinds of olives, and feta cheese. Check for seasonal specials, such as Middle Eastern turkey stuffing and an edible almond Christmas wreath.

Antiques

Hall & Winter. 78 Bond Street, between Atlantic Avenue and State Street, 797-4330. Hours are by appointment only. No credit cards.

Their workshop-showroom is modestly tucked away on an unpretentious street in Brooklyn, but Hall & Winter have a stellar reputation for selling eighteenth- and early-nineteenth-century English and American furniture in pristine condition. Dining room sets, armoires, and secretaries from their collection appear in more than a dozen exclusive national antique shows every year. Richard Hall and Roger Winter are pros, able to reel off the vital statistics and provenance of each piece—that a certain desk, for example, was a nineteenth-century cabinetmaker's interpretation of a George II original, purchased seventy-five years ago by a Park Avenue family and subsequently by a Greenwich banker. Prices are commensurate with quality. They also have a showroom in New Hope, Pennsylvania. A full restoration service is available on the premises.

The following antique and second-hand shops are listed in order of their addresses on Atlantic Avenue.

Times and Moments. 349 Atlantic Avenue, between Bond and Hoyt streets, 497-4529. Tues.–Sun., 12:30–6 p.m.; closed Mon. Checks accepted. No credit cards.

If you're interested in bric-a-brac from the Depression up through the 1950s, you'll love this collection of items ranging from flatware to appliances.

Horseman Antiques. 351 Atlantic Avenue, between Bond and Hoyt streets, 596-1048. Daily, 10 a.m.–6 p.m. Major credit cards.

There's four floors of turn-of-the-century and Art Deco pine and oak furniture here, plus a fairly large collection of stained glass. In addition you will find an eclectic collection of new brass headboards and beds. If you're in the mood, come by on a Sunday evening in the winter or Tuesday in the summer for the weekly auction of floor items. Prices here are moderate, which may be one reason this store has been in business for some thirty years.

In Days of Old, Limited. 357 Atlantic Avenue, near Hoyt Street, 858-4233. Wed.–Sat., 11 a.m.–5 p.m.; Sun., 1–5 p.m. Major credit cards.

Lots of late Victorian oak, walnut, and mahogany pieces are sold here—armoires, desks, and tables—along with turn-of-the-century lighting fixtures. The friendly owner has restored several Brooklyn brownstones himself, and he has an eye for unusual pieces. This is a good place for people redecorating or renovating their own homes in period style.

City Barn Antiques. 362 Atlantic Avenue, between Bond and Hoyt streets, 855-8566. Tues.–Sun., 11 a.m.–6 p.m.; closed Mon. Checks accepted. No credit cards.

Original mission oak and Arts and Crafts–era furniture is the strong suit here, along with a fairly good collection of old stained glass pieces and period lighting fixtures displayed in several adjoining rooms. Prices start at about $500. Be sure to ask if you're looking for a particular piece; they may have what you want in storage or be able to find one for you.

Atlantic Attic. 366 Atlantic Avenue, between Bond and Hoyt streets, 643-9387. Thurs.–Sun., noon–6 p.m. Major credit cards.

Open mostly on weekends, this shop specializes in Victorian and Federal-style furniture. As in other Atlantic Avenue antique shops, you've got to sift through many items you may want to find the one perfect piece that's right for you. Custom framing also is available.

Time Trader Antiques. 368 Atlantic Avenue, between Bond and Hoyt streets, 852-3301. Mon.–Fri., 11 a.m.–7 p.m.; Sat. and Sun., noon–6 p.m. Major credit cards.

The excellent and fairly priced merchandise here spills over into no fewer than seven storefronts (308, 328, 368, 369, 373, and 443 Atlantic Avenue). This is one of the largest importers of English and European furniture in the tristate area. There are original armoires, sofas, chairs, and tables, Victorian to Deco, as well as less-expensive reproduction pine and oak furniture. Delivery is available and they're open seven days a week.

Circa Antiques. 374 Atlantic Avenue, between Bond and Hoyt streets, 596-1866. Tues.–Fri., noon–5 p.m.; Sat.–Sun., 11 a.m.–6 p.m. Major credit cards.

There are restored American tables, chairs, and beds of walnut, rosewood, and other fine woods here. Prices for sets range from $1,000 to $7,000. The store has been here for seventeen years, so you can be assured of its good reputation.

Bird Dog Antiques. 394 Atlantic Avenue, between Bond and Hoyt streets, 875-7027. Sat.–Sun., noon–5 p.m. Sometimes open on weekdays; call for information. No credit cards.

They know their classic American oak furniture here, as well they should —they've specialized in it for more than twenty years. Some pieces are in mint condition, some are restored. Prices are in the middle range.

Rene's Antiques. 400 Atlantic Avenue, between Bond and Hoyt streets, 237-0559. Daily, 1–7 p.m. Checks accepted. No credit cards.

This store sells more than standard oak furniture. The selection of interesting, high-quality finds from the late Victorian era through 1950s era includes furniture, chandeliers, and table lighting, plus such architectural details as marble fireplaces and Victorian door frames from old Brooklyn brownstones. If you are thinking about renovating your apartment or brownstone, ask to see owner Rene's portfolio; a former jeweler, he also consults on restorations in Brooklyn and Manhattan.

Time & Tide Antiques. 411 Atlantic Avenue, between Bond and Nevins streets, 858-1767. Wed.–Sun., noon–5 p.m. No credit cards.

This shop's offerings include wonderful, inexpensive, rural Americana, from tables and chairs to small tabletop items, such as candlesticks and wooden bowls. The two owners have a sharp eye for the odd, interesting piece.

Upholstered Room. 412–416 Atlantic Avenue, between Bond and Nevins streets, 875-7084. Wed.–Sun., noon–6 p.m.; closed Mon. and Tues. Major credit cards.

This is a classy collection of eighteenth- and nineteenth-century antique furniture. One room has high Victorian pieces, including high-quality tables, sofas, and chairs. The back room features period furniture perfect for that historically correct renovated brownstone. The styles range from American Federal to Empire. Everything is in mint condition and accordingly priced in the $1,000-and-up range.

Prophecies 423 Atlantic Avenue, between Bond and Nevins streets, 855-4285. Daily, 10 a.m.–6 p.m. Checks accepted. No credit cards.

Here's a fascinating shop if you like curiosities and don't mind rummaging around. The diverse collection of American folk art and architectural objects changes but likely includes carved mantels, doors, and columns from nineteenth-century Brooklyn brownstones and churches, memorabilia from the old Coney Island amusement park, maritime paintings, and subway oddities, such as a device that rotates destination signs. Maybe that's why movie prop managers like to shop here.

Interesting Neighborhood Shops

Dress Rehearsal. 105 Atlantic Avenue, near Henry Street, 858-0967. Tues.–Thurs., noon–7 p.m.; Fri., noon–6 p.m.; Sat., 11 a.m.–6 p.m.; Sun., noon–5 p.m.; closed Mon. By appointment after hours. Major credit cards.

The owner describes the style here as " 'L.A. Law'–style clothes for executive women." Indeed, the specialty in this small, tasteful shop is sophisticated executive women's clothing, featuring both American and European updated classic dresses starting at $180. Many name brands are discounted. This store is located several long blocks toward the water from the antique stores listed above.

The Gift Room. 412 Atlantic Avenue, between Bond and Nevins streets, 875-7084. Wed.–Sun., noon–5 p.m. Major credit cards. ✳

Here's a new idea in merchandising: At Halloween this little gift and notions store is filled with great ghoulish stuff. On Valentine's Day it is all hearts and cupids. We're not talking about a few cardboard hangings—the store undergoes a complete metamorphosis. The same holds for other important holidays, including Christmas, Hanukkah, and Easter. With a surprise in every nook and cranny, it is a wonderful place to bring the kids. But watch those sticky fingers, because the shop is attached to a store filled with expensive antiques.

James Glass Studio. 176 Atlantic Avenue, between Clinton and Court streets, 596-6463. Mon.–Fri., 9 a.m.–5 p.m. No credit cards.

This is one of the many places in Brooklyn to get stained glass repaired or to commission an original piece. The reasonably priced stained glass lamps make great gifts. All work is done on the premises.

Karl Lighting. 396 Atlantic Avenue, between Bond and Hoyt streets, 596-1419. Sat. and Sun., noon–5 p.m. Call for a weekday appointment. Checks accepted. No credit cards.

Beautifully crafted stained glass custom lighting sells here for 25 percent less than prices at many upscale boutiques. You can spend from $200 to $2,000.

Rashid Sales Company. 191 Atlantic Avenue, between Clinton and Court streets, 852-3295 or 852-3298. Mon.–Sat., 9:30 a.m.–7 p.m.; Sun., noon–7 p.m. Major credit cards.

Besides recordings of classical Middle Eastern music, this store imports the latest books and periodicals from the Middle East. Satellite editions of the influential Arabic newspaper *El Ahram* are available daily.

Scott Jordan Furniture. 280 Atlantic Avenue, near Smith Street, 522-4459. Tues.–Fri., 11 a.m.–6 p.m.; Sat. and Sun., noon–5 p.m. Major credit cards.

Buy yourself an heirloom for the future. Craftsman Scott Jordan makes new furniture along the lines of simple antique Shaker pieces. Everything is done in solid hardwoods, and only dovetailed joints are used—a rarity today. The quality of the workmanship shows in every bed (including canopy-style), table, and chair. Of course, such quality comes at a price, reasonable but not inexpensive. Catalogs are available.

Scuba Network. 290 Atlantic Avenue, corner of Smith Street, 802-0700. Mon.–Fri., 11 a.m.–7 p.m.; Sat., 10 a.m.–6 p.m. Major credit cards. ✳

Amid the antique dealers and Middle Eastern food merchants is this huge store catering to water lovers. You can get all the gear you'll need for snorkeling or scuba diving, or sign up for classes before your next trip south. They also carry plenty of bathing suits and other beach paraphernalia. There are four Scuba Networks in Manhattan, so if you don't find what you want here, they probably can get it.

Vesture. 141 Atlantic Avenue, between Clinton and Henry streets, 237-4126. Daily, 10 a.m.–6 p.m. Major credit cards.

Attention hat lovers! Don't be put off by the odd window displays. This is where you'll find more than a hundred different kinds of hats—from classic to downtown hip—designed by the owners and made on the premises. You could go to the Soho and Tribeca boutiques where these hats are sold, but why pay retail when you can get it wholesale? Note the great collection of affordably priced hatboxes.

FULTON FERRY WATERFRONT AND DUMBO (Down Under the Manhattan Bridge Overpass)

Where it is: From Court Street along the waterfront to the area under the Brooklyn and Manhattan bridges.

How it got its name: Robert Fulton's *Nassau*, the first steam-powered ferry, plowed the waters of the East River between Manhattan and a landing here. The ferry transported both people and farm produce. Since the 1980s, "DUMBO" has come into vogue, in the tradition of Manhattan's Soho (South of Houston Street) and Tribeca (Triangle Below Canal Street).

Special events: Indoor/Outdoor Art Show, Brooklyn Waterfront Artists Coalition (May).

How to get there:
   By foot: Walk over the Brooklyn Bridge; exit the footpath at Tillary Street.
   By car: Once across the Brooklyn Bridge, take the first exit, turn right, then turn left past the entrance to the BQE.
   By subway: 2 or 3 train to Clark Street. Walk toward the Brooklyn Bridge.
   Cab services: Promenade (858-6666), Atlantic (797-5666) or Janice (797-5773). Cost is about $12 from Grand Central Station, $15 from Sheepshead Bay.

ABOUT THE NEIGHBORHOOD

Whether you are interested in history, great views of Manhattan, or just a respite from the urban fray, a trip to the Fulton Ferry waterfront can be just what the doctor ordered. If you're traveling with children, the open spaces are wonderful for an urban romp. Among the notable sites on Old Fulton Street are the **Eagle Warehouse and Storage Company**, a huge 1893 red brick factory converted into stylish co-ops; **Bargemusic**; the **River Cafe**; a wonderful little secret park; and of course, the **Brooklyn Bridge** (you're right underneath it).

In the past decade, abandoned industrial loft space in this old manufacturing center has been resuscitated by numerous artists, priced out of Manhattan, who fell in love with the space, views, and light here. Their work is sometimes shown at several galleries, including the **Anchorage**'s fifty-five-foot-high stone chambers underneath the Brooklyn Bridge and the **New Waterfront Museum**.

Historical Notes

Originally a waterfront hamlet, the Fulton Ferry area was the site from which Brooklyn's Dutch settlers embarked for Manhattan. In those days, boats were powered by oars, sails, or even horses walking on treadmills. The little hamlet became a bustling commercial and residential center in the nineteenth century, when Robert Fulton's first steam ferry, the *Nassau*, began transporting people and produce across the East River. Many historical figures are associated with the area: Thomas Paine lived in a house at the corner of Sands and Fulton streets, Talleyrand once lived in a Fulton Street farmhouse opposite Hicks Street, and Walt Whitman set type for the first edition of *Leaves of Grass* in 1855 at 170 Fulton Street, on the corner of Cranberry. With the completion of the Brooklyn Bridge in 1883, however, the neighborhood's demise came quickly.

PARKS AND PLAYGROUNDS

Brooklyn Bridge. Walkway entrance is at Adams and Tillary streets. ✳

Walk it, drive it, bike it, or just admire it—the Brooklyn Bridge soaring over the East River is one of the greatest of New York City's bridges. An architectural beauty designed by John A. Roebling, it was at the time of its completion in 1883 the world's longest suspension bridge, connecting Manhattan at City Hall Park to Brooklyn's Cadman Plaza. It is also an icon of the borough as well as the picturesque subject of paintings, photos, and movie sets, not to mention a few time-worn jokes. With spectacular views of Manhattan's skyline, the river, and the Statue of Liberty, the bridge is the place for one of the most romantic and inspiring strolls in all New York.

The opening of the Brooklyn Bridge in 1883 was the first of several major changes that transformed Brooklyn from a rural farming area with scattered neighborhoods, such as Brooklyn Heights, Fort Greene, and Bedford, into a major Manhattan suburb. The second big change was the extension of the subways from Manhattan into Brooklyn, starting with the IRT in 1905. Land speculators and developers brought new residents to such neighborhoods as Carroll Gardens, Cobble Hill, and Boerum Hill. Indeed, in 1898, the once-independent Brooklyn merged to become part of New York City, for better and worse.

Empire Fulton Ferry Park. New Dock Road, by Water Street and the East River, (212) 977-8240. ✳

You'll almost forget you're in New York City when you visit this sizeable grassy meadow along the East River, sandwiched between the Brooklyn and Manhattan bridges. While the kids run around, you can treat yourself to a 360-degree view—of Manhattan in front, fabulous Civil War–era spice warehouses and turn-of-the-century industrial lofts behind, and the bridges on either side. Relatively undiscovered, this is a wonderful place for a picnic with or without kids. The park is at the end of the block on New Dock Street. You can walk, drive, or ride the B41 bus from Brooklyn Heights to the end of the line at the **Eagle Warehouse** apartment building (see page 136).

Harry Chapin Playground. Columbia Heights, along Middagh Street. ✳

Like many of Brooklyn's best-kept secrets, this immaculate little playground is tucked away, almost unseen yet providing an enviable view of Manhattan across the East River. Go one-half block past the **Eagle Warehouse** apartment building and then left up Everit Street.

POINTS OF CULTURAL INTEREST

Anchorage. Cadman Plaza West and Front Street, under the Brooklyn Bridge, (212) 619-1955. Call for a schedule. Summers only. ✳

Feeling cramped? For adventure, visit the art gallery housed in eight fifty-five-foot-high stone chambers that hold the Brooklyn Bridge suspension cables. Recently restored, the chambers provide a playful atmosphere for equally playful audio, visual, and performance artwork. Many shows are installed by Creative Time, a well-known Manhattan-based arts organization that mounts interdisciplinary works in other nontraditional places, such as the dunes of Battery Park City. Admission is free, and you're near **Empire Fulton Ferry Park** and its impressive view overlooking the East River (see page 135).

Bargemusic. Fulton Landing, at the end of Cadman Plaza West, 624-4061. Call for scheduled concerts. Tickets cost $12 to $15. Checks accepted. No credit cards.

The New York Times says of Bargemusic: "Some of the finest chamber music around can be heard in a setting spectacular enough to be an event all its own." Since 1978 this renovated Erie Lackawanna coffee barge has been the site of floating concerts on the East River. Noted performers play Mozart, Bach, Beethoven, Brahms, and the like year-round. The lovely wood-paneled hall has great acoustics, and since the boat is just 102 feet long, you virtually sit in the musicians' laps. Located to the left of the Brooklyn Bridge as you face Manhattan and a short walk from several good restaurants, this little gem offers a uniquely romantic and musical evening. Reservations are a must.

Eagle Warehouse. 28 Old Fulton Street, corner of Elizabeth Place, 855-3959.

In 1980 this elegant medieval-style warehouse was renovated into expensive cooperative apartments, many with spectacular views of Manhattan, the Brooklyn Bridge, and the East River. Built in 1893, it is one of Brooklyn's few remaining buildings by Frank Freeman, who was dubbed "Brooklyn's greatest architect" by the late Brooklyn historian Elliot Willensky in his *AIA Guide to New York*. The arched entry bears large bronze letters reading EAGLE WAREHOUSE AND STORAGE COMPANY; atop the building is a huge clock, now situated in a studio loft. The Eagle does not stand alone as a reminder of the busy shipping past of the Fulton Street docks. The waterfront area is scattered with nineteenth-century warehouses; note the unusually large site occupied across the street by the circa 1885 Empire Stores, stretching from 53 to 83 Water Street.

New Waterfront Museum and **AMMO Artists Exhibition Space.** Museum: AMMO Exhibition Space: 135 Plymouth Street, 184 Front Street, under the Brooklyn Bridge, 858-1900. Call for hours.

Curious about the much-heralded Brooklyn waterfront art scene? In a small area between the Brooklyn and Manhattan bridges a growing number of professional artists have been drawn to the large lofts in these industrial warehouses. Relatively low rents and great light are the attractions, and now several local exhibition spaces also have opened in the area. Visitors should head for either the Artists Exhibition Space, housed in an old munitions factory, or the New Waterfront Museum. Both are "alternative exhibition spaces" run by a nonprofit artists group called AMMO. Other galleries within walking distance are the **Rotunda Gallery** (see page 115) and **BACA Downtown** (page 108).

NOTABLE RESTAURANTS

Harbor View. 1 Old Fulton Street, near Water Street, 237-2224. Tues.–Sat., noon–11:30 p.m. Major credit cards.

Any restaurant that's been in business for 140 years must be doing something right. Although the clientele has changed from blue collar to white collar, the Italian food is still good and hearty, the prices are moderate, and there's live music on weekends. Across from the better-known **River Cafe** (see below), Harbor View also has a view of Manhattan. Weekend reservations are recommended.

Parker's Lighthouse. 1 Main Street, between Plymouth and Water streets, 237-1555. Mon.–Thurs., 11:30 a.m.–2:30 p.m. and 5:30–10 p.m.; Fri. and Sat., 11:30 a.m.–2:30 p.m. and 5:30–11 p.m.; Sun., 11 a.m.–3 p.m. and 5–9:30 p.m. Major credit cards.

Unlike the vast majority of New York restaurants, Parker's is both spacious and clean, and the seafood—blackened Cajun fish and coconut shrimp, for example—is exceptionally tasty. But what most people come for is the view across the East River; the lights of lower Manhattan and the Brooklyn Bridge combine to make this a favored spot for romantics. The owners also run the Top of the Sixes restaurant in Manhattan. The Sunday brunch, a $16 all-you-can-eat extravaganza, is filling and lots of fun. Parker's has a large, airy bar, so if you want to, come early and hang out. Weekend reservations are recommended.

River Cafe. 1 Water Street, at the end of Cadman Plaza West, 522-5200. Mon.–Sat., noon–2 p.m. and 6:30–11 p.m.; Sun., 11:30 a.m.–2 p.m. and 6:30–11 p.m. Major credit cards.

Famous for its breathtaking view of the Manhattan skyline, the River Cafe has an excellent menu, lots of romantic ambience, and valet parking as well. Don't be put off by the whine of cars crossing the Brooklyn Bridge overhead; it's all part of the charm. This is the perfect place to celebrate a special occasion or to have a drink before heading off to eat somewhere else. But nothing at the River Cafe comes cheap. Dinner is a fixed price of $55; brunch and lunch are a la carte, with most entrées costing about $17. Jackets are required, ties preferred. Reservations are necessary.

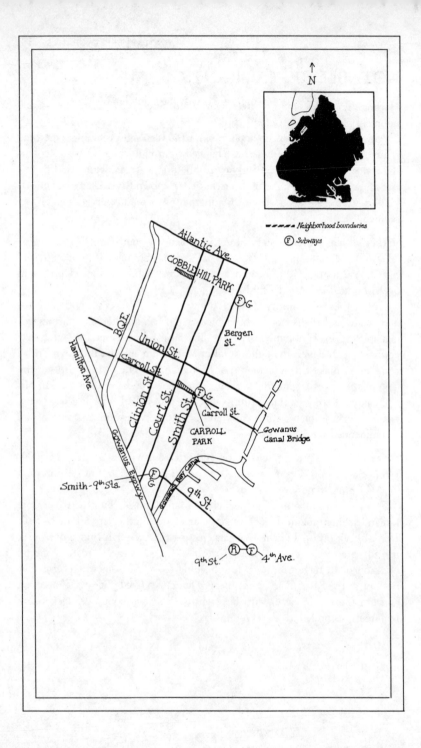

CARROLL GARDENS AND COBBLE HILL

Where it is: Combined, these two neighborhoods are bounded by Atlantic Avenue and 4th Place, and Henry and Hoyt streets.

What's nearby: Atlantic Avenue, Brooklyn Heights, and Park Slope.

How to get there:
> *By car:* Take the first exit off the Brooklyn Bridge, to Court Street. Stay on Court Street and cross Atlantic Avenue.
>
> *By subway:* F or G train to Carroll Street for Carroll Gardens, or to Bergen Street for Cobble Hill. Other subway stops are farther away but within walking distance: take the 2, 3, 4, or 5 train to Borough Hall, or the M or R train to Court Street.
>
> *Cab services:* Cobble Hill Car Service (643-1113) or Atlantic (797-5666). Cost is about $13 from Grand Central Station, $13 from Sheepshead Bay.

How each got its name: Originally a section of Red Hook or South Brooklyn, Carroll Gardens was named after Maryland's Charles Carroll, the only Roman Catholic signer of the Declaration of Independence, in honor of the Maryland regiment that fought nearby in the Revolutionary War. Cobble Hill: in the 1950s a real estate broker discovered that this area had been designated "Cobles Hill" in a 1766 map of New York. The name referred to a long-gone hill near the intersection of Court Street and Atlantic Avenue.

ABOUT THE NEIGHBORHOODS

Carroll Gardens

For those who know Brooklyn, a trip to Carroll Gardens is usually motivated by a craving for freshly made Italian food, nostalgia, or both. That doesn't mean that the many official historic landmarks and rows of nineteenth-century brownstones aren't reason enough to visit. But what brings people back to this part of Court Street time and again is an ethnic authenticity—the taste of fresh pasta and mozzarella; the aroma of coffee newly roasted in an old cast-iron roaster; and the sight of men playing bocci, gesticulating with their hands in a language understood in Sicily. Although locals swear that the best Italian cooking still comes from mama's kitchen, there are a half dozen good family-style restaurants here to fill the belly and satisfy the soul.

Carroll Gardens is not the biggest Italian neighborhood in Brooklyn; Bensonhurst, with its nonstop influx of new Italian immigrants, claims to be the true Little Italy of New York City. But Carroll Gardens' magic is that it remains so very Italian, despite its location, which is within walking distance of gentrified brownstone Brooklyn and ethnically mixed downtown.

The strict Italian character of Carroll Gardens has been diluted in recent years by professionals, artists, and others attracted to the brownstone housing and sunny openness of this residential area. Yet what differentiates Carroll Gardens from other brownstone neighborhoods, such as Brooklyn Heights and Park Slope, is the palpable sense of continuity. Many descendants of Carroll Gardens' original Italian families have stayed in the neighborhood— children, parents, and grandparents often live down the street from one another, if not under the same roof. Their homes are row upon row of neat brownstones with flowering, well-tended front gardens. Gentrification has made inroads, but it has not overwhelmed the style here.

Points of nonculinary interest include the nineteenth-century "socially enlightened" **Workingmen's Cottages** and **Tower Buildings** built by philanthropist Alfred Tredway White; a landmark 1880s bridge; and **Cammareri's Bakery**, where scenes from the movie *Moonstruck* were filmed.

Cobble Hill

Historically, Cobble Hill shares more with wealthy nineteenth-century Brooklyn Heights than it does with working-class Carroll Gardens. Defined by a twenty-block officially designated landmark district north of DeGraw Street, its elegant brownstones were built by members of the upper middle class, including distinguished architect Richard Upjohn. A large contingent of young urban professionals now occupies these buildings. After a period of decline

Cobble Hill has come full circle, thanks to an activist community and the brownstone revival movement.

In Cobble Hill, visitors can wander lovely tree-lined streets past pre–Civil War architecture; rest in lovely Cobble Hill Park; and marvel at the notable Verandah Mews, where Thomas Wolfe lived, before gentrification.

For Brooklynophiles Only

We know that to some of you it's almost a crime to violate neighborhood boundaries by lumping them together. But the irregular lines of demarcation between Cobble Hill and Carroll Gardens can make sticking with the "official" boundaries confusing for visitors. To that end, locations of interest in Cobble Hill near Court Street are included with Carroll Gardens listings. Restaurants and shops that are officially in Cobble Hill's Atlantic Avenue section are included in the Atlantic Avenue section of the previous chapter (pages 123–133).

Historical Notes

The first Europeans to settle here were seventeenth-century Dutch farmers. Middle- and upper-middle-class English folk moved in through the early 1800s. But it was the sailors and longshoremen—many of them Italian—who immigrated to America between the 1850s and World War I and labored on the nearby docks that gave Carroll Gardens its flavor. In those days the entire area was simply called "Red Hook," which covered much of Carroll Gardens and parts of nearby Boerum Hill (but not more rarified Cobble Hill). The ports of the Atlantic and Erie basins, the busy State Barge Canal Terminal, and connecting railways made this one of the nation's busiest shipping centers for more than a century. It is no accident that the headquarters of the Longshoreman's Union is right here on Court Street. Red Hook was immortalized in Arthur Miller's *A View From the Bridge*; its worst aspects were epitomized by Al Capone, who lived here before moving to Chicago.

After World War II both Carroll Gardens and Cobble Hill declined as the lure of the suburbs took hold. Shipping and related businesses shifted to more modern facilities in the New Jersey ports when containerization revolutionized the industry. The newly built Belt Parkway and Brooklyn Battery Tunnel adversely affected whole swaths of the area. However, in the 1960s both neighborhoods revived, fueled by activist residents and an influx of younger newcomers. (Indicative of the most recent changes are the churches-turned-condominiums at 360 Court Street and 450 Clinton Street.) Commercial change may again roil the area, and the redevelopment of downtown Brooklyn will most likely attract another wave of residents to these neighborhoods in the 1990s.

Food Shopping and Eating

In Carroll Gardens, shopping is straight out of the old world. You buy bread at the bread bakery, pastry at the pastry bakery, sausage at the pork store, meat at the butcher shop, fruit at the fruit stand, and fresh pasta at the pasta shop. Walk down Court Street or the small commercial strip on Henry Street and you'll find more than a dozen small family-owned food stores—**Caputo's Bake Shop, D'Amico Foods, G. Esposito Pork Store**, and **Pastosa Ravioli** among them—that have been riding Brooklyn's downs and ups since World War II. **Staubitz Market**, Brooklyn's most upscale butcher shop—selling such items as free-range poultry and no-nitrate bologna—is also on Court Street. Tucked away where you'd least expect to find it is one outstanding French bakery, **Marquet Patisserie**. Almost nobody leaves this neighborhood without bringing home food for a feast.

You have your choice of nearly a dozen reliable Italian restaurants that serve tasty, family-style food at moderate prices, including the modern, renovated **Nino's**, old-fashioned **Monte's Venetian Room**, and the Victorian **Café on Clinton**. Note that many stores are closed on Sunday.

Food for an Italian Feast
antipasti
fennel sausage
fresh mozzarella
homemade ravioli and sauce
special prosciutto bread
cannoli and almond cookies
espresso

Kidstuff

There's not much out of the ordinary here for kids, but there are plenty of playgrounds, bookstores, and pizza places to satisfy little stomachs. There's also a nice little movie theater on Court Street, the **Cobble Hill Cinema**.

ENTERTAINMENT

Most of the "entertainment" in this area is food-related; see pages 145–150 for restaurants and specialty food shops.

Cobble Hill Cinema. 265 Court Street, corner of Butler Street, 596-9113. Call for show times.

This is a nice place to catch a movie and dinner. There are lots of dining choices within walking distance: neighborhood Italian restaurants, trendy Cobble Hill cafés, and Middle Eastern restaurants on Atlantic Avenue.

PARKS AND PLAYGROUNDS

Carroll Park. Carroll Street, corner of Court Street. ✳

The main park in Carroll Gardens has swings and seesaws as well as a bocci game or two on nice afternoons. It's a very safe, neighborhood environment, and while there's not much shade in hot weather, the sprinkler keeps kids cool.

Cobble Hill Park. Entrances are on Clinton Street and Henry Street, between Congress Street and Verandah Place. ✳

One of the first "vest-pocket" parks in New York City, this park was developed in response to community activists' efforts to prevent construction of a supermarket on the site, which would have dwarfed the surrounding three- and four-story brownstones. Renovated in the spring of 1990, it is now one of the loveliest little parks in brownstone Brooklyn, featuring antique-style benches and tables as well as a kiddie play area and marble columns at the entrances. It is near Thomas Wolfe's Verandah Place home, one of his many residences in the borough. For snacks, see the listing for the **Cobble Hill Deli** or the Italian delis along Court Street (pages 147–150).

Red Hook Pool. Bay and Clinton streets, corner of Henry Street, 965-6579. Open from the last Sat. in June to Labor Day, daily, 11 a.m.–7 p.m. Admission is free, but bring your own lock. ✳

Run by the New York City Department of Parks and Recreation, this more-than-Olympic-size swimming pool in nearby Red Hook offers a welcome respite from those sweltering days of summer. Since its extensive renovation in the mid-1980s, the clientele has changed, reflecting the gentrification of the area: once there were gang fights here, but now kids and parents come from middle-class Brooklyn Heights, Park Slope, and Prospect Heights as well as the local area to swim. On weekends the pool is extremely busy and parking is difficult.

Small children can splash in a separate wading pool. The nearest subway is a hike away, at the corner of Smith and 9th streets, but you can pick up the number 77 bus there; it goes directly to the pool. Get off at Clinton and Bay streets.

POINTS OF CULTURAL INTEREST

Brooklyn Public Library. Clinton Street, near Union Street, 625-5838. Call to check hours. ✳

Beloved by locals, this comfy library has a special area with toys and books for preschoolers. Conveniently located only a block from the Court Street commercial center, it is in the midst of a quiet, lovely tree-lined residential area full of nineteenth-century brownstones. Books borrowed here can be returned to any Brooklyn branch library.

Carroll Gardens Homes. 1st Place through 4th Place, between Henry and Smith streets.

It is no accident that Carroll Gardens has the word *garden* in its name. The homes on these blocks have unusually large front yards, thanks to an innovative surveyor, Richard Butts, who mapped out this area for development way back in 1846. He broke from tradition and provided for big front yards in addition to standard-size backyards. Today these yards show the results of the proverbial Italian green thumb and make this a beautiful area for strolling.

Cobble Hill Homes. Along Clinton Street, near Henry Street.

Take a walk along Clinton Street to get a taste of the history of this neighborhood. Number 296 Clinton was the residence of Richard Upjohn and his son, both famed turn-of-the-century architects who built **Grace Church** in Brooklyn Heights (see page 114). Numbers 301 through 311 Clinton Street are Italianate-style houses built around 1850 by lawyer and developer Gerard Morris. Number 334 was built in 1850 by established Brooklyn architect James Naughton, who also built the architecturally acclaimed **Boys and Girls High School** in Bedford-Stuyvesant (see page 34). Number 340 is the widest house in the area, built for Dr. Joseph Clark in 1860. Verandah Place, between Clinton and Henry streets, is a lovely mews full of carriage houses, one of which was inhabited for a time by writer Thomas Wolfe.

East Coast Film Cars. 757 Hicks Street, near West 9th & Huntington streets, 624-6881. ✳

Near the Brooklyn Battery Tunnel, this business supplies the cars for TV and movie shows; many are parked outside. Passersby have seen the *Ghostbuster* vehicles, and the owners have been known to open the shop for kids and cameras on occasion. Drive by—you never know what famous four-wheeler you might see!

Carroll Street Bridge. Carroll Street, at 2nd Avenue.

Recently declared a landmark and renovated, this historic bridge spans the Gowanus Canal, built in 1889 as part of Brooklyn's network of industrial waterways. The waters of the canal have become polluted and no longer carry heavy industrial barge cargo, but the bridge is unusual: it opens by sliding along the tracks on the shore. It is the oldest of four such bridges in the country. This is in walking distance of **Monte's Venetian Room** restaurant, the name of which reflects wishful thinking. (But the food is good; see page 146.)

Kane Street Synagogue. 236 Kane Street, between Court and Clinton streets, 875-1550.

The congregation housed here, Beth Israel, founded in 1856, claims to be the oldest Jewish congregation in Brooklyn. Its fate followed that of the neighborhood, prospering through the 1920s, languishing until the 1960s, and coming to life again as the brownstone gentrification movement brought in a younger membership. The original synagogue was located on the site now occupied by the Brooklyn House of Detention; the current synagogue building was erected in 1855 as a Dutch Reformed church.

Workingmen's Cottages. 1-25 and 2-26 Warren Place, between Hicks and Henry streets.

If you're interested in politics, history, or architecture, make a short detour off the main Court Street commercial strip and visit one of the nation's first low-rent housing units, built for workers. The structure's design was inspired by London's Victorian apartment buildings. Philanthropist Alfred Tredway White built these units in 1877, incorporating modern concepts of ventilation. The tiny cottages—less than twelve feet wide—line a lovely mews, Warren Place. The apartment buildings nearby, Tower Buildings, are at 417–435 Hicks Street, 136–142 Warren Street, and 129–135 Baltic Street. Other apartments, called the "Home Buildings," are at 439–445 Hicks Street and 134–140 Baltic Street, at Hicks Street. All were restored in 1986.

NOTABLE RESTAURANTS

Almontaser Restaurant. 218 Court Street, between Warren and Baltic streets, 624-9267. Sun.–Thurs., 11:30 a.m.–10:30 p.m.; Fri. and Sat., 11:30 a.m.–11:30 p.m. No credit cards.

What a mix: imagine a wonderful Middle Eastern menu that also includes coq au vin and something known as "turkey babagalo," a dish topped with pineapple and peach chunks resting on a bed of rice. Reflecting traditions of Yemen rather than Lebanon, these Middle Eastern dishes are spicy. Entrées are priced under $12.

Café on Clinton. 268 Clinton Street, between Warren and Congress streets, 625-5908. Dinner daily, lunch Wed.–Fri., brunch weekends. Mon.–Tues., 5 p.m.–11 p.m.; Wed.–Sun.,11 a.m.–3:30 p.m. and 5–11 p.m. Major credit cards.

The warmth pours forth from this intimate little restaurant's oak and exposed brick walls. The pressed-tin ceilings are beautifully restored. There are fewer than a dozen tables for eating plus seats for about eight at the small bar. A real treat is the $12.95 lobster every Tuesday night. Don't miss the hand-wrought iron brain-teaser puzzles hanging from a rack to the right of the bar. They'll keep you busy for hours. The menu features fresh-from-the-market grilled fish plus Mexican, Oriental, and Italian dishes. Entrée prices range from $7 to $15.

Casa Rosa. 384 Court Street, between Carroll and President streets, 625-8874 or 787-1907. Tues.–Sat., 11:30 a.m.–midnight; Sun., 1–10 p.m. Major credit cards. ✳

This is one of several restaurants on Court Street within walking distance of the **Cobble Hill Cinema** (see page 143). For $15 per person you can get solid, simple Italian fare that includes an antipasto, main course, and coffee.

Marco Polo Restaurant. 345 Court Street, corner of Union Street, 852-5015. Mon.–Thurs., 11:30 a.m.–11 p.m.; Fri., 11:30 a.m.–midnight; Sat., 3 p.m.–midnight; Sun., 1–10:30 p.m. Major credit cards.

A local favorite, this traditional Italian restaurant was rated one of Brooklyn's best by the *New York Daily News* in 1990. The extensive menu includes about fifteen seafood and fifteen meat entrées each, with such specialties as *porcini* mushroom pasta and black pasta with scallops and shrimps. Dinner entrées cost about $13 to $20. The pasta is homemade, and breads come from **Caputo's** down the street (see page 148). There's live piano music seven nights a week, and free valet parking. Weekend reservations are recommended.

Monte's Venetian Room. 451 Carroll Street, between Nevins Street and 3rd Avenue, 625-9656 or 624-8984. Daily, noon–10 p.m. Major credit cards.

Tucked away on a nondescript residential street, Monte's lays claim to being the oldest Italian restaurant in Brooklyn, having opened in 1906. The hand-painted Venetian scenes on the walls of the single, small dining room lend romance along with a familial ambience. The waiters become your friends, recommending the kitchen's best dishes.

Nino's. 215 Union Street, between Clinton and Henry streets, 858-5370. Mon.–Fri., noon–10 p.m.; Sat.–Sun., 1 p.m.–10 p.m. Major credit cards. ✳

Here is one good reason to dig a bit deeper into Carroll Gardens. Newly renovated, Nino's is a spiffy Sicilian restaurant known for its ample use of fresh vegetables. Dinner entrées are about $12 for fish and $8 for pasta dishes served with excellent homemade sauces. The decor is attractive, with blonde wood, green and white tablecloths, and a working fireplace. An upstairs room seats eighty for special occasions.

Red Rose. 315 Smith Street, between President and Union streets, one block from Court Street, across from Carroll Street Park, 625-0963. Mon.–Sat., 4:30–10 p.m.; Sun., 1–10 p.m. Major credit cards. ✳

Slightly off the beaten path, this cozy, old-fashioned restaurant has a definite appeal for its food and its low prices. You can have a bowl of soup and pasta for less than $10, and the food is well prepared and fresh. Come early on Sunday and you'll dine among the older Italian crowd; later arrivals represent the more gentrified neighborhood locals.

Pizza and Other Quick Meals

Ferdinando's. 151 Union Street, near Hicks Street, 855-1545. Mon.–Thurs., 10 a.m.–5 p.m.; Fri.–Sun., 10 a.m.–8 p.m. No credit cards. ✳

Seventy-five years old and slightly out of the way, this restaurant will give you some feel for the Red Hook of yesteryear, an Italian immigrant community of dock and factory workers. There's a certain romance in the old tiled floors and pressed-tin ceiling. But what has kept this *focacceria* going are its lunch specialties, such as rice balls with ricotta and *panelli*, a stuffed Sicilian bread.

Joe's. 349 Court Street, between Union and President streets, 625-3223. Daily, 6 a.m.–7:30 p.m. ✳

This is an old luncheonette that attracts the locals for breakfast or lunch. The prices are low, the food is hearty, and both the owners and the clientele couldn't be more down-to-earth. Joe's also makes a mean cup of espresso.

Leonardo's Brick Oven Pizza. 383 Court Street, corner of 1st Place, 624-9620. Daily, noon–midnight. No credit cards. ✳

This is the best pizza place in the neighborhood if you like thin crust pizza with lots of different toppings, cooked in an old-style brick oven. There is outdoor seating in good weather, and the staff is more than tolerant of young children.

Sam's Restaurant. 238 Court Street, between Kane and Baltic streets, 596-3458. Wed.–Mon., noon–10:30 p.m. No credit cards. ✳

For sixty years this cozy local spot has been turning out Italian food, so no wonder the *rollatini*, spaghetti, and brick-oven pizzas are excellent. You can't get more authentic than this. Prices are low.

SHOPPING

Specialty Food Shops

Cammareri Brothers Bakery. 502 Henry Street, between Sackett and Union streets, 852-3606. Daily, 6 a.m.–7 p.m.

This is a bakery with a double claim to fame. Moviegoers will be interested to know that this is where Cher met her lover's baker-brother in *Moonstruck*. Antique buffs will be pleased to know that the rare old-fashioned coal oven turns out about five thousand loaves of bread a day. Everyone will enjoy the fresh baked goods. The bakery is located a few blocks off Court Street, the main commercial strip.

Caputo's Bake Shop. 329 Court Street, between Union and Sackett streets, 875-6871. Daily, 6 a.m.–7 p.m. No credit cards.

This fourth-generation family bakery is *the* place for bread in the neighborhood. About ten different kinds are baked on the premises, and you can make a meal out of a special bread filled with salami and provolone cheese. This is a must for picnickers.

Cobble Hill Deli. 264 Clinton Street, corner of Verandah Place, 858-0840. Mon.–Sat., 8 a.m.–8 p.m.; Sun., 8 a.m.–5 p.m. No credit cards.

This is the perfect place to go if you want fixings for a picnic in Cobble Hill Park. While you're in the area, take a walk up Verandah Place to see a beautiful private lane of three-story brick houses. You can almost picture the old sailors of Brooklyn returning here to their homes after a month at sea.

College Bakery. 239 Court Street, between Warren and Baltic streets, 624-5534. Tues.–Sun., 7 a.m.–8 p.m. No credit cards.

Not much of the original German population is left in this neighborhood, but one survivor is this sixty-year-old, family-run German bakery which makes old-fashioned whipped cream birthday cakes, chocolate layer cakes, and rye and sourdough rye breads. This is also the local source for a high-fiber European Malsovit diet bread that people buy by the dozen.

Court Pastry Shop. 298 Court Street, between DeGraw and Douglass streets, 875-4820. Daily, 8 a.m.–8:30 p.m. No credit cards.

Wonderful traditional Italian sweets are the treat here, from cannoli to *sfogliatella* (huge lobster-tail pastries filled with cream) to *pistachiotta* (pistachio-filled sweet pastry) and *sfinge*, also known as "Saint Joseph's pastries." Seasonal holiday treats like *strufoli* and *cassata* also are available.

D'Amico Foods. 309 Court Street, between DeGraw and Sackett streets, 875-5403. Mon.–Sat., 9 a.m.–7 p.m.; closed Sun. No credit cards.

Walk through the door and a huge old-fashioned cast-iron coffee roaster and grinder immediately give you the flavor of this authentic Italian grocery store. More than fifty different kinds of coffee are roasted on the premises. You'll also find large jars of olives and pimentos, spices, cheeses, and Italian biscuits. Don't forget to try a cup of coffee before you leave.

G. Esposito Pork Store. 357 Court Street, near President Street, 875-6863. Mon.–Sat., 7 a.m.–6 p.m. No credit cards.

Esposito's family-owned shop has been selling homemade sausages since 1922. Among the seven varieties are specials flavored with fennel, pepper and onion, and cheese with parsley. You can pick up all of the ingredients for a feast—three kinds of fresh mozzarella cheese; delicious milk-fed veal; rice and prosciutto balls; eggplant, olive, or mushroom salad; and, if you're in the mood, pigs' feet.

Marquet Patisserie. 235 Smith Street, between Douglas and Butler streets, 852-8915. Tues.–Fri., 7 a.m.–7 p.m.; Sat., 8 a.m.–7 p.m.; Sun., 8 a.m.–5:30 p.m.; closed Mon. No credit cards.

The New York Times has rated this "one of the finest pastry shops in New York City." Started by neighborhood residents Jean-Pierre Marquet and his wife Lynne Guillot, this little shop turns out thin lemon tarts, petite macaroons, and spectacular croissants filled with almond cream and apples. Despite its out-of-the-way location, connoisseurs come from Manhattan and all over Brooklyn to buy these treats.

Mazzola's Bakery. 192 Union Street, corner of Henry Street, 643-1719. Daily, 6 a.m.–7:30 p.m. No credit cards.

More than fifty years in the same location, Mazzola's specializes in breads. Bread with a filling of provolone and pepperoni (and the unfortunate name of "lardbread") is delectable, as is the extra-fluffy *torrese* bread and magnificent raisin bread.

Monkeyswedding. 225 Court Street, between Warren and Baltic streets, 852-7326. Tues.–Fri., 8 a.m.–8 p.m.; Sat., 8 a.m.–6 p.m.; Sun., noon–5 p.m.; closed Mon. Major credit cards. ✳

Homemade luncheon salads, lemon squares, and brownies are sold at this small, friendly store, along with a huge assortment of tea, pottery, baskets, and other sundry kitchen items.

Pastosa Ravioli. 347 Court Street, near Union Street, 625-9482. Mon.–Sat., 9 a.m.–6 p.m.; Sun., 9 a.m.–12:30 p.m. No credit cards.

Since the original shop opened twenty-five years ago, another dozen have been launched by Ajello family members throughout the greater New York area. Daily specials include freshly made pasta, ravioli, and lasagne. Other items include sauces, prosciutto balls, meatballs, and a variety of salads. Everything is excellent.

Staubitz Market. 222 Court Street, between Baltic and Warren streets, 624-0014. Mon.–Sat., 9 a.m.–1 p.m., 2–7 p.m. House credit cards only.

Brooklyn's most upscale butcher shop, Staubitz carries a wide selection of "health food meats": no-nitrate turkey and hot dogs; mousses, pâtés, and sausages by Les Trois Petits Cochons; hormone-free chicken and veal; and a good selection of standard and kosher meats. The store also sells top-quality gourmet foods, such as imported cheese, pasta, chutney, barbecue sauce, fresh-ground coffee beans, and bread. Call in your freezer order and they'll pack it for instant storage. Local delivery is available.

Interesting Neighborhood Shops

Bookcourt. 163 Court Street, between Pacific and Dean streets, 875-3677. Mon.–Sat., 10 a.m.–11 p.m.; Sun., 11 a.m.–8 p.m. Major credit cards. ✳

Comfortable and filled with a good selection of contemporary paperbacks and new hardcovers, this pleasant bookstore also has an attractive children's room in the back with cute seats for the little browser.

Cobble Hill Community Bookstore. 212 Court Street, corner of Warren Street, 834-9494. Mon.–Sat., 10:30 a.m.–9:30 p.m.; Sun., noon–8 p.m. Major credit cards. ✳

This is one very full store, with an overwhelming selection of kids' books as well as toys. The owners will order books on request, and they regularly discount hardcover books. Once related to Park Slope's Community Bookstore, the affiliation no longer exists.

Home Pottery. 231 Court Street, between Warren and Baltic streets, 797-3924. Daily, 11 a.m.–8 p.m. Major credit cards.

This shop sells pottery, jewelry, and crafts made exclusively by Brooklyn artists. There are lovely items here, from salad bowls and garlic jars to unusual candelabra. All are handmade by members of a local pottery cooperative.

Johnnie's Booterie. 208 Smith Street, between Baltic and Butler streets, 625-5334. Mon.–Sat., 10 a.m.–6:30 p.m. Major credit cards. ✳

A second-generation family business, Johnnies' hallmark for more than fifty years has been experienced service and careful attention to fitting children's shoes. Most of the shoes are moderately priced Stride Rites. High-flying munchers take note: one block down is **Marquet Patisserie**, one of New York City's most fabulous French bakeries (see page 149).

Kane-Miller Book Publishers. 307 Court Street, between Sackett and DeGraw streets, 624-5120. Mon.–Fri., 10 a.m.–5 p.m. No credit cards. ✳

Here's a special place for books for kids up to age ten. Kane-Miller publishes English translations of illustrated foreign children's books—and the product is first rate. Some titles come from Europe, but others come from Ghana, Venezuela, even Sri Lanka. Retail customers can purchase seconds here at 50 percent off.

Laughing Giraffe at Monkeyswedding. 234 Court Street, corner of Baltic Street, 852-3635. Tues.–Sat., 11 a.m.–6 p.m.; closed Sun. and Mon. Major credit cards. ✳

One of the two owners of this children's toy store is also the owner of the **Monkeyswedding** bakery across the street (opposite). Some "educational" toys plus more pedestrian offerings—crayons, paper, and other basics—fill the shelves. You won't find a cozier environment or more helpful sales staff.

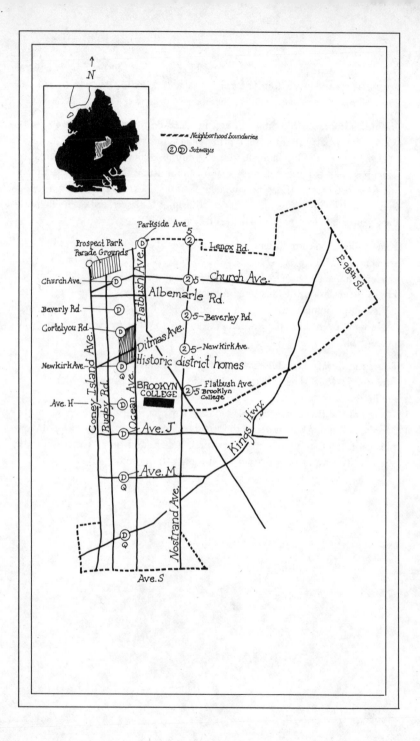

N

Neighborhood boundaries
② ⑩ Subways

Parkside Ave.
Prospect Park Parade Grounds
Lenox Rd.
E. 98th St.
Church Ave.
Church Ave.
Albemarle Rd.
Beverly Rd.
Beverley Rd.
Cortelyou Rd.
Ditmas Ave.
Newkirk Ave.
Newkirk Ave.
Historic district homes
Flatbush Ave.
Ave. H
BROOKYN COLLEGE
Brooklyn College
Coney Island Ave.
Rugby Rd.
Ocean Ave.
Ave. J
Kings Hwy.
Ave. M
Nostrand Ave.
Ave. S

FLATBUSH

This chapter gives a bird's-eye view of just three strikingly different areas within what used to be called, simply, Flatbush: East Flatbush, Midwood, and Prospect Park South. This is not the whole of Flatbush, just a sampling. But among them you can eat, shop, take in a play or stroll to your heart's content.

How to get there: As you might expect from its central Brooklyn location, there are many ways to get to Flatbush. A detailed map will help you get your bearings.

By car: One easy, if not elegant, route is to follow Flatbush Avenue south. For Brooklyn College, continue south on Flatbush, turn right on Bedford Avenue, and follow it to Avenue H (call for detailed directions). For Prospect Park South and Ditmas Park, the best route is south on Coney Island Avenue, turning left onto Albemarle Road, Beverley Road, Cortelyou Road, or Ditmas Avenue. You also can follow this route to Brooklyn College, turning left on Avenue H. The best way to Midwood is via Ocean Parkway. In general, Ocean Parkway is the most attractive and fastest thoroughfare in Flatbush.

By subway: D or M trains to Newkirk Avenue (Ditmas), to Church Avenue (Prospect Park South), or to Avenue J, Avenue M, or Kings Highway (Midwood). Or take the 2 or 5 train to Flatbush Avenue (Brooklyn College), or the 2 or 5 train to Church Avenue (East Flatbush).

Cab services: Avenue J Airport Service (251-3200), Best Way Car Service (252-6363), Prompt Car Service (284-2288), or Shalom Cars (236-5777). Cost is about $8 to $12 to Brooklyn Heights, $20 to $25 to Grand Central Station.

ABOUT THE NEIGHBORHOOD

The string of neighborhoods known collectively as Flatbush is one of Brooklyn's most famous regions. It is no longer the mostly Jewish area it was in the first half of the 20th century, and some old-timers bemoan the fact that "the neighborhood has changed." In fact, Flatbush remains largely middle- and working-class but now encompasses a varied and truly international population distributed among many sub-neighborhoods.

There is a wonderfully urbane incongruity in Flatbush of the 1990s. Hungering for Caribbean flavors and sounds? Take Flatbush Avenue to the Caribbean community in East Flatbush. West Indians from more than thirty Caribbean nations reside here. Sample Guyanese codfish cakes and ginger beer at **Sybil's Bakery & Restaurant**, or indulge in Jamaican fruit turnovers at **Hammond's Finger Lickin' Bakery**. If music is your interest, check out the latest in African and Caribbean music trends at the **African Record Center**—and then take a ten-minute car ride to the original **Sam Ash**, now a nationally known discounter of musical instruments. If you're shopping for top-notch jewelry, handbags, and home decorations, you'll love the prices in Midwood at such boutiques as the **Yellow Door** and **Carole Block** on Avenue M, and famous **Jimmy's** and **Chuckies** on Kings Highway. The largest community of non-European Jews outside of Israel lives in Midwood, too; try the food at **Mansoura's Oriental Pastry** or **Negev Caterers**. Speaking of nourishment, you'll find some for the mind at lectures, concerts and kids programs at **Brooklyn College**, and Judaica at places like **Hecht's Hebrew Book Store**. After all this culture shock, you may need a respite—a half dozen blocks down Coney Island Avenue from Prospect Park is the peaceful residential area of Prospect Park South and a bit further, Ditmas Park. Even Brooklynites are surprised to find block after block of turn-of-the-century urban mansions here.

Kidstuff

There are *terrific* shows for kids at **Brooklyn College**. You're in the heart of the city here, so of course there are urban playgrounds and basketball courts. The huge wholesale **Terminal Market** also may be of interest. But unless you happen to live here (or Grandma does), Flatbush is not kiddie heaven.

POINTS OF CULTURAL INTEREST

Brooklyn College. Intersection of Hillel Place and Campus Road, 434-1900.

Old flicks, theater, dance, lectures—all are available at Brooklyn College. For generations of Brooklyn kids the American Dream started on this site, which was once used to host the Barnum and Bailey Circus. Since its inception in 1930 Brooklyn College has been one of New York City's great educational resources, and is still one of the "best buys in American public education," ranking high in the list of the nation's better colleges. Students reflect Brooklyn's wide spectrum of ethnic groups.

Brooklyn Public Library—Midwood. East 16th Street, near Avenue J, 377-7972. Call to check hours.

This library is central to the shopping on Avenue J, so it is a good place to stop for a read with kids. Brooklyn residents: remember, any book you check out here can be returned at your local branch library.

Brooklyn Terminal Market. Main gate is on Foster Avenue, near East 85th Street. (Take exit 13 off the Belt Parkway, go north on Rockaway Parkway, then left on Foster Avenue to the main gate.) Daily, 8 a.m.–6 p.m. Cash only.

This market actually is in Canarsie, close to Flatbush. This big, bustling wholesale food and plant market, in operation since 1945, is a great place for showing kids where the store owners go shopping—call it Economics 101 or Introduction to Wholesaling. Many of the establishments here are open to the public. Lots of people like the pickles and ambience here better than what they find on Manhattan's Lower East Side. Of particular interest to gardeners are the spring shrubs and plants sold at the lowest possible prices by Tony Pagano at stall 62 (968-7400) and fruit vines (watermelons, wine grapes) and Christmas firs at Anthony Visconti and Sons, stall 14 (241-7776).

Erasmus High School Museum. 911 Flatbush Avenue, between Church and Snyder avenues, 282-7803. By appointment.

Once called "the Eton of High Schools," Erasmus may be Brooklyn's most famous high school. Its alumni include Barbra Streisand, Alexander Hamilton, chess master Bobby Fisher, Oscar Brand, Beverly Sills, Mickey Spillane, Eli Wallach, Neil Diamond, basketball player Billy Cunningham, and artist David Levine, among others. Opened by the Flatbush Reformed Dutch Church in 1786, it became a public school in 1896. Inside the original Georgian-Federal building with a columned porch, visitors can spend at least half an hour in the museum viewing old yearbooks, desks, and framed photos of famous alumni.

NBC Studios. East 14th Street, off Avenue M, 780-6400. ✳

Some of the earliest silent films were made in this building, the old Vitagraph Studios. Mary Pickford had a house built on the corner of nearby Ditmas Avenue and Rugby Road so she could live it up in style while filming here. The original *Peter Pan* was filmed here during the 1950s. Sammy Davis, Jr., recorded shows here in the 1960s, and this also was the base of operations for "The Cosby Show" during its heyday in the mid-1980s. The soap opera "Another World" has been videotaped and edited here for twenty-six years, and periodically the two state-of-the-art studios broadcast "Saturday Night Live." Tours are limited to school groups and last only fifteen minutes; call NBC public relations in Manhattan, (212) 664-4444, for information.

Wyckoff House Museum. Clarendon Road and Ralph Avenue, at East 59th Street, 629-5400. Fri.–Sun., 10 a.m.–3 p.m., or call for an appointment.

One of the oldest buildings in New York City, and restored to reflect the life-styles of wealthy Dutch settlers of the 1650s, this historic oasis is worth visiting. Today there are lectures, weekend craft sessions, children's story hours, and outdoor programs held on a large lawn area. Standing here all those years, the Wyckoff House is a reminder of all the social configurations Brooklyn has witnessed: from a rural Dutch colonial farming settlement to a retreat for wealthy nineteenth-century industrialists, to a haven for Jewish, Italian, and other immigrants in search of the American dream, to today's urbanized hodgepodge of yentas, yuppies, Caribbean islanders, African-Americans, and Eastern European refugees. Cultural events are held here, including summer concerts. For free brochures, contact the Flatbush Development Corporation, 1418 Cortelyou Road, Brooklyn, NY 11226, or call 469-8990.

EAST FLATBUSH

Special events: The colorful annual West Indian American Day Carnival, New York's largest Caribbean celebration, takes place not in East Flatbush but along Eastern Parkway in Crown Heights (Brooklyn's other big Caribbean population center) on Labor Day.

ABOUT THE NEIGHBORHOOD

Many Americans know something of the Caribbean: since the advent of discount airfares, vacationers by the millions have fallen in love with it. Music born of the islands seems almost as American as apple pie, from Harry Belafonte's calypso "Day-O" in the "Banana Boat Song" to the reggae and salsa beats that influence modern jazz and permeate rock and roll. This cultural and human traffic travels a two-way street; today Brooklyn is home to hundreds of thousands of pizza-eating, subway-riding islanders from more than thirty different nations.

The biggest attraction for visitors to Caribbean East Flatbush is unquestionably culinary. The enticing fruit and vegetable markets are exotic, with piles of mangos and coconuts, huge plantains, and innumerable mysterious-looking roots. A quick trip along Church Avenue will bring you to small, informal, and inexpensive eating establishments bubbling over with the true flavors of the Caribbean. The food and ambience bear the stamp of authenticity.

Some of the ingredients of this West Indian cuisine deserve a note because they reflect so clearly the combined African and Indian origins of West Indian culture as it is today. *Bammy* is a flatbread made of the cassava root (also the basis of tapioca), which is indigenous to the West Indies; Columbus reportedly feasted on cassava bread given to him by the local Indians. On the other hand, a spinach look-alike called *callaloo* is an indigenous African vegetable said to have been introduced to the Caribbean islands by enterprising African slaves. An okra dish with the wonderful name *coo-coo* also has African origins. And exactly what goes into the soft drinks labeled "Agony: Peanut Punch Plus" and "Front End Lifter and Magnum Explosion Combo," which are sold at some of the bakeries, is anybody's guess.

Historical Notes

For decades Caribbean islanders have come to Brooklyn seeking a better life. Of 300,000 West Indian immigrants who arrived in the United States between 1900 and the 1930s, tens of thousands ended up in Brooklyn. Many had a strong work ethic, and they scrimped and saved and eventually bought homes in neighborhoods such as Bedford-Stuyvesant, East Flatbush, and Crown Heights. Following World War II the flow of immigrants picked up again. Since 1960 more than 600,000 Caribbean immigrants have sought their fortunes in New York City. Unlike the first wave of mostly uneducated farmers, among the most recent arrivals are professional and technically skilled workers.

West Indians are considered the second-largest immigrant group in New York City (after Italians), but they are hardly one united community. Rivalries and tensions are said to run strong, which is not surprising given the diversity of their backgrounds and native tongues: English in Trinidad, Jamaica, Grenada, and Barbados; Dutch in Aruba and Curaçao; Spanish in Puerto Rico and the Dominican Republic; and French and Creole dialects in Martinique, Guadeloupe, and Haiti.

Note: This isn't a Caribbean resort, so don't wear your latest mink-lined leather coat; sneakers and jeans are fine.

ENTERTAINMENT, NOTABLE RESTAURANTS, AND SPECIALTY FOOD SHOPS

> ### Food for a Caribbean Feast
> jerk chicken, curried goat, or shrimp
> steamed red snapper
> johnny cakes (fried yeast balls)
> fried *bammy*
> carrot juice with nutmeg
> vanilla mango ice cream

B and H Fruit and Vegetable. 5012 Church Avenue, corner of Utica Avenue, 345-7839. Daily, 8 a.m.–8 p.m.

To get the flavor of the neighborhood, check out the wonderful Korean-run multiethnic grocer next to **Hammond's Bakery** (opposite). It sells not only the standard array of grapes, carrots, and kiwis one finds everywhere in New York, but also breadfruit, a boggling array of yams with such foreign names as *dasheen* and *edo*, plus salted beef, plantain flour, and an international assortment of packaged goods.

Cheffy's Jamaican. 740 Nostrand Avenue, corner of Park Place, 363-9515. Mon.–Sat., 11 a.m.–10 p.m.

If you're in the mood for authentic Jamaican foods, the locals say you should try Cheffy's. This hole-in-the-wall restaurant is one of several in the area serving fried dumplings, oxtail stew, fish cakes, cow's feet or goat curry, and more. A full meal runs less than $10 per person.

Flatbush Food Cooperative. 1318 Cortelyou Road, between Argyle and Rugby roads, 284-9717. Mon.–Fri., 9:30 a.m.–8 p.m.; Sat. and Sun., 9:30 a.m.– 7 p.m.

This health food cooperative specializes in organic foods. There is a big selection of organic produce and specialty natural and kosher foods. The co-op is owned and operated by members (who get discounts off shelf prices), but you don't have to be a member to shop here.

Glen's Jerk Chicken. 3125 Church Avenue, between 31st and 32nd streets, 287-7380. Daily, 7 a.m.–2 a.m.

Anyone who knows anything about West Indian food knows about spicy jerk chicken and pork (so named for the slow barbecue technique). A whole chicken at Glen's is about $9, and there is also a full menu of specialties, such as fried dumplings, oxtail stew, fish cakes, cow foot curry, *bammies*, fried plantains, red snapper, and soursop juice. Glen's three locations are sandwiched between familiar-looking local stores—a driving school, a dress shop, and a hair stylist—but don't be surprised to find pictures of Haile Selaisse, posters of Jamaica, and Bob Marley reggae music. This is Rastafarian country.

Hammond's Finger Lickin' Bakery. 5014 Church Avenue, near Utica Avenue, 342-5770. Mon.–Sat., 8:30 a.m.–7:30 p.m.; Sun., 10:30 a.m.–4:30 p.m.

While cruising Church Avenue in search of a Caribbean taste or two, stop here for Jamaican treats: cinnamon buns, tropical fruit turnovers, beef patties, and more. All goodies are under $1. The food made at this small bakery is traditional and very tasty. There's another Hammond's at 1436 Nostrand Avenue.

Hanna Town Bakery. 3222 Church Avenue, near New York Avenue, 287-5956. Mon.–Sat., 8 a.m.–8 p.m.

Here you'll find Jamaican *hardo* bread (a dense white bread good for toast and excellent for sopping up stews), coconut turnovers, and spice buns, plus an interesting line of imported goods: Jamaican cream sodas, Kola Champagne, Tamarindo drink, and British Ginger wine. Don't miss the little packets of Mrs. Lunn's Tropical Pepper Shrimp Snacks.

Island Restaurant and Club. 875 Utica Avenue, near Church Avenue, 485-7947. Tues.–Sun., 5 p.m.–midnight; live music Thurs.–Sat. Major credit cards.

This restaurant and club is a bit of Trinidad in New York, which means it is a little bit French, a little bit Spanish, and a little bit Indian. The decor aspires to high tech, the crowd a good mix of well-dressed, mature adults as well as people in their early twenties. On Thursday, Friday, and Saturday there is live music, from rhythm and blues to reggae to oldies. Menu items start at about $8 and include Caribbean and seafood entrées with colorful names like "Calypso Chicken" and "Reggae Fish." Early in the evening you are likely to find families here celebrating birthdays and other special occasions.

Sybil's Bakery and Restaurant. 2210 Church Avenue, near Flatbush Avenue, 469-9049. Mon.–Sat., 8 a.m.–midnight; closed Sun.

This clean, friendly West Indian (Guyanese) restaurant and bakery is centrally located if you happen to be driving down Flatbush to the beach or **Kings Plaza Shopping Center** (page 102) or are setting out to explore Caribbean Brooklyn. The bakery section is filled with an exotic array of pastries, such as coconut sweet bread, doughy cheese rolls, glazed jelly-filled triangles, and *salaras*, red coconut cookies. Sit at the counter, or at one of the green and white tables for a meal of baked chicken, stewed fish, codfish cakes, and goat *roti* curry. Try a few drinks: cane juice, sorrel, ginger beer, *mauby* (from a bark akin to cinnamon). There are Guyanese newspapers, too, for a change of perspective.

Interesting Neighborhood Shops

African Record Center Makossa Distribution. 1194 Nostrand Avenue, between Hawthorne and Fenimore streets, 493-4500. Daily, 9 a.m.–8 p.m.

New York City's largest importer and producer of pan-African sounds for twenty-five years, this shop is a central resource for many musicians. You'll find a wealth of compact discs, records, and tapes here from Nigeria, Ghana, Zaire, Cameroon, Ethiopia, and South Africa by such prominent third world artists as Fela Kuti, Franco, and OK Jazz group, whom Makossa Distribution Company helped launch. There's also an extensive collection of popular Haitian music. If you're interested but unfamiliar with the music, come in and chat with the knowledgeable staff, who will play demonstration tapes for you.

Dorsey's Picture Frame and Art Gallery. 553 Rogers Avenue, between Hawthorne and Fenimore streets, 771-3803. Daily, 1–8 p.m.

Framing is the business at hand at Dorsey's, but there's also a small display of artwork by Caribbean and Afro-American artists. Check it out if you're in the area. The owner is charming.

Discmart Black Mind. 610 New York Avenue, corner of Rutland Road, 774-5800. Mon.–Sat., 10 a.m.–8 p.m.

Both books and records are sold at Discmart, one of Brooklyn's premier black book shops. There is a good selection of African writers and sounds, some produced by Makossa Distributing Company, in addition to Caribbean and Haitian imports.

Loehmann's. 19 Duryea Place, off Flatbush Avenue near Beverley Road, 469-9800. Mon., Tues., Fri., and Sat., 10 a.m.–5 p.m.; Wed. and Thurs., 10 a.m.–9 p.m.; closed Sun. Major credit cards.

Like a tough old lady this seventy-year-old pioneer of discounted designer shopping lives on—in spite of nouveau discount competition from Vermont to California. There are two ways to "do" Loehmann's. One approach favored by hard-core shoppers is to dedicate an hour every week to scoping out the latest shipments (at least that way you won't drown in the racks and racks of picked-over merchandise). The other is to go on a fundraiser "shopping night" (a popular ploy) with your civic, church, or synagogue group, when your purchases are tax-deductible (call the store about arranging such a visit). Loehmann's is located on a small road off a low-income shopping strip. Macy's is a block away, and nearby is the shell of the once-famous Loew's Kings Theater, one of the nation's most ornate Depression-era movie theaters.

MIDWOOD

Special events: Believe it or not, a Mardi Gras along Avenue M (June).

How it got its name: From the Dutch *Midwout* or "Middle Woods." In fact, many streets are still tree-lined.

ABOUT THE NEIGHBORHOOD

Drive along Ocean Parkway on a Friday or Saturday evening and you'll see a constant flow of well-dressed Jewish families going to one of Midwood's many synagogues. Dubbed "kosher yuppie land" by one New York daily, Midwood recently has undergone a youthful gentrification. Demand for housing within walking distance of the Sephardic synagogues is so strong that the price of some homes has shot past the million-dollar mark.

For those so inclined, there is a great deal of Jewish cultural life here. There is also good shopping. And, yes, this is where actor-director Woody Allen went to high school.

Midwood is home to both Sephardic (Middle Eastern and South European) and Ashkenazi (Northern European) Jews. The Ashkenazi presence is visible in Midwood's old German bakeries and the world-famous Flatbush and Mirrer yeshivas (religious schools). Members of the wealthy Jewish community that has settled around Ocean Parkway are mainly Syrians from Aleppo and Damascus. Their style and affluence is apparent in the stunning $7 million Sephardic Community Center and Sha'are Zion Synagogue on Ocean Parkway.

The Orthodox Jewish Syrian community is tight-knit, and to outsiders the "SY," as they call themselves, may appear clannish. Arabic and French are spoken along with English, young people marry within the community, and many people work in family businesses. Their year is punctuated by highly formal holidays and customs; many of the fancy local clothing stores are fueled by the Syrian demand for orthodox elegance.

On the other hand, Avenue J reflects old Jewish Flatbush. In its past Avenue J served a thriving German and Eastern European Jewish community; it still helps to know a little Yiddish here. In the clothing shops you are likely to hear talk of *hassanas* (weddings) and *shidduchs* (arranged marriages) as well as bar mitzvahs. Typical of Brooklyn, where Jews and Italians have lived side by side for decades, the neighborhood used to be partly Italian.

Avenue M is a thriving shopping street with a mix of local stores and expensive boutiques catering to both the affluent Syrian community and es-caped-to-the-suburbs ex-Brooklynites—many of whom still make shopping expeditions back to Brooklyn in search of good prices and storekeepers who know them on a first-name basis. Incongruously located next door to a kosher fast-food joint called *Chapanosh* (which in Hebrew translates to "Grab-a-Bite") is the old Vitagraph movie studio, now used by NBC. Silent movie stars Mary Pickford and Laurel and Hardy were filmed at the Vitagraph; later, Perry Como, Steve Allen, and recently "The Cosby Show" were all produced here. The nearby Edward R. Murrow High School specializes in communications.

Nearby, Coney Island Avenue between Avenues J and M is chockablock with no-frills discount shops ranging from interior design and silver shops to the one-of-a-kind **Miss Pauline's Bras and Girdles**. Many of these stores have such minimal window displays that they hardly look like retail shops at all. But the merchandise is good, the service is great, and of course many prices are discounted—not to mention that the experience of shopping here is different from what you'll get at any bland suburban mall.

Kings Highway, which intersects Ocean Parkway, has been a major shopping thoroughfare for decades. The decorative two-story buildings that line the avenue date from the 1930s, when the strip was first built. The local Middle Eastern influence is clearly visible: note the decorative Alexandria at 809 Kings Highway, now a kosher catering hall. The section of Kings Highway from about East 2nd Street to East 9th Street is part of the Syrian Jewish enclave; among expensive clothing shops, Middle Eastern grocery stores carry the names of Israeli and Lebanese cities: Bat Yam, Holon, and Beirut. On Saturday most stores in this area are closed for the Sabbath. From East 9th Street farther along Kings Highway, the numerous clothing and shoe stores serve the general public and are open on Saturday.

ENTERTAINMENT

Brooklyn Center Cinema. Whitman Hall, Brooklyn College, intersection of Hillel Place and Campus Road, 780-5295 or 780-5298. Call for show times. Tickets are only $4.

Film buffs! In an era when many Manhattan revival theaters are closing down, Brooklyn's Walt Whitman Hall is going strong. This is Brooklyn's first and only retrospective movie house, complete with a forty-foot-wide by two-story-high CinemaScope screen. Here's the hitch: showings are less frequent than at commercial houses. Call to get on the mailing list, or watch local listings. The B41 or B44 bus stops at Avenue H, a stone's throw away from here.

Brooklyn Center for the Performing Arts at Brooklyn College (BCBC). Intersection of Hillel Place and Campus Road, 434-1900. Call for a schedule of performances. Major credit cards. ✳

More than eighty excellent musical, dance, and theater performances make their way here each year. Well-known names include Alvin Ailey, José Limon, the Shanghai String Quartet, and the King Singers. Even Mel Tormé comes to Brooklyn College! Theater productions range from Rodgers and Hammerstein's *Oklahoma!* to a Yiddish version of Gilbert and Sullivan's *HMS Pinafore*, to reggae and calypso shows. You can buy a BCBC subscription series or get single tickets for Saturday evening and Sunday afternoon performances. Get a calendar and directions by writing to the Conservatory Concert Office, c/o BCBC, Box 163, Brooklyn, NY 11210. For information on the "Family Time" series call 434-1900.

Kent Triplex Movie Theater. 1168 Coney Island Avenue, near Avenue H, 338-3371. Call for show times. ✳

This local triplex is close to both the Ditmas Park and Midwood areas and not far from Prospect Park. Ticket prices are reduced substantially for matinees.

Kingsway RKO Cinema. 946 Kings Highway, corner of Coney Island Avenue, 645-8588. Call for show times. ✳

Smack in the middle of Kings Highway you'll find this large movie theater—a good stop for a midafternoon break from shopping.

PARKS AND PLAYGROUNDS

Colonel David Marcus Park. Avenue B, between East 3rd Street and Ocean Parkway. ✻

This spacious and newly renovated playground is a wonderful find. Worthy on its own of a visit, this lovely kiddie spot also happens to be a short drive away from several interesting shopping areas, such as Avenue M and Kings Highway. It is also on the way to the **New York Aquarium, Coney Island**, and **Brighton Beach**.

Kolbert Playground. Avenues L and M, between East 17th and East 18th streets. ✻

Here's a microcosm of the neighborhood: Russians playing checkers and chess, mothers with baby strollers, and elderly women chatting on the benches. There's a big renovated playground for the kids and a large basketball area for teenagers. Located within walking distance of most of Avenue M shopping in a pleasant middle-class neighborhood behind Edward R. Murrow High School, this is a fine place for a picnic lunch—and people watching.

Ocean Parkway Mall. Ocean Parkway, from Prospect Park to the Atlantic Ocean. ✻

Adults will enjoy the six-mile bike ride along wide, flat Ocean Parkway, though crossing all of those side streets can be slow going. Still, Ocean Parkway is one of the finest boulevards for riding or strolling in New York City. It was designed by Frederick Law Olmsted and Calvert Vaux, creators of Central Park and Prospect Park. Along the way you'll pass through a middle- and upper-middle-class, largely Orthodox Jewish area (many people will be strolling to and from synagogue on Friday evening and Saturday). Once you arrive at the boardwalk it is only another few minutes' ride to the **New York Aquarium, Coney Island amusement park**, and **Nathan's** to the right (see pages 85–87), or to the left along Brighton Beach Avenue to the Russian emporium, **M & I International Foods**, and **Mrs. Stahl's Knishes** (see page 82).

NOTABLE RESTAURANTS

Carmel Classic. 923 Kings Highway, at Coney Island Avenue, 336-2500. Mon.–Fri., 2 p.m.–midnight; weekends, 2 p.m.–3 a.m.; Sat., closed until after sundown. Major credit cards. ✻

This unusual restaurant has Chinese, Moroccan, and Israeli foods, all kosher—and that's just for starters. The restaurant also offers Moroccan and Israeli music and dancing. Weekend evenings can run late here. It's also a popular spot for parties, bar mitzvahs, and weekend gaiety.

Caraville. 1910 Avenue M, near East 19th Street, 339-2540. Daily, 6 a.m.–midnight. *
Caraville isn't a kosher deli but instead a classic New York Greek diner. The extensive menu has offerings ranging from crabmeat salad to Italian veal dishes, pancakes to fountain items. You can get lunch here for under $10 and dinner entrées for under $14. Unlike many diners, the waiters are uniformed, the floor is carpeted, and the owners have style: on the restaurant's tenth anniversary, locals feasted on $5 lobsters, which is what they had cost on the restaurant's opening day.

Gourmet Cafe. 1622 Coney Island Avenue, between Avenues L and M, 338-5825. Mon.–Thurs., 11:30 a.m.–10 p.m.; Sun., noon–10 p.m.; closed Fri. and Sat. Major credit cards. *
This small, modern restaurant serving kosher vegetarian food is modestly priced and conveniently located on a major thoroughfare. The menu includes excellent soups made from vegetable broth and fresh veggies, croissant sandwiches, salads, soy-based goulash, Italian dishes, such as manicotti and eggplant parmigiana heros, apple crisp, whole grain peach muffins, cappuccino, ice-cream sodas, and more. Lunch specials cost around $5; a three-course dinner is about $12.

Weiss Kosher Dairy Restaurant. 1146 Coney Island Avenue, near Avenue H, 421-0184. Sun.–Thurs., noon–10 p.m.; closed Sat. during the day but open after sundown.
Sometimes you need a slightly fancy kosher dairy restaurant, and Weiss's fits the bill. There's good food and a nice old-fashioned *parve* ambience. A dinner of lemon sole runs about $13, or you can get blintzes for about $7. There is a parking lot across the street.

SHOPPING

Specialty Food Shops
For a taste of what nourishes the traditional Jewish body and soul, try the following:

Chiffon's Bake Shop. 1373 Coney Island Avenue, between Avenue J and Avenue K, 258-8822. Mon.–Thurs., 6 a.m.–8 p.m. Fri., closes early; closed Sat. *

Your Jewish grandmother would be at home here. Chiffon's has been turning out its baked goodies for years. The smell and taste of these rye breads, *challahs*, and cheesecakes suggest that they've been baked the same way, using the same recipes, for generations.

Isaac's Bake Shop. 1419 Avenue J, between East 14th and East 15th streets, 377-9291. Sun.–Thurs., 8 a.m.–7 p.m. Fri., closes early; closed Sat.

Noted in particular for its *challahs*, this kosher bakery sells enormous loaves perfectly suited to huge, hungry families. If *challah* isn't your thing, the dense loaves of kosher rye bread, *babkas*, cookies, and pastries are good choices. Isaac's gets very crowded on Thursday and early Friday, but whenever you visit, don't be surprised if the elderly ladies behind the counter call you "sweetheart." ✱

Mansoura's Oriental Pastry. 515 Kings Highway, between East 3rd and East 4th streets, 645-7977. Sun.–Thurs., 8 a.m.–7 p.m.; Fri., closes early; closed Sat.

This is a fifth-generation family business, run by Sephardic bakers from Aleppo, Syria. Their centuries-old recipes for birds nest, a honey- and pistachio-filled pastry, plus chocolates, Turkish delight, and candies are worth a taste. On Sunday only, "real food" is served at the half dozen tables: *bastorma* (spiced salami) and *bureka* (triangles of phyllo with spinach or cheese), falafel and *kibbe* (a spiced chopped meat dish).

Negev Caterers. 1211 Avenue J, between East 12th and East 13th streets, 258-2875. Sun.–Thurs., 9 a.m.–6 p.m.; Fri., closes early; closed Sat.

Here's a sure-fire way to impress a Jewish mother-in-law: pick up some authentic kosher take-out food from this shop—a spin-off from its Manhattan parent on West 72nd Street in the heart of the Jewish Upper West Side—and pass it off as your own cooking. Appetizers include an array of smoked salmon, herring, and whitefish salads. Entrées range from kosher garlic and honey roast chickens to pickled tongue or pastrami. There are also traditional soups: cabbage, matzoh ball, and *kreplach*. Special holiday dishes can be ordered. Call in advance for delivery on orders over $25.

Ossie's Avenue J Fish Store. 1215 Avenue J, near East 12th Street, 258-3129. Sun.–Thurs., 8 a.m.–6 p.m.; Fri., 8:30 a.m.–2:30 p.m.; closed Sat.

So you want to make your own gefilte fish from scratch? Ossie's sells ready-to-cook ground raw fish balls, and if you want to follow your bubba's recipe, they also sell ground codfish, whitefish, and pike. Everything here is kosher, so it gets busy near Jewish holidays. This store also has take-out soups, appetizing whitefish salad, and egg, tuna, and salmon salads.

Stern's Bakery. 1201 Avenue J, corner of East 12th Street, 377-9443. Sun.–Fri., 8 a.m.–6 p.m.; closed Sat. ✳

There's a pleasant atmosphere in this old-fashioned German Jewish bakery, but beware of the long lines on Friday and before holidays. Stern's has been in the family for three generations; the founder's picture is on the wall behind mounds of *rugalach*, honey cakes, *hamantaschen*, cheesecake, cookies, and almond cakes.

There are several Judaica shops in the area as well, including the following:

Eichler's Religious Articles, Gifts and Books. 1429 Coney Island Avenue, between Avenues J and K, 258-7643. Sun.–Wed., 10 a.m.–7 p.m.; Thurs., 10 a.m.–9 p.m.; Fri., 10 a.m.–3 p.m.; closed Sat. Major credit cards.

This is one of several Brooklyn shops specializing in Judaica. If you're not ready for tomes of the Talmud in Aramaic, you can still find Passover *hagadas*, holiday tapes in English and Hebrew, *tifilin* and best of all for the non-Orthodox, reference manuals on how to teach your kid to be a Jewish *mensch*. If you know what you want, call and they'll ship it UPS. Browsers are welcome. Don't be surprised if you there's a heated philosophical discussion going on between customers. There's another store in Borough Park at 5004 13th Avenue (633-1505).

Hecht's Hebrew Book Store. 1265 Coney Island Avenue, between Avenues I and J, 258-9696. Sun.–Thurs., 10 a.m.–6 p.m.; Fri., 10 a.m.–2:30 p.m.; closed Sat.

If it's Judaica you want, you'll find it at Hecht's. There are books in both Hebrew and English, plus cassettes, records, and religious items, such as *tallisim* (fringed prayer shawls) and imprinted skull caps for weddings and bar mitzvahs. There are also plenty of gift items, from crystal to silver trays.

Women's Clothing and Accessories

Bangles and Beads. 1515 Avenue M, near East 15th Street, 339-7600. Mon.–Sat., 11 a.m.–6 p.m.

It takes a personality to open a store in what Anita, the owner, calls a "sneeze of a shop" underneath the elevated subway tracks. More than seventy years old, the place was originally a cabbie stand; the original antique clock is still outside. Possibly Brooklyn's smallest shop, Bangles and Beads is crammed with costume jewelry, from $15 earrings to $200 necklaces.

Carole Block. 1413 Avenue M, between East 14th and East 15th streets, 339-1869. Mon.–Fri., 10 a.m.–6 p.m.; Sun., noon–5 p.m.; closed Sat. Major credit cards.

With one of the largest selections of fine Italian leather handbags this side of Manhattan, this store lets you browse through top-tier bags by Genny, Gianfranco Ferre, Desmo, Braccialini, Gianni Versace, Moschino, and Carlos Falchi. They also carry smaller leather goods, such as wallets and cases. Prices range from $50 to over $1,000. Carole Block has been in business for more than twenty years, and the service is excellent.

Chuckies. 1304 Kings Highway, near East 13th Street, 376-1003. Mon.– Sat., 10 a.m.–7 p.m.; Sun., noon–5 p.m. Major credit cards.

Like its other store in Manhattan's East 60s, Chuckies sells top-of-the-line imported shoes for both women and men. Among the popular designers likely to be represented are Stephanie Kelian and Donna Karan for women. Men's shoes by Charles Jourdan, Montana, and others are in the companion store at 1222 Kings Highway on the next block. Some lines are discounted.

Head to Hose. 1717 Avenue M, near East 17th Street, 692-0820. Sun.–Fri., 10:30 a.m.–6 p.m.; Fri., closes early; closed Sat. Major credit cards. ✳

If you agree that good things come in small boxes, check out the pretty, high-quality accessories here, from hair ornaments and hats to decorative stockings and socks for women and kids. The hosiery selection includes top brands, such as Donna Karan. Once you establish your favorite brand and size, you can phone in orders for quick delivery by UPS.

Jimmy's. 1226 Kings Highway, near East 13th Street, 645-9685. Mon.–Sat., 10 a.m.–6 p.m.; Thurs., 10 a.m.–9 p.m.; Sun., noon–5 p.m. Major credit cards.

Jimmy's is in a class all by itself in Brooklyn. The specialty at this two-generation store is top-of-the-line, this-season fashion by European designers, such as Ungaro, Valentino, Versace, Gottier, and Ferre, for both women and men. Accessories include bags and shoes by Prada and Manaolo Blahnik. What makes shopping here different from shopping at a fancy Manhattan boutique is the family-style service: regular customers are greeted on a first-name basis and if you're in a pinch tailoring can be done on the spot.

June's Collection. 519 Kings Highway, between East 2nd and East 3rd streets, 376-4899. Sun.–Thurs., 10 a.m.–6 p.m.; Fri., closes early; closed Sat. Major credit cards.

Women's accessories are the raison d'être at June's. The store has a huge selection of decorative hair ornaments and moderately priced costume jewelry arranged by colors. There is also a good selection of attractive swimwear, lingerie, evening bags, and hosiery. Most name-brand merchandise is discounted about 20 percent off the list price.

Lupu's. 1494 Coney Island Avenue, between Avenues K and L, 377-3793. Mon.–Sun., 10 a.m.–6 p.m.; Wed., open late; closed Sat.

Of the half dozen discount women's clothing stores which accommodate local Orthodox styles (long hems, long sleeves, loose cuts) on the two-block strip from Avenue J to Avenue L, Lupu's carries the broadest selection of classic sportswear and daytime dresses. Everything is heavily discounted in comparison with department store prices for the same merchandise.

Marion's Boutique. 515 Kings Highway, between East 2nd and East 3rd streets, 375-9055. Sun.–Fri., 11 a.m.–6 p.m.; closed Sat. Major credit cards.

Who in Brooklyn buys at these prices? You'd be surprised. The casual outfits and sporty suits in very feminine styles ranging from $250 to $500 are popular among those who travel the ladies' luncheon circuit. They also have some attractive cocktail dresses.

Miss Pauline's Bras and Girdles. 1478 Coney Island Avenue, between Avenues K and L, 252-7310. Mon.–Thurs., 10 a.m.–4 p.m.; Fri., closes early; closed Sat. and Sun.

When was the last time you really were *fitted* for a bra? This hole-in-the-wall shop has been in the business of fitting for thirty years. Miss Pauline's inventory of American and European undergarments is discounted about 15 percent, but it's the philosophy that permeates this shop that makes it special: if they had a motto it would be "Make the Best of What You've Got!" So, in four tiny dressing rooms the saleswomen patiently measure, test, and consult. They'll even have their on-site seamstress take a tuck for free while you wait. Fan mail from all over waxes enthusiastic. One letter gushed: "Thanks again for the D-lightful bra you mailed me." Mail order is available.

Sarachelle. 1715 Avenue M, near East 17th Street, 377-4002. Sun.–Thurs., 10 a.m.–6 p.m.; Thurs., 10 a.m.–8 p.m.; Fri., 10 a.m.–3 p.m.; closed Sat. Major credit cards.

If you want to put on the Ritz with the full array of feminine ammo but don't want to spend thousands of dollars, this may be your kind of place. Fancy evening wear runs from $200 to $600 in sizes 4 to 14. A little black cocktail dress is at the conservative end of this spectrum, with lots of pretty numbers flaunting sequins, beads, and off-the-shoulder straps. Perfect for dress-to-kill weddings, sweet sixteen parties, New Year's Eve, or any special occasion. Service is excellent, and tailoring can be done on the premises.

Men's Clothing

Clothing Connection. 508 Kings Highway, near East 2nd Street, 375-5893. Sun.–Thurs., 10 a.m.–6 p.m.; Fri., 10 a.m.–2:30 p.m.; closed Sat. Major credit cards.

Updated classic Italian suits in fine lightweight wools are sold here at a 20 to 30 percent discount, including names such as Marzotto and Lubiam. This is one of only a handful of Brooklyn men's stores where style counts. No tailoring is done on the premises.

Crown Clothiers. 1434 Coney Island Avenue, near Avenue J, 252-6666. Sun.–Thurs., 10 a.m.–7 p.m.; Fri., closes early; closed Sat. Major credit cards.

Crown has a complete line of medium- and high-quality men's wear that includes a big selection of sports jackets and slacks, suits, sweaters, leather jackets, and accessories. The merchandise is discounted 15 to 25 percent from retail and includes names such as Le Baron, Bartolini, Oleg Cassini, London Fog, and Preswick and Moore. The salespeople are easygoing and knowledgeable. Tailoring is available on the premises.

Clothing for Kids

Haas Children's Wear. 1306 Avenue M, near East 13th Street, 627-0100. Sun.–Fri., 11 a.m.–6 p.m.; closed Sat. Major credit cards. ✳

One of several children's clothing shops in the neighborhood, Haas offers attractive discounts on middle- and top-tier items from layette to preteen sizes. Toddler outfits begin at about $40. Name brands include Lacoste, Mousefeathers, Petit Boy, and many other American and European brands.

Marcelle's Children's Wear. 505 Kings Highway, between East 3rd and East 4th streets, 339-6991. Sun.–Fri., 10 a.m.–6 p.m.; Fri., closes early; closed Sat. Major credit cards. ✳

Marcelle's carries some unusual brands of Italian and French children's clothes, including Le Mur, Chappointu, and Pito. Outfits start at around $50 and move up from there. From layette to teenager there's a complete look, starting with underwear and pajamas and ranging to swimsuits, jackets, and coats. Seasonal sales are a good time to pick up a bargain on this high-quality merchandise.

Tuesday's Child. 1904 Avenue M, between East 19th street and Ocean Avenue, 376-3864. Sun.–Fri., 10 a.m.–6 p.m.; Thurs., 10 a.m.–8 p.m.; closed Sat. Major credit cards. ✳

Exclusive, expensive, and elegant imported children's clothing ranging from layette through junior sizes for both girls and boys fill this upscale establishment. Many items are manufactured in Italy especially for the store and are not available even in the best Manhattan shops. Styles range from camp clothes and everyday wear to tuxedos and ballet slippers. Classic designs include such items as sailor dresses, white baby gowns, pink-lace dresses for girls, and classy print shirts for boys. Outfits start at $60. The store also will help you outfit children for special occasions, such as weddings, bar mitzvahs, and communions.

Zeldy's Place. 1815 Avenue M, near East 18th Street, 252-9313. Mon.–Fri., 10:30 a.m.–6 p.m.; Sun., 11 a.m.–5 p.m.; closed Sat. Major credit cards. *

Zeldy's stocks a full line of top- and middle-tier children's clothing from layette through junior boys and girls, with discounts of up to 30 percent on American and imported brands, such as Carter's, Mousefeathers, Le Tigre, Little Me, Trimfit, and Rifle pants. Typical of the neighborhood, the sales staff is outgoing and friendly.

Gift Stores

Discount Variety Store. 1917 Avenue M, between East 19th Street and Ocean Avenue, 338-1237. Sun.–Fri., 10 a.m.–6 p.m.; closed Sat. *

A throwback to the five and dime of your childhood, this variety store with the old-fashioned sign outside sells housewares, cosmetics, dishes, toys, and just about everything else. As you might expect, the prices are from another era as well.

Presentations. 1324 Avenue M, corner of East 13th Street, 627-1022. Sun.–Wed., 10:30 a.m.–5:30 p.m.; Thurs., 10:30 a.m.–7 p.m.; Fri., 10:30 a.m.–2:30 p.m.; closed Sat. Major credit cards. *

Here's a place that will take phone orders and arrange delivery of gift packages for special occasions, such as children's birthday parties, over-the-hill parties, and weddings. They've got everything from fifty-cent pencils to jellybean-filled champagne bottles. For delivery you need a $25 minimum order and two weeks' lead time.

Special Effects. 1822 Avenue M, near East 19th Street, 645-5119. Mon.–Fri., 10:30 a.m.–6 p.m.; Sun., 11 a.m.–5 p.m.; closed Sat. Major credit cards. *

This little shop carries a nice assortment of juvenile gift items, such as rocking horses, colorful wall hangings, and lamps. As an added service, just about everything can be personalized with the child's name free of charge, including bikes, mirrors, and towels.

Yellow Door. 1308 Avenue M, between East 13th and East 14th streets, 998-7382. Mon.–Fri., 10 a.m.–5:45 p.m.; Sun., 11 a.m.–5 p.m.; closed Sat. and on weekends during the summer. Major credit cards.

A woman of any age would love a gift or a gift certificate from this shop. Perfect items for weddings, anniversaries, Mother's Day, or birthdays include fine crystal, unusual table linens, and decorative boxes. The Yellow Door also has a huge selection of high-fashion costume jewelry in the $50 to $700 range, all by well-known designers. They also carry a small selection of antique silver items. Prices range from moderate to expensive; many items are sold below typical retail prices.

PROSPECT PARK SOUTH

How It Got Its Name: The houses here were designed to be an extension of nearby and then-elegant Prospect Park. The entrances to this tony residential enclave carry the initials *PPS* engraved in brick.

Special events: House tour of a dozen private historic houses (May).

ABOUT THE NEIGHBORHOOD

If you have the idea that Brooklyn is all old brownstones, a trip to Prospect Park South will turn that notion on its head. You'll think you're dreaming when you first spot elegant Victorian mansions with spacious porches, decorative turrets, bay windows, stained glass, and well-kept lawns throughout Prospect Park South. Busy two-career couples of the 1990s can only imagine the pampered life-style lived here. The architecture says it all: sweeping mahogany-banister staircases lead to sumptuous bedroom suites; steep backstairs ascend from the kitchen to third-floor servants' rooms.

Take your pick from among many delicious fantasies: the so-called Japanese house (131 Buckingham Road); the lovely home where the movie *Sophie's Choice* was filmed (101 Rugby Road); the "Honeymoon Cottage" (305 Rugby Road), built for one of the Guggenheim daughters; and for gardeners, the private botanic gardens at the rear of 145 Argyle Road. Or walk down Albemarle Road, off Stratford Road, to see former homes of the industrial elite. Number 1519 Argyle Road was built by the president of the American Can Company in 1905; down the street at 1505 is a Queen Anne–style home built by Elmer Sperry, of Sperry-Rand fame, back in 1900. The architect of Manhattan's famous Chrysler Building designed the Spanish-style home at number 1215 for the Fruit of the Loom family.

For an excellent series of self-directed walking tours contact the **Flatbush Development Corporation** (469-8990) and ask for their excellent "Flatbush Tour" brochure. In May, this organization sponsors a four-hour shuttle bus tour of a dozen private homes that are restored and original mansions dating from the turn of the century.

Flatbush Reformed Church. 890 Flatbush Avenue, at Church Avenue, 284-5140.

There's a bit of Old New York right here. The original church was built in 1654 by the order of Governor Peter Stuyvesant, and the existing structure was built in 1796. Note the wonderful stained glass windows, including many Tiffany originals. The church has hosted a Sunday service every week for the last 325 years.

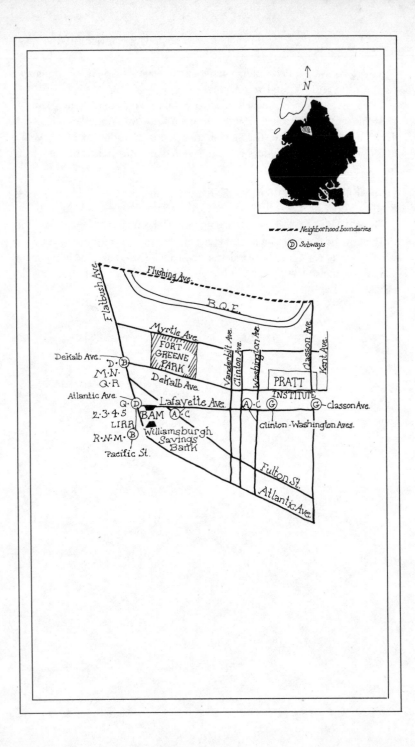

N

Neighborhood boundaries
(D) Subways

Flushing Ave.
B.Q.E.
Flatbush Ave.
Myrtle Ave.
FORT GREENE PARK
Vanderbilt Ave.
Clinton Ave.
Washington Ave.
Classon Ave.
Kent Ave.
DeKalb Ave. — D·(B)
M·N·Q·R
DeKalb Ave.
PRATT INSTITUTE
Atlantic Ave. — Q·(D)
Lafayette Ave.
(A)·C (G)   (G)— Classon Ave.
2·3·4·5
LIRR
BAM (A)·C
Clinton-Washington Aves.
R·N·M·(B)
Williamsburgh Savings Bank
Pacific St.
Fulton St.
Atlantic Ave.

FORT GREENE
AND
CLINTON HILL

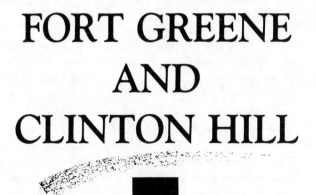

Where it is: Bounded by the Brooklyn Navy Yard on the north, Atlantic Avenue on the south, Bedford-Stuyvesant to the east, and Flatbush Avenue on the west.

What's nearby: Atlantic Avenue, Bedford-Stuyvesant, Brooklyn Heights, Carroll Gardens, Cobble Hill, downtown Brooklyn, Park Slope, and Waterfront.

How to get there:

By car: From Flatbush Avenue turn left onto Myrtle Avenue or Fulton Street.

By subway: The 2, 3, 4, 5, D, or Q train to the Atlantic Avenue stop, or the B, M, N, or R train to Pacific Street.

Cab services: Atlantic Avenue Car Service (797-5666) or Janice Car Service (797-5773). Cost is about $7 from Brooklyn Heights, $15 from Grand Central Station.

How each got its name: *Fort Greene* is named for Nathaniel Greene, a general in the Battle of Long Island during the Revolutionary War. *Clinton Hill,* literally up a hill from Fort Greene Park, was a fashionable nineteenth-century residential area named for New York governor DeWitt Clinton. The boundary between Fort Greene and Clinton Hill is Vanderbilt Avenue.

Special events: Brownstone tour through the interiors of restored private landmark homes (May).

ABOUT THE NEIGHBORHOODS

With its rows of renovated nineteenth-century brownstones and sycamore-lined streets, Fort Greene looks similar to Brooklyn's other landmark brownstone neighborhoods. But there is more here than initially meets the eye. Fort Greene is probably the most artistic and most racially integrated of Brooklyn's many middle class areas. Its sophisticated mix of residents has generated an upbeat creative energy here in the past decade. The neighborhood is home to many African-American artists, designers, filmmakers, and musicians who, along with foreigners and yuppies, were drawn to Fort Greene by its proximity to Manhattan and its fabulous, relatively affordable housing stock.

Many visitors to Brooklyn have actually been to Fort Greene without knowing it. Just five minutes from the Manhattan Bridge, it is home to the **Brooklyn Academy of Music**, nationally acclaimed for its avant-garde **Next Wave Festival**, as well as the numerous opera, dance, and children's programs. But BAM is not the only reason to visit Fort Greene.

Architecture buffs will find a stunning diversity of styles in Fort Greene and neighboring Clinton Hill, once a silk-stocking, mansion-filled retreat for wealthy industrialists. Fort Greene also has a small and eclectic group of shops and restaurants. From **Chris Cakes**, a stupendous hole-in-the-wall bakery, to **Sheila's Restaurant & Jazz Room**, a sophisticated Cajun-Southern style restaurant housed in a beautifully renovated brownstone, to tasteful home furnishings with an African motif at **Blackberry**, there is plenty here for the casual explorer. Fashion-conscious women will discover that the area is sprinkled with stylish clothing boutiques, such as **V. J. Jones** and **Studio 14A**, many run by a new generation of young African-American women entrepreneurs. In nearby Prospect Heights, the **Spiral Art Gallery**, which shows the work of contemporary black artists, is a five-minute drive from Fort Greene.

Don't be surprised if during your wanderings the sounds of jazz come wafting through the air. Fort Greene is home to a host of prominent musicians, including saxophonists Branford Marsalis and Steve Coleman, trumpet master Lester Bowie, and vocalist Betty Carter. It is also home to filmmaker Spike Lee, whom *Village Voice* critic Nelson George has called the "central energy source" for the African-American creative set based here. Lee's **40 Acres and a Mule** production company is headquartered in renovated Firehouse 256 along

DeKalb Avenue. Lee employs local residents, uses Brooklyn as a backdrop in his films, and bluntly articulates an African-American perspective that has achieved a rare critical and financial success. Lee has not bailed out to the suburbs or Manhattan; he plows his resources and energy back into the neighborhood.

Sundays are particularly good days for music during services at the **Institutional Church of God in Christ**. This is where you can hear gospel music by the nationally known Institutional Choir, the same group that performed in Europe and on Broadway in the award-winning show *Gospel at Colonus*. There are lectures, art exhibits, and a collegiate oasis of green at **Pratt Institute**. **Fort Greene Park**, a thirty-acre masterpiece designed by the team of Olmsted and Vaux (creators of both Central Park and Prospect Park) is a tranquil, natural boundary to the neighborhood—and its underused tennis courts are a well-kept secret among the net set.

After years of relative quiet, Fort Greene is an area on the brink of change. Already rising nearby is the **MetroTech Center**, a commercial center in Brooklyn Heights, just a few blocks from Fort Greene, that will bring an enormous influx of business, workers, and traffic to this part of Brooklyn. Add to that a proposed multimillion-dollar Atlantic Terminal commercial and residential development and this quiet neighborhood is sure to see a new surge of interest in its homes, amenities, and artistic energy.

Historical Notes

It all started with the Fulton Ferry. Improved transportation between Manhattan and Brooklyn Heights in the 1830s sparked the suburbanization of then-rural Brooklyn. Development began in the Heights and rapidly spread to nearby Fort Greene, where, from its early beginnings, a free black community of shipbuilders lived before the Civil War. Fort Greene's Hanson Place Baptist Church was an important stop for slaves fleeing the south on the Underground Railroad. The first European residents were mid-nineteenth century immigrants from Ireland, Germany, and England, as street names reminiscent of London (South Portland, South Oxford, Cumberland, and Waverly) attest. Many of contemporary Fort Greene's elegant row homes were built during this period, from 1850 to 1870.

Lower Fort Greene was settled by the middle and working class. But the neighborhood's most desirable residential location—up the hill on Clinton and Washington avenues—was the site of sumptuous villas with great lawns, backed by elegant carriage houses like those that still line Waverly Avenue. Clinton Hill became known as a fashionable district of great mansions designed by famous architects of the era. Charles Pratt of the Standard Oil Company catalyzed the neighborhood by building a home at 252 Clinton Avenue in 1874. Each of Pratt's sons also was presented with a fine home along the avenue as a wedding present. Other merchants and industrialists who followed Pratt's lead included Cuban coffee magnate John Arbuckle, members of the Underwood family of typewriter fame, lace manufacturer A. G. Jennings, and D. R. Hoagland, a baking soda merchant.

At the turn of the century the area down the hill was developed further. Fulton Street thrived, and the **Brooklyn Academy of Music** (BAM) was built in 1906 along with the Martyrs Memorial in Fort Greene Park (1907) and the Masonic Temple (1907). In her essay "Brooklyn From Clinton Hill," Pulitzer Prize–winning poet Marianne Moore captured the elegance of the era from her home at 260 Cumberland Street.

In the Depression years much of the era fell into disrepair, and during World War II many brownstones were subdivided into rooming houses to accommodate the seventy thousand workers laboring at the nearby Brooklyn Navy Yard. Many mansions in nearby Clinton Hill were razed; a precious few were incorporated into Pratt Institute and St. Joseph's College. Gentrification began in the late 1960s and 1970s, leading to renovation and rising real estate values. The area bounded by Willoughby and Vanderbilt avenues and South Elliot Place, Fulton Street, and Fort Greene Park is now a landmark district.

Fort Greene has survived and thrived for years as a racially and economically mixed area—a record of which the community is justifiably proud.

Kidstuff

Although much of Fort Greene will appeal mainly to adults, **Fort Greene Park**'s rolling hills and playgrounds, plus the special events run by the Urban Park Rangers, are a child's treat. **BAM** has many programs geared toward the young, and at the **Williamsburgh Savings Bank** you can open an interest-bearing savings account for your child for only $2.

ENTERTAINMENT AND POINTS OF CULTURAL INTEREST

Brooklyn Academy of Music. 30 Lafayette Avenue, corner of Ashland Place, 636-4100. Call for a schedule. Major credit cards. For most performances a BAMBUS travels between 51st Street and Lexington Avenue in Manhattan and BAM. *

Less than one mile from the Brooklyn Bridge, BAM is one of Brooklyn's most famous cultural institutions. BAM's ten-week Next Wave Festival, started in 1983, is considered the country's top forum for avant-garde performance art. Under the creative direction of Harvey Lichtenstein since 1967, BAM has presented works by many of the leading musicians, dancers, and theater artists of the past two decades, from Peter Brook to Philip Glass, Laurie Anderson, and Twyla Tharp. There is also opera from February through June, DanceAfrica in the spring, and excellent children's shows throughout the school year. Call to get on the mailing list. Advance purchase for performances is recommended.

Opened in 1861, BAM is the oldest performing arts center in America. In its present location since 1908, BAM once hosted the likes of Enrico Caruso, Isadora Duncan, Mary Pickford, Gustav Mahler, even Gertrude Stein. Recently BAM renovated the nearby nine hundred-seat **Majestic Theater** (see below).

The nearest subways are the 2, 3, 4, 5, D, M, and Q (Atlantic Avenue stop), or the B, N, and R (Pacific Street stop).

BAM Majestic Theater. 651 Fulton Street, corner of Ashland Place, 636-4100. Call for a schedule.

Back in 1904 when the Majestic Theater opened, there were twenty large theaters in Brooklyn, with resonant names like the Star, Billy Watson's Pearl, the Novelty, the Gaiety, the Unique, and the Folly. Very few of them are still standing; most have been razed, some are churches, and the Prospect Theater on 9th Street between 5th and 6th avenues in Park Slope became a supermarket. In its early years the eighteen hundred–seat Majestic was considered an important "tryout" house for Broadway-bound theatrical productions. Subsequently it hosted everything from Shakespearean plays to opera, vaudeville, and movies. Then it lay dormant for two decades. A cooperative effort by the city and the Brooklyn Academy of Music led to the theater's restoration. The facade has been preserved but the interior has been remodeled after Peter Brook's Parisian theater, Les Bouffes du Nord. Watch BAM listings for a schedule of programs.

Institutional Church of God in Christ. 170 Adelphi Street, between Myrtle and Willoughby avenues, 625-9175. Sunday services, 11:30 a.m.–2:30 p.m. ✳

Looking for some real-live gospel music? During Sunday services you can hear this renowned group, the fifty-person Institutional Radio Choir, which has broadcast for years every Sunday evening at 10 p.m. on New York's

WWRL–1600 AM. This was the gospel choir in the Broadway show *Gospel at Colonus*. You can count on a fabulous performance.

New York Experimental Glass Workshop. 647 Fulton Street, near Flatbush Avenue, 625-3685. Call to check hours. ✻

Established in 1977 and recently relocated from Manhattan's Mulberry Street to a fabulous seventeen thousand square foot space in a renovated 1918 Brooklyn theater, the Glass Workshop is one of the nation's premiere organizations for artists working in the glass arts. It provides the only studio in New York City where one can learn to blow glass, paint on glass, and create neon art. Parts of the studio are open to the public, with a gallery space and a working facility that visitors can tour. Terrific educational opportunities are available through a range of lectures, demonstrations, weekend workshops, seminars, and other programs.

Paul Robeson Theater. 40 Greene Avenue, between Carlton and Adelphi avenues, 783-9784.

This building, which used to be a Polish Catholic church, is now a community cultural center serving African-American audiences. It produces a range of entertainment, including theater, dance, and movies. This small theater is within five blocks of BAM and is a ten-minute drive from Park Slope and Prospect Heights. Call to get on the mailing list.

Penny Bridge Players. 520 Clinton Avenue, between Atlantic Avenue and Fulton Street, 855-6346. Call for a schedule of performances. Tickets are $6 for adults and $2.50 for children. ✻

A wonderful local theater group for kids, the Penny Bridge Players perform classics like *Cinderella* for the four- to eleven-year-old set. Plays are performed at the beautiful **Church of St. Luke and St. Matthew**, near **Pratt Institute** (see below).

Pratt Institute. 200 Willoughby Avenue, at DeKalb Avenue and Hall Street, 636-3600. ✻

More than a century old, Pratt was founded by nineteenth-century industrialist Charles Pratt, a pragmatist whose students studied not Latin but mechanical drawing, sewing, and typing. The Pratt Institute Free Library was opened to serve students and local residents and was the first in the nation to open a children's room. Today, the institute is a leading school of design, advertising, and other applied arts. The campus quadrangle is a lovely green oasis, and there is a refreshing energy in the air generated by the artistic student body. It's worth a visit, for kids as well as adults.

Lectures featuring architects, artists, critics, and writers are common at Higgins Hall, located in the Multi-Media Center at Lafayette Avenue and St. James Place. Call 636-3491 for information. About nine professional exhibitions a year of "provocative" and "risky" contemporary art can be seen in the Schafler Art Gallery in the Main Building, Mon.–Fri., 9 a.m.–5 p.m. Call 636-3517 for information.

Spiral Art Gallery. 637 Vanderbilt Avenue, between Prospect Place and St. Marks Place, 783-2891. Tues., 1–8 p.m.; Sat., 11 a.m.–8 p.m.; Sun., 1–5 p.m.

Although it is located in Prospect Heights, about seven blocks away from Fort Greene, this gallery is part of the Fort Greene scene. Small, and graciously outfitted with carpet and piano, the gallery highlights such well-known African-American artists as Ernie Chrichlow and has about a half-dozen different shows during the year. Prices range from $200 for drawings to over $900 for original paintings.

Other points of interest include the following:

Brooklyn Public Library. 380 Washington Avenue, corner of Lafayette Avenue, 857-8038. Call to check hours. ✳

Besides a good, standard selection of children's books here, many focus on African-American traditions and literature. Looking for a children's book on black cowboys? This is the place.

Church of Saint Luke and Saint Matthew. 520 Clinton Avenue, between Atlantic Avenue and Fulton Street, 855-6346.

Described as a "voluptuous Victorian valentine," the Church of Saint Luke and Saint Matthew is distinguished by a long porch, sculpted teak columns, and Tiffany windows. Built by Episcopalian industrial barons, the hundred-year-old church today has white clergy and a West Indian congregation. It is not far from **Pratt Institute** and just a few blocks from the mansions along Clinton Avenue where some of the church's original congregants lived in splendor.

Emmanuel Baptist Church. 279 Lafayette Avenue, between Washington Avenue and St. James Place, 622-1107. By appointment.

The facade of this large French Gothic church, with its twin towers and triple entrance, is reminiscent of a medieval cathedral. Completed in 1887, it is a notable landmark contributing to the nineteenth-century ambience of the neighborhood. The construction of the church was financed by Charles Pratt, founder of **Pratt Institute**.

Fort Greene and Clinton Avenue house tours. 783-8454 or 857-9471. Annual spring tours; book in advance. House tour tickets are about $10.

Brooklyn's elite lived in this area in the late 1800s and the Victorian and Romanesque Revival architecture is among the finest in the nation. This annual tour of the interiors of half a dozen or so homes is great for architecture buffs. If you miss the once-a-year tour, you can just walk along tree-lined streets past turn-of-the-century houses to see why dyed-in-the-wool Manhattanites fall in love with Brooklyn. In Fort Greene, try South Oxford Street and South Portland Avenue, between Lafayette and DeKalb avenues. In Clinton Hill, stroll down Clinton Avenue and take in the beauty of the several dozen mansions. The original Pratt residence, at number 241 Clinton, is now the official residence of the Roman Catholic bishop of Brooklyn and Queens. Nearby are three residences of Pratt's sons: numbers 245 and 232, now St. Joseph's College, and number 229, now a foreign student residence of **Pratt Institute**. As you look down Clinton Avenue you'll also catch a view of the Brooklyn Navy Yard. If this whets your appetite, make a note of the next annual house tour.

Hanson Place Seventh Day Adventist Church. 88 Hanson Place, corner of South Portland Avenue, 783-9354. Daily, 10 a.m.–4 p.m.

Monumental in scale, this Greek Revival and Italianate church is of the same 1850–60s architectural generation as **Borough Hall** and the landmark **State Street Houses** (pages 111 and 125) in Boerum Hill. The site also marks a once-welcome destination for southern slaves traveling the Underground Railroad to Fort Greene's well-established free community of blacks, many of whom were employed in shipbuilding at the nearby navy yard.

Lafayette Avenue Presbyterian Church. 85 South Oxford Street, corner of Lafayette Avenue, 625-7515.

Pulitzer Prize–winning poet Marianne Moore called this her church. Famous for its Tiffany windows, the window in the Underwood Chapel dates from 1920 and was one of the last completed by the Tiffany firm. Depending on your bent, today you can find spiritual uplift, social action, or great music here. During services there is fabulous music in the great European and American choral tradition, accompanied by a four-keyboard organ. This is also the site of many community group meetings.

Steele House. 200 Lafayette Avenue, off Vanderbilt and Clinton avenues.

As though plucked from some small Massachusetts town, this nineteenth-century yellow-frame house stands out from the surrounding brownstones and churches in the area. Indeed, it is a landmark of architectural interest, since successive owners combined Federal, Greek Revival, and Italianate styles. Originally built for Joseph Steele, it was later owned by the first president of Brooklyn Union Gas.

Williamsburgh Savings Bank Building. 1 Hanson Place, between Atlantic and Flatbush avenues, 270-4447. Mon.–Fri., 9 a.m.–5 p.m.; closed Sat., Sun., and bank holidays.

Brooklyn's tallest building offers breathtaking views of much of Brooklyn and beyond from its top floors. Take the elevator forty-five stories up and gaze away. The building has one of the world's largest four-face dial clocks and is home to one of Brooklyn's oldest financial institutions, the Williamsburgh Savings Bank, established in 1851. This landmark 1929 building designed by McCormick and Helmer, completed just a few years before the Depression, resembles the grand Bowery Savings Bank opposite Grand Central Station in Manhattan. Note the mosaic mural on the ground floor.

PARKS AND PLAYGROUNDS

Fort Greene Park. Washington Park, next to Brooklyn Hospital, near DeKalb and Myrtle avenues, 965-8900. ✳

Thought to have the world's only all-marble bathrooms, this Olmsted-designed park is topped by the Prison Ship Martyrs Monument, a 148-foot tower said to be the world's tallest free-standing Doric column. The park also contains six beautiful and underused tennis courts. (Call 965-8993 for permit information.) The Urban Park Ranger station that now occupies the marble facilities has information on special events and weekend tours. One of the park's specials is a ten-minute nighttime haunted walk at Halloween, guaranteed to frighten even the bravest souls.

Underwood Playground. Washington Avenue, corner of Lafayette Avenue. ✳

This big, lovely playground is one of the nicest outside of Fort Greene Park itself. The land used to be the site of a mansion belonging to typewriter baron John T. Underwood. As the story goes, his widow had it demolished when she saw the surrounding neighborhood deteriorate, so that her precious home would not fall into the "wrong hands." As is apparent from other mansions in the vicinity, things never got that bad.

NOTABLE RESTAURANTS

Caribbean Pavilion. 570 Fulton Street, off Flatbush Avenue, 260-8021. Mon.–Fri., 7 a.m.–11 p.m.; Sat. and Sun., 7 a.m.–midnight. ✱

Across from the **BAM Majestic Theater** (see page 179), this new spanking-clean restaurant looks like a midwestern hamburger chain. But instead of milkshakes on the menu, you'll find pea and cow's foot soups and a terrific specialty, red snapper chowder, on Friday and Sunday. Delicious curried chicken is just $7, and standard beef or chicken patties are $1. There are plenty of side dishes to choose from, including fried plantains and sweet potato pudding. If you haven't tried Caribbean cuisine, this is a good place to do so.

Cellars. 250 DeKalb Avenue, at Vanderbilt Avenue, 789-7630. Sun.–Thurs., noon–10 p.m.; Fri.–Sat., noon–midnight. Major credit cards.

When television crews come to Brooklyn to get the middle-class "African-American perspective" on an important social issue, they'll often stop at this local establishment. Order southern specialities like fried chicken, black-eyed peas, and a tropical drink and you'll be set. Entrée prices hover around $10.

Greene Avenue Grill. 13 Greene Avenue, between South Oxford and Cumberland streets, 797-2099. Daily, 7 a.m.–10:30 p.m.; Sunday brunch, 11 a.m.–4 p.m. Major credit cards.

New, impeccably modern, and offering a tasty southern-style food, this fashionable restaurant–bar–meeting place has become extremely popular with local artists and professionals. Dinner options include burgers, glazed chicken in apricot sauce, great southern-style fries, potato salad, and homemade corn bread. The atmosphere is informal and warm. Prices for entrées range from $5 to $12.

Harper Valley. 745 Fulton Street, between South Portland Avenue and South Elliott Place, 596-2367. Mon.–Sat., noon–10 p.m. ✱

Harper Valley is close to **BAM** (page 178) in the heart of Fort Greene. The appeal of this simple seven-table restaurant is its contemporary approach to traditional southern cooking. Chef and owner Zester Harper substitutes herbs for salt, minimizes the use of molasses, and has a light hand with those pork rinds. Vegetarians appreciate the vegetable platter, a $6 do-it-yourself assemblage of any four of eighteen dishes, such as candied yams, succotash, string beans and corn, okra and tomatoes. Southern specials include a Georgia-style barbecued chicken, ribs, and southern-fried fish in cornmeal; all come with two vegetables for less than $9. Regular customers swear by the peach cobbler and other desserts.

Joe's Place. 624 Waverly Avenue, near DeKalb Avenue, 622-9244. Thurs.– Sun., 4–11:30 p.m. Major credit cards.

Located in a former carriage house, this Italian restaurant's charm is most evident outdoors on a warm evening. Low lighting, plants, and an old wooden fence make for a European atmosphere. The food is moderately priced, with entrées under $15, and tasty but far from gourmet. Stick with the simpler pasta dishes for the best meals. Because of its romantic setting, Joe's keeps the locals coming back.

Kinch Kakes Cafe and Bakery. 662 Fulton Street, near South Elliott Place, 797-0523. Mon.–Thurs. and Sat., 7:30 a.m.–8 p.m.; Fri., 7:30 a.m.–10 p.m.; Sun., 11 a.m.–5 p.m. Major credit cards. ✱

Just one and a half blocks from **BAM** (page 178), Kinch Kakes has been nicely renovated in the last year. Caribbean, Creole, and American foods are served, and there are baked goodies to take out. The ambience is simple but modern. You'll get tasty codfish cakes, beef *pelau* (a rice mixture with raisins, almonds, tomato, and beef), and *coo-coo* (a cornmeal and okra cake), plus lots of handouts about local African-American cultural events. The Sunday brunch for less than $10 includes spicy buffalo wings, apple-filled pancakes, and braised gizzards in sherry. Once a month there is a jazz brunch.

Mike's Coffee Shop. 328 DeKalb Avenue, across from Pratt Institute, 857-1462. Mon.–Fri., 7 a.m.–8:30 p.m.; Sat. and Sun., 8 a.m.–6 p.m. ✱

Right across from **Pratt Institute** (page 180), this place attracts a university crowd. A clean, pleasant ambience with standard coffee shop fare and good prices, Mike's is a good place to come with a friend or kids, or for settling in with a newspaper. Just about everything on the menu costs less than $5.

Ms. Ann's Southern Cooking. 86 South Portland Avenue, between Lafayette Avenue and Fulton Street, 858-6997. Call to check hours.

Ms. Ann makes magic with southern spices. Call before you make a special trip here; she's only open Wednesday through Saturday and is known for taking long holidays on short notice. The ambience tends toward dingy, but she makes the best Cornish game hen we've had in ages.

Sheila's Restaurant & Jazz Room. 271 Adelphi Street, corner of DeKalb Avenue, 935-0292. Mon.–Sat., 5 p.m.–11 p.m.; Sun., brunch, 11 a.m.– 3 p.m., and dinner, 5–10 p.m. Major credit cards.

Large, tasty helpings of Creole, West Indian, and southern cookery in a spacious renovated brownstone are just part of the attraction here. Live jazz often starts as early as 7:30 p.m.: expect a $5 to $10 cover charge per person. Or skip dinner (which is tough to do) and head upstairs to the bar, where you can hear the music without paying a cover charge. The restaurant occasionally has special music and dinners on Mother's Day, Father's Day, and other holidays. Weekend reservations are recommended.

SHOPPING

African International Market. 96 DeKalb Avenue, between Rockwell and Ashland places, 260-9078. Daily, 10 a.m.–8 p.m.

An eclectic array of Nigerian staples and artifacts, from dried cod and powdered yams to medicinal powders, drums, masks, wooden cups, and clothing can be found here. It's an adventure just perusing the shelves.

And Why Not. 700 Fulton Street, between South Portland Avenue and South Oxford Street, 802-1663. Daily, noon–7 p.m. Major credit cards.

Owner Paula Neil, one of a number of African-American entrepreneurs in the area, originally worked in the foreign currency markets but traded it in for a clothing shop catering to working women who also like to play. Prices are moderate, with many items starting at $50.

Blackberry/ND Design. 767 Fulton Street, near South Portland Avenue, 522-7355. Mon.–Sat., noon to 7 p.m.; Sun., 11 a.m.–5 p.m. Major credit cards.

Outstanding hand-crafted leather bags with Afro-centric themes are made and sold at this one-of-a-kind shop. Small pouches and made-to-order leather bags with insets of African *kente* cloth from $150 up are a specialty and have been featured in major national fashion magazines. There are also decorative imports from Africa and a large selection of leather settees from Morocco and Nigeria.

Chris Cakes. 142 DeKalb Avenue, near South Elliott Place, 596-7331. Tues.–Sun., 7:30 a.m.–6:30 p.m.; closed Mon. *

There's only room to take one step inside this tiny hole of a bakery. That's all you'll need, though. Just try to decide between German chocolate cake, rum cake, pineapple upside-down cake, sticky buns, or the ever-changing selection of muffins. You can wash it down with some iced tea or lemonade (if there's any left).

Christine's. 197 DeKalb Avenue, between Carlton and Adelphi avenues, 237-2437. Tues.–Sun., 1–10 p.m.; closed Mon.

Not easy to spot, this small takeout store and bakery also has a tiny restaurant on the floor above. Sweets and treats include West Indian fruitcake, turnovers, rum and coconut-lemon-orange pound cakes, plum pudding, and coconut cream pies. During holidays bring in your own turkey, chicken, or duck and the staff will clean, stuff, and roast it for $25. Or order a full dinner to go that includes turkey, ham, or Cornish game hens, yellow rice, candied yams, and greens. If you want to impress your spouse or guests with your culinary skill, they'll even serve it up on your own dishes and platters from home.

General Greene's Emporium. 88 South Portland Avenue, between Lafayette Avenue and Fulton Street, 643-4221. Wed.–Fri., 11:30 a.m.–7 p.m.; Sat., 10 a.m.–6 p.m.; Sun., noon–5 p.m. Major credit cards.

This beautiful store stocks fine teas, coffees, preserves, pottery, and cookware. You could find many of these items in more expensive top-tier shops, but why bother? The employees are helpful and there is almost always something on sale, when discounts run as high as 40 percent.

Jazz It Up. 606 Vanderbilt Avenue, between Saint Marks Avenue and Prospect Place, 638-2078. Mon.–Sat., 10:30 a.m.–8 p.m. Major credit cards.

An unusual hair and clothing boutique with full personal shopping services, this friendly, stylish shop is located in nearby Prospect Heights, a five-minute drive from Fort Greene. Outfits run from sexy black Lycra for evening wear to career dresses. Prices range from $65–$130. The two African-American women who run the store also will give you a complete makeover if you wish. It includes a manicure, pedicure, hair styling, and makeup, not to mention the clothes, of course.

South Portland Antiques. 698 Fulton Street, near South Portland Avenue, 596-1556. Mon. and Tues., 2–7:30 p.m.; Wed.–Sun., noon–6:30 p.m.

If the Atlantic Avenue antique shops don't have what you want, look here.

You can find American furniture—particularly dressers, chairs, and chests—at fairly inexpensive prices. The stock is replenished frequently, so keep trying.

Status. 140 DeKalb Avenue, near South Elliott Place, 596-6333. Mon.–Sat., 9 a.m.–8 p.m.

Film director Spike Lee's influence can be felt at several Fort Greene clothing stores, but this one carries the greatest selection of T-shirts and other fashions of the type that appear in Lee's films. Status also specializes in batik and tie-dyed African wear.

Sticks-n-Stones. 110 DeKalb Avenue, between Ashland Place and Saint Felix Street, 522-5383. Mon.–Sat. and sometimes on Sun., 10 a.m.–7 p.m. Major credit cards.

Right next to **Yolly's** (opposite), Sticks-n-Stones puts the words of the African-American movement on your chest. There's interesting jewelry, lots of T-shirts with such slogans as "Um From Brooklyn," and a lot of spunk. If you want to know what's going on in activist African-American circles in Fort Greene, Bedford-Stuyvesant, and Harlem, check out the notices here advertising everything from art to black Muslim celebrations.

Studio 14A. 14A Saint James Place, between Lafayette and DeKalb avenues, 857-4335. Daily, noon–6:30 p.m.; Fri., noon–8 p.m.; closed Tues. Major credit cards.

Here's a find: located in a brownstone and comfortably outfitted with Persian rugs, this lovely shop has stylish, classic clothing at moderate prices, with outfits well under $150. There's also a good selection of accessories and lingerie. This is one of a handful of local boutiques and it's worth a visit.

V. J. Jones. 138 DeKalb Avenue, near South Elliott Place, 237-2613. Mon.–Fri., noon–8 p.m.; Sat. and Sun., 11 a.m.–8 p.m. Major credit cards.

Here's a terrific collection of clothing for women ready to show off their figures. Racks hang heavy with contemporary "goin' out clothes," from sassy dresses to black Lycra jumpsuits and specialties by local designers. Many are designed by V. J. Jones herself, who was trained at nearby **Pratt Institute** (page 180) and was once a buyer for Bloomingdale's. Hats (many by Eric Javits), unusual jewelry, and other accessories are also in good supply at this tiny shop. Don't be surprised if you're offered wine and cheese while you shop; this is a friendly place.

Yippee! General. 80 Lafayette Avenue, corner of South Portland Avenue, 802-9155. Mon.–Fri., 11 a.m.–7 p.m.; Sat., 10 a.m.–6 p.m.; Sun., 11 a.m.–6 p.m. Major credit cards.

Amid the balloons, candies, and sundry gifts you'll find toys, T-shirts, flowers, cards, and more. This local landmark is also a focal point for Fort Greene's community organizing activities. Ask the proprietors for a copy of their monthly newsletter, which comes complete with discount coupons to local shops and classifieds offering everything from apartments to astrologers to meetings of the local La Leche League.

Yolly's Thrift Shop. 110 DeKalb Avenue, between Ashland Place and St. Felix Street, 237-0267. Mon.–Sat., noon–7 p.m.; Sun., noon–6 p.m. Major credit cards.

Used clothing with a flair for fashion is the trademark at Yolly's. Trendy men's and women's clothing and accessories from sweaters to sequins, can be found amid the clutter. This is a must for young thrift shop afficianados.

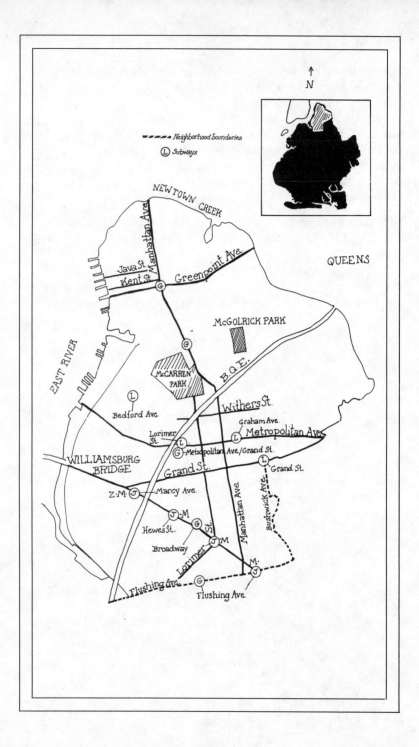

GREENPOINT AND WILLIAMSBURG

Where it is: North of the Williamsburg Bridge, south of Newtown Creek, along the East River.

What's nearby: Manhattan is directly across the Williamsburg Bridge.

How to get to Greenpoint:
By car: From Manhattan cross the Williamsburg Bridge and drive northeast, turning left on Manhattan Avenue to enter Greenpoint. From the BQE, take exit 33 to Magrenes Boulevard. After four traffic lights, turn left onto Nassau Avenue.
By subway: From Manhattan ride the L crosstown train from 14th Street to the Lorimer Street stop and transfer to the G subway heading north. Get off at the Nassau Avenue or Greenpoint Avenue stops.

How to get to Williamsburg:
By car: From Manhattan, cross the Williamsburg Bridge and you're there.
By subway: G train to Metropolitan Avenue, or L train to Lorimer Street.
Cab services: Greenpoint Car Service (383-2727) or Havemeyer Cars (486-6060). About $9 from Brooklyn Heights, $11 from Wall Street, and $12 from Grand Central Station.

Special events: Feast of Giglio, Our Lady of Mount Carmel Church, July.

How each got its name: Not surprisingly, Brooklyn's northernmost point was once covered in trees, hence "Green Point," now Greenpoint. Williamsburg was named in 1810 after the man who surveyed the area, Colonel John Williams, reputedly a grandnephew of Benjamin Franklin. The original spelling included an *h* at the end; only a few places, such as the Williamsburgh Savings Bank, still use the old spelling.

ABOUT THE NEIGHBORHOODS

Appearances and names can be deceiving. Although Greenpoint was originally named for the lush vegetation early settlers found here, today it has the look and feel of the industrial town it became. Still, Greenpoint's pleasures are many. An architecturally significant historic district (between Java and Calyer streets and Franklin and Manhattan avenues) encompasses quiet row house streets worthy of a quick stroll when a peaceful diversion is your goal. You'll also find utterly fantastic and inexpensive Polish food to take home from the **Honeymoon Bakery and Sweet Shop** and the **W. Nassau Meat Market** or to eat in at the **Polska Restaurant**.

At first glance you might imagine that the grit and grime clinging to some of Greenpoint's buildings remains from the area's industrial past. Manhattan Avenue is still working class and most of its buildings unremarkable, yet behind its dull facade the neighborhood is thriving. Usually thought of as a Polish preserve, Greenpoint in fact is like much of Brooklyn, multiethnic with Irish and Italian immigrants in abundance. Still, besides English, the predominant spoken and written language here is Polish.

Williamsburg, too, is home to a diverse population: Hasidic Jews, Puerto Ricans, Italians, and, most recently, artists who have renovated old industrial lofts into studios. Williamsburg has an odd array of attractions—one of the earliest and still-finest low-income housing complexes in New York City, the **Williamsburg Houses**, dating from the 1930s; **Peter Luger**, one of the best steak houses on the East Coast; and the small, avant-garde **Williamsburg Music Center**.

To get a quick idea of Williamsburg's ethnic and historic flavor, travel along Bedford Avenue or Rutledge Road. Here you'll find many nineteenth-century mansions like that built by the founder of the company that became the Jack Frost sugar empire. These elegant homes are now occupied by synagogues and yeshivas. Or, plan to take a day in July to attend the famous **Feast of Giglio**

Our Lady of Mount Carmel. Top it off with an old-fashioned family-style Italian meal at **Crisci's** or **Bamonte's** and, on your way home, a drive past the original **Williamsburgh Savings Bank** building.

Historical Notes

Greenpoint and Williamsburg were part of the mid-seventeenth-century town known as Boswijck (Bushwick), meaning the "wooded district." Real development began only in the early and mid-1800s. One interesting note: the streets running roughly perpendicular to the East River are named alphabetically, from Ash to Box, Clay, Dupont, Eagle, Freeman, Green, Huron, India, Java, Kent, Milton, Noble, and Oak streets.

Greenpoint became a center for what were known as the five "black arts": glass and pottery making, printing, refining, and the manufacture of cast iron. Charles Pratt's Astral Oil Works refined kerosene here. The iron gunship *Monitor*, launched in 1862 from a site near the intersection of Oak and West streets, was fabricated in Greenpoint by Continental Iron Works at West and Calyer streets. Greenpoint's only better-known offspring, actress Mae West, was born here in 1893.

We can't actually prove this bit of Greenpoint lore, but it is said that Brooklyn's famous and distinctive accent was born here in "Greenpernt."

Williamsburg was first developed by middle-class Irish and Germans; the locals ran fancy hotels frequented by the Vanderbilts, Whitneys, and other wealthy Manhattanites. When the Williamsburg Bridge opened in 1903, a huge migration of working-class immigrants, mostly Jews escaping overcrowding on the Lower East Side of Manhattan, settled in Williamsburg—indeed, the *New York Tribune* of that era refers to the bridge as "Jews Highway." While many of the original Jewish families have moved away, there is still a highly visible Jewish presence in the area, including forty thousand Satmar Hasidim who fled Europe in 1946. You can't miss the long black coats and earlocks worn by the men and the long-hemmed, long-sleeved styles worn by the women.

Kidstuff

Monsignor McGolrick Park is an enormous expanse of green, with all of the urban amenities—playground, ball fields, sprinklers, and concerts in the summertime. A few bakeries and shops, such as **Zapakone**, which specializes in folk art, also may be of interest to young ones.

ENTERTAINMENT

Clubs and performance arts spaces. Greenpoint and Williamsburg have been home to a number of popular dance and performance clubs in recent years. Unfortunately, these places come and go; two of the best known, Quiet Life and Lizards Tail, were closed in the spring of 1990 after a crackdown on illegal clubs by the New York City Fire Department. At the time of this writing, some other clubs and gallery spaces frequented by locals include Brand-Name Damages, at 301 Bedford Avenue; the Blue Cafe, at 507 Vandervoort Avenue; Minor Injury, at 1073 Manhattan Avenue; Art Farm, at 23 Bushwick Ave; and El Centro Cultural, at 308 Bedford Avenue. One of the most stable is Epoche, at 397 Wythe Avenue. For current information look for an underground paper called *Word of Mouth* (15 Grand Street, Brooklyn, N.Y. 11211).

Teddy's Bar and Grill. North 8th Street, near Berry Street, 384-9787. Daily, 9 a.m.–11 p.m. Dinner is served Tues.–Sun. No minimum or cover charge.

For a great bar scene with live entertainment from Wednesday through Saturday, try Teddy's in Williamsburg. The crowd is mixed; half are neighborhood regulars, mostly blue-collar workers, others are artists who recently moved into the neighborhood. Depending on the evening, you may catch some jazz (Joel Forrester of Microscopic Sextet has been a regular), country, or reggae music. On Saturday night Teddy's has dancing with music by a disc jockey. Live music starts weeknights at 8:30, Fridays at 10:30, Saturdays at 11 p.m. For food there are burgers and light snacks.

Williamsburg Music Center. 367 Bedford Avenue, at South 5th Street, 384-1654.

On the first three Sundays of the month you can catch a jazz performance here at 6 p.m. by local singers and instrumentalists. The series is supported by **BACA**, the **Brooklyn Arts Council** (see page 108).

PARKS AND PLAYGROUNDS

Monsignor McGolrick Park. Along Nassau and Driggs avenues, between Monitor and Russell streets, 389-5455. ✳

There's a lot of space for running around at this nine-acre park. History buffs also will be interested in the Shelter Pavilion in the center of the park. Built in the early 1900s, the lovely curved structure is reminiscent of French eighteenth-century formal gardens. In fact, it was designed after the Trianon at Versailles. Note also the statue of the naked sailor pulling on his mooring rope, a memorial to a leading figure in local shipbuilding lore.

POINTS OF CULTURAL INTEREST

Astral Apartments. 184 Franklin Avenue, between Java and India streets.

When Charles Pratt's Astral Oil Works refined kerosene in Greenpoint, his workers lived in this huge apartment house built in 1886. Note the patterned brickwork, brownstone lintels and arches, and multiple entrances.

Cathedral of the Transfiguration of Our Lord. 228 North 12th Street, at Driggs Avenue.

Even in this city of churches, you can't miss this official landmark Greek Orthodox beauty, built in 1921. Its five copper-clad, onion-shaped domes, typical of Russian Byzantine style, tower over the neighborhood. When the structure was built, Greenpoint was one of several thriving industrial belts in Brooklyn, with a large Greek Orthodox population working in nearby factories.

Our Lady of Mount Carmel Church. 275 North 8th Street, 384-0223. By appointment.

This church organizes the Giglio, one of New York City's most famous Italian festivals-cum-street fairs, held in July. The highlight of the festival is a procession in which several hundred men reenact an early medieval procession, complete with bands and dancing in the street, by carrying a sixty-five-foot painted wooden spire for a mile and a half.

Williamsburg Houses. Maujer Street to Scholes Street, Leonard Street to Bushwick Avenue.

Built in 1937, this public housing project was the first of many to be built in New York City. Many experts still consider it to be the best, with low, four-story buildings with courtyards, columned entrances, and other visual amenities.

NOTABLE RESTAURANTS

Bamonte's. 32 Withers Street, between Union and Lorimer streets, 384-8831. Wed.–Mon., noon–11 p.m.; open until 1 a.m. on weekends; closed Tues. Major credit cards.

Classic Italian fare is served at this big, popular old-fashioned restaurant known for its white-shirted waiters, dim lighting, and big portions. The kitchen is glass-enclosed, so you can see what's cooking. Meat entrées cost around $15 and the pasta, which is excellent, costs less. Call for directions.

Crisci's. 593 Lorimer Street, near Metropolitan Avenue, 384-9204. Tues.– Sun., 11:30 a.m.–11 p.m.; closed Mon. Major credit cards.

Crisci's is out of a scene from some old-time movie. The Formica tables and elder statesmen-cum-waiters set the tone for a meal of moderately priced family-style Italian food. Pronounced "Kreh-she," it's been around since 1902 and is a Williamsburg favorite. Entrées, from dishes of baked clams to chicken in wine and garlic, are enormous and most cost less than $15.

Efe's Continental Restaurant. 17 Kent Avenue, corner of North 13th Street, 384-9194. Daily, noon–11 p.m. Major credit cards.

What is the attraction of this tiny Turkish-European restaurant, completely off the beaten track in an industrial area? A spectacular view of Manhattan (best from outside at dusk), hearty entrées of chops, kebabs, and chicken dishes for under $10, *and* belly dancing make things so busy that reservations are recommended on the weekends.

Peter Luger Steak House. 178 Broadway, near Driggs Avenue, 387-7400. Mon.–Sat., noon–midnight; Sun., 1–10 p.m. No credit cards.

You don't have to step too far into Brooklyn to get to Peter Luger: just pop over the Williamsburg Bridge and you're there. In business since 1887, Williamsburg's most famous restaurant deserves a visit from everyone who loves steaks. The portions are enormous, the atmosphere is noisy and informal, and the waiters can be a classic pain in the neck. The steaks, grilled on the bone, are considered the absolute best. Plan to spend $40 to $50 per person, bring cash, and expect bare oak floors and tabletops. Weekend reservations are highly recommended.

Polska Restaurant. 136 Greenpoint Avenue, near Manhattan Avenue, 389-8368. Daily, noon–9 p.m. ✳

Talk about good homemade food! Generous servings of entrées, such as chicken cutlets, blintzes with strawberries, goulash with barley, and beef Stroganoff, cost less than $8. The $2 homemade soups—Russian borscht, sour soup, vegetable soup—are excellent, as are the potato pancakes and pirogi. A taste of the old country, this little restaurant with its plastic flowers and calendars on the walls seems appropriately located between the renovated Polish Slavic Credit Union and Polstar Publishing.

Polska Restaurant/Happy End Snack Shop. 924 Manhattan Avenue, corner of Kent Street, 389-8368. Daily, noon–9 p.m. ✳

There are a few tables in the back of this restaurant, but the action is at the counter, where you can munch a pirogi or homemade kielbasa while the neighborhood regulars saunter in and out. Don't miss the blintzes or red borscht, one of the specialties. The waitresses may call it dinner, but Polska serves from noon to nine every day. Prices start at $4. Don't confuse this with the better-publicized Polska Restaurant on Greenpoint Avenue (see listing above).

SHOPPING

Specialty Food Shops

Food for a Polish Feast
sweet pickles and pickled mushrooms
kielbasa sausage
stuffed cabbage and horseradish
huge loaf of rye bread
babka

Galleria Pastry Shop. 600 Metropolitan Avenue. 782-3777. Daily, 8 a.m.– 9 p.m.; Sun., 11 a.m.–5 p.m. ✳

Straight out of Italy, this slick, modern *pasticceria* in Williamsburg has a cappuccino-espresso bar, lots of mirrors, and out-of-this-world pastries. It's across the street from Tedone Latticini, which some consider one of the best places in Brooklyn for homemade Italian cheeses.

Honeymoon Bakery and Sweet Shop. 837 Manhattan Avenue, corner of Noble Street, 389-5252. Mon.–Sat., 7:30 a.m.–7 p.m.; Sun., 7:30 a.m.–4 p.m. ✳

You may not see the number over the door, but you can't miss the enormous pink awning that shelters the entrance to the Honeymoon. The cookies, cakes, candies, and breads are distinctly Italian and delicious. For those with tired feet there is one tiny table with two chairs where you can take a quick rest.

J and Z Pastry. 223 Bedford Avenue, between North 4th and North 5th streets, 782-2104. Daily, 6:30 a.m.–7 p.m.; Sun., 8 a.m.–7 p.m. ✳

If you need a break, try the excellent apple cake, cheesecake, and danish at this little Polish bakery in Williamsburg. You won't be disappointed.

Piekarnia Rzeszowska. 948 Manhattan Avenue, corner of Java Street, 383-8142. Daily, 10 a.m.–8 p.m. ✳

The selection may be limited to a few butter rolls and fruit-filled pastry breads, but once you've seen and tasted the gigantic (the bakery calls them "extra-large") *babkas*, you won't wish for anything more. You can fill a shopping bag here for less than $10; the extra-large babka is just $3.50. As in many shops in Greenpoint, there's also a small selection of Polish magazines and cassettes.

Polish and Slavic Credit Union–Bakery. 138 Greenpoint Avenue, 383-6268. Daily, 8 a.m.–6 p.m.; closed Sun.

Inside a small public lunchroom there is a bakery that many claim has the best breads, *babka*, sweet charlotte, and poppy seed cake in Greenpoint. Try the fruit breads.

R. Nassau Meat Market. 121 Nassau Avenue, near McGuinness Boulevard, 383-3476. Mon.–Fri., 8 a.m.–8 p.m.; Sat., 8 a.m.–6 p.m.; closed Sun.

Don't be shy. Even if you don't know what something in the window is, wander in and ask. These Greenpoint butchers are so friendly you are likely to get several samples of their freshly made spicy meatloaf or some other Polish specialty. This shop is great for bacon, sausages, and kielbasa, plus things to go with them, such as *babka*, huge loaves of fresh rye bread, imported mustard, horseradish, canned cherries, and other goodies.

Tedone Latticini. 597 Metropolitan Avenue, 387-5830. Mon.–Sat., 8 a.m.–5:30 p.m.; closed Sun. No credit cards.

For seventy years Tedone has been making excellent homemade cheeses and antipasti here, along with cold cuts, serving Williamsburg's Neapolitan Italian-American community.

W. Nassau Meat Market. 915 Manhattan Avenue, between Greenpoint and Kent avenues, 389-6149. Mon.–Sat., 8 a.m.–8 p.m.; closed Sun.

A vast array of kielbasa sausages hangs in the window here, along with a tongue-numbing variety of hams and other cold cuts. Between the stuffed cabbage, hot horseradish, pickled mushrooms, and enormous fresh loaves of bread, you may want to make this your last stop in Greenpoint. Load up and head home or to the park for a wonderful meal.

Interesting Neighborhood Shops

Architectural Salvage Warehouse. 337 Berry Street, between South 4th and South 5th streets, 388-4527. Hours change, so call for a recorded message. Checks accepted. No credit cards.

Whether you're meticulously restoring a brownstone to nineteenth-century splendor or searching for an interesting architectural artifact for your modern apartment, come to this warehouse one block north of the Williamsburg Bridge. The New York City Landmarks Preservation Commission retrieves items from city-owned buildings that are poised for demolition and sells them here. The selection includes doors, spindles, shutters, handrails, windows, and iron fences. Prices range from $10 for a piece that needs work to several hundred dollars. While much of what you'll find is run-of-the-mill, there's always the chance you'll stumble on an old mantle or mirror that will make the search worthwhile.

Goltex Company. 117 Nassau Avenue, between Ekhart and Leonard streets, 389-4192. Tues.–Sat., 10 a.m.–6 p.m.; Sun., 11 a.m.–5 p.m. No credit cards.

Where can you find Polish home video rentals and fine imported sheepskin coats under the same roof? Only in Greenpoint. In what may be the city's oddest use of retail space, you'll find a huge stock of men's and women's handsome $400–$800 coats hanging from ceiling racks, while the eye-level space is filled with shelves of video rentals. This is a great find for bargain hunters in need of warm winter outerwear.

Ksiazki Books. 140 Nassau Avenue, between Newell Street and McGuinness Boulevard, 383-3501. Mon.–Fri., 11 a.m.–8 p.m.

Can you imagine the difficulty of struggling to make your way in a new country when there is a revolution going on back home? It's no wonder there are several thriving Polish bookshops in Greenpoint's community of newly arrived immigrants. This bookstore sells periodicals, literature, and socio-political analyses of the current state of East-West relations, as well as some books in English. It is located within a block of a good kielbasa store, **Goltex** discount shop (page 199), and a bakery.

Nathan Borlan. 157 Havermeyer Street, near South 2nd Street, 782-0108. Sun.–Thurs., 10 a.m.–5 p.m.; Fri., closes mid-afternoon; closed Sat. Checks accepted. ✹

Nathan Borlan is right over the Williamsburg Bridge from Manhattan. It is Williamsburg's most famous store, and you shouldn't miss it, especially if you are looking for boys' and girls' clothing in classic styles—at discount prices. The family-run business is in its fifth decade of operation. Some of the same high quality merchandise you'll find here is sold at Manhattan's better department stores for 30 percent more—which is why shoppers flock here when looking to purchase big-ticket items such as winter coats. The branch store at 575 Kings Highway (336-3500) specializes in boys' wear. Both stores have a wide range of styles and prices, from children's through preteen sizes. There's a parking lot near the Williamsburg store; call to hear a tape that outlines detailed travel directions.

Panacea Herb and Spice House. 735 Manhattan Avenue, between Norman and Meserole streets, 383-8953. Mon.–Fri., 10 a.m.–7 p.m.; Sat., 10 a.m.–6 p.m.; Sun., 11 a.m.–4 p.m.

At first glance you may think this is an ordinary spice shop with bilingual (English and Polish) labels, but look closer for a few rarities. While many of the loose teas are your garden-variety mints or fruits, you'll also find Periwinkle, Street Benedict Thistle, Mistletoe, and Hemp Nettle. The personable owner, Jerzy Kapuscik, also stocks a selection of henna powders at $19.99 per pound and can tell you which "color" you'll need.

Pol-Am Bookstore. 946 Manhattan Avenue, corner of Java Street, 389-7790. Mon.–Fri., 11 a.m.–7 p.m.; Sat., 10 a.m.–5 p.m.; Sun., 11 a.m.–4 p.m.

Behind an unassuming facade, this shop sports an enormous selection of Polish works—books, records, cassettes, and compact discs as well as greeting cards, videotapes, and maps. Unless you read or speak Polish it may take you awhile to find the small selection of English language books. Anyone interested in Polish history, politics, or cinema will find plenty to choose from here.

Zakopane. 714 Manhattan Avenue, between Norman and Meserole streets, 389-3487. Daily, 10 a.m.–7 p.m. ✹

The jumble of wooden bowls, jewelry boxes, embroidered skirts and blouses, enormous carved eagles, and human figurines make this a must stop in Greenpoint—if only for browsing. Everything is imported from Poland. Don't miss the bright, hand-painted wooden eggs at about $1.50 each. These beauties look nice displayed in a bowl on a table and make unusual party favors for kids.

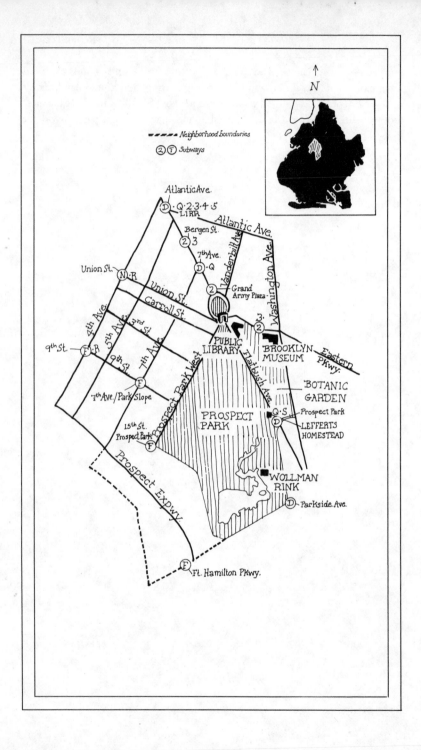

N

↑

Neighborhood boundaries

② Ⓕ Subways

Atlantic Ave.
Ⓓ · Q · 2 · 3 · 4 · 5
LIRR

Bergen St.
② ③

7th Ave.
Ⓓ · Q

Atlantic Ave.

Union St.
Ⓝ · R

Union St.

Carroll St.

4th Ave.

5th Ave.

3rd St.

7th Ave.

② Grand
Army Plaza

Washington Ave.

Vanderbilt Ave.

②

PUBLIC
LIBRARY

BROOKLYN
MUSEUM

Eastern
Pkwy.

9th St.
Ⓕ · B

9th St.

7th Ave./Park Slope

Ⓕ

Prospect Park West

Flatbush Ave.

PROSPECT
PARK

BOTANIC
GARDEN

Q · S
Ⓓ

Prospect Park
LEFFERTS
HOMESTEAD

15th St.
Prospect Park
Ⓕ

WOLLMAN
RINK

Prospect Expwy.

Ⓓ · Parkside. Ave.

Ⓕ
Ft. Hamilton Pkwy.

PARK SLOPE

Where it is: Between Flatbush Avenue and 17th Street, sloping down from Prospect Park to 4th Avenue.

What's nearby: Carroll Gardens, Brooklyn Heights, Fort Greene, and Sunset Park.

How to get there:

By car: Take the Manhattan Bridge and continue on Flatbush Avenue approximately two miles, then turn right on 7th Avenue; turn right. Or take the Brooklyn Bridge: take the second exit and immediately turn left onto Tillary Street, then right onto Flatbush Avenue. Continue as noted above.

By subway: The 2 and 3 trains go to Grand Army Plaza and the D train goes to 7th Avenue, both at the north end of Park Slope. The F train will take you to the 7th Avenue stop at 9th Street, toward the southern end of the neighborhood.

Cab services: Brownstone Cars (789-1536) or Denise Car Service (439-4943). Cost is about $15 from Grand Central Station and $6 from Brooklyn Heights.

Special events: Irish-American Parade (March); brownstone tour through the interiors of restored private landmark homes (third Sunday in May); Cherry

Blossom Festival (May); Children's Halloween Parade, 7th Avenue (October); Fireworks (New Year's Eve). Call 788-0055 for year-round events in Prospect Park.

How it got its name: Any neighborhood that slopes downhill from Prospect Park could logically be known as Park Slope.

ABOUT THE NEIGHBORHOOD

The saying goes that when city-loving couples in Manhattan decide to have children they move to fertile Park Slope. Given the stroller gridlock that grips the neighborhood sidewalks on a sunny weekend, that probably is not far off the mark. What draws new residents and visitors alike are the well-preserved brownstones and townhouses on Park Slope's many tree-lined streets, as well as the proximity to some of Brooklyn's grandest attractions: **Prospect Park**, the main branch of the **Brooklyn Public Library**, the **Brooklyn Museum**, and the **Brooklyn Botanic Garden.**

The official *Guide to New York City Landmarks* calls Park Slope "one of New York City's most beautiful residential areas." It boasts twenty-four blocks of landmark buildings and charming shops. Huge **Prospect Park** is enticing, with its open fields, jogging paths, pedal boats, the **Wollman Skating Rink**, and just-renovated **Prospect Park Carousel**. Nearby, the **Brooklyn Museum** has world-class exhibits of Egyptian artifacts and nineteenth-century American paintings, among others. Visitors travel far and wide to the **Brooklyn Botanic Garden** for its renowned cherry blossom festival and to enjoy the new and acclaimed **Steinhardt Conservatory**. The imposing and decorative **Central Library**, which is wonderful to look at, has two floors of excellent collections. Elegant **Grand Army Plaza**, which joins Eastern Parkway and Prospect Park, successfully fulfills its designer's dreams that it beautifully mimic the Arc de Triomphe in Paris.

In contrast to Polish Greenpoint, Russian Brighton Beach, and Italian Carroll Gardens, Park Slope does not have a predominant ethnic flavor— except perhaps yuppie. The style is casual, and the residents—count among them lawyers, writers, therapists, and businesspeople—tend to be well educated, liberal, and usually from somewhere in America other than Brooklyn. To suit their tastes, the neighborhood bristles with bookstores, nouvelle cuisine takeouts, upscale toy stores, handicraft specialty shops, and even a spectacular Victorian hostelry, **Bed and Breakfast on the Park**. Like a college town, Park Slope's trees and phone poles are papered over with notices announcing concerts, social action group meetings, lost dogs, and stoop sales (the vertical equivalent of yard sales).

You certainly won't go hungry in this neighborhood or its environs. There's excellent Chinese food at **Kar Chinese Cuisine** and simple Latino dishes at **El Re de los Castillos de Jagua**, good neighborhood Italian food at **Laura's**, Mexican cuisine at the **Santa Fe Bar and Grill**. Along Fifth Avenue you can buy fresh artichoke or spinach pasta at the unique **Morisi's Pasta**, excellent fresh Italian sausage and imported cheese at the anchor store of the **A. S. Fine Foods** empire, and imported Eastern European specialty items at **Eagle Provisions**. Two local bakeries, **Faith's Bakery** and **Cousin John's Cafe**, produce such spectacular delicacies that they supply some of the toniest eateries in Manhattan.

Architecture lovers will revel in the beautiful nineteenth-century homes and churches here. Amid spires, turrets, bay windows, and rows and rows of evenly matched brownstone stoops are architectural treasures reflecting Italianate and French Second Empire to Greek and Romanesque Revival styles. Among the most outstanding are the mock-Venetian palazzo **Montauk Club** and the parkside mansion in which **Woodward Park School** is now housed. Just walk along Montgomery Place, Carroll Street, or 6th Avenue to get a sense of the variety and beauty here. The landmark district goes from Park Place to Union Street between 6th and 8th avenues, then from Union Street to 4th Street between Prospect Park West and 7th Avenue.

Whether you come by subway, car, or bicycle, you can walk through most of Park Slope in well under an hour. But don't come with expectations of a quick foray; the sights can keep you occupied for a full day.

For Brooklynophiles Only

Some of the listings in this chapter legitimately belong in the neighborhoods of Prospect Heights, Prospect Gardens, Windsor Terrace, or Crown Heights. We've included them here because they are relatively close to Park Slope and often are combined with visits to this neighborhood. Our apologies to purists.

Historical Notes

Settled in the seventeenth century by Dutch farmers, Park Slope remained the province of two large families until the mid-1800s, when developers began subdividing the area into neat rows of streets and avenues. The Litchfield family's mansion still presides over Prospect Park; today it is the headquarters for the Parks Department.

When developers first began selling homes here in the mid-1800s, German and English upper-middle-class families settled in the brownstones in what is now Park Slope's landmark district. The area came to be known as a "streetcar suburb," a pleasant place to live with easy access to Manhattan, just two miles away. (The description is still apt today.) Park Slope even gained its own version of Central Park: completed in 1873, Prospect Park was the masterwork of Calvert Vaux and Frederick Law Olmsted, the team that had collaborated on Manhattan's rural jewel. In the latter quarter of the nineteenth century Italian and Irish working-class immigrants settled in more modest homes in what came to be known as the "South Slope" below broad, tree-lined 9th Street.

Just before the turn of the century the impressive new mansions being built across from Prospect Park on Prospect Park West and Plaza Street came to be dubbed "Millionaires Row" or "Brooklyn's Gold Coast." Development in the area continued after World War I with large apartment buildings rising on Plaza Street. After World War II the entire neighborhood went into decline—but, as with the rest of brownstone Brooklyn, a revival started in the 1960s that led to the renovation of many homes in Park Slope and the surrounding areas.

Kidstuff

Park Slope is a delightful place for children. **Prospect Park** has it all, from ball fields to a skating rink to tennis. The **Central Library**, a wonder to visit, has an extensive children's book collection and video department. Toys and books abound at the **Brooklyn Museum Children's Shop, Al's Toyland**, and **Little Things**. The **Botanic Gardens** and the **Brooklyn Museum** cannot be beat for educational, interesting expeditions.

ENTERTAINMENT

Landmark Pub. 7th Avenue, corner of 2nd Street, 768-4306. Weekend evenings.

The Landmark looks like a bar where time stands still. The windows are broken and the exterior looks like it hasn't seen a spot of paint other than graffiti for decades. But don't let that stop you. Inside, the decor is eclectic —toys, bottles, and coffee cans to bang in time with the music are scattered everywhere, and an old bed's headboard separates the bar from the tables. The beer is cold, and live music on the weekends makes this a local hot spot for the younger set. Though bustling with energy today, this may be a passing fancy; call ahead first.

Plaza Twin Cinema, 314 Flatbush Avenue, near 7th Avenue, 636-0170. Call for show times. ✳

Located virtually on top of the D and F trains' 7th Avenue subway stop, the Plaza Twin is Park Slope's only movie house. With two screens, it shows plenty of first runs and kiddie hits.

Puppetworks. 338 6th Avenue, corner of 4th Street, 965-3391. Weekends; call for show times. Tickets are $5 and under. ✳

The true art of puppetry might be lost if it were not for marionette makers and performers like these seasoned professionals who have helped create, among other things, Macy's annual Christmas and Easter puppet shows for fifteen years. The new seventy-seat theater is a vast improvement over the tiny former space, and now it's air conditioned as well. For preschoolers through sixth-graders, the extensive year-round repertoire under the direction of Nicholas Coppola includes classics such as the *Wizard of Oz, Pinocchio,* and *Sleeping Beauty.* Productions run about forty-five minutes and are well reviewed by everyone from *The New York Times* to the *New York Post.* You can also have your child's birthday party here.

Spoke the Hub. Gowanus Arts Exchange, 295 Douglass Street, between 3rd and 4th avenues, 596-5250. Call for show times. Tickets are under $10. ✳

Part of an up-and-coming art scene, Spoke the Hub is an innovative outfit that produces adult and children's dance and performance works. One of a half dozen "pre-preview" theaters in New York City that showcase emerging artists, Spoke's Outback Series, now in its fourth year, features both new and established artists. (Don't be surprised if some of the performers you see here make it to Manhattan's Dance Theater Workshop or BAM's Next Wave Festival.) Call to get on the mailing list, or watch listings in the *Village Voice.* Extra bonus: every six weeks the large open space turns into a local disco, where exuberant crowds boogie to rock, reggae, and all-around funky music. (See page 214 for the **Gowanus Arts Exchange** and page 245 for the "Groundhog" children's series at Spoke the Hub.)

PARKS AND PLAYGROUNDS

Prospect Park. The main entrance is at Grand Army Plaza, at the intersection of Flatbush Avenue, Prospect Park West, and Eastern Parkway, 287-3400 or 965-8900. Call 788-0055 for information on special events. ✳

Olmsted and Vaux, who designed Manhattan's Central Park, said they considered Prospect Park their best work. Designed in 1860, the 526 acres of rolling green lawns, wooded areas, streams, brooks, and lake make this a great environment for biking, walking, romancing, and just fooling around. In winter there is ice skating at the outdoor **Wollman Rink** and cross-country skiing in **Long Meadow** after a snowfall. In autumn the foliage is gorgeous, and the Urban Rangers put on a Halloween haunted walk for kids that follows a safe path into a ravine and across bridges and rocky ledges. Check for the Autumn Fest in the Boat House.

In the summer there's plenty to do here. Rent a pedal boat for a ride around **Prospect Lake** near the Lincoln Road–Parkside Avenue entrance. Listen to performances of the Metropolitan Opera in June or the New York or Brooklyn Philharmonic in August, or attend a Celebrate Brooklyn concert at the bandshell every Friday through Sunday night from July 4 through Labor Day. On Sunday afternoon, concerts from Hot Prospects in the Picnic House are great for kids. The park drive is closed to cars on summer weekdays, 10 a.m. to 3 p.m. and 7 p.m. to 10 p.m., and from 7 p.m. Friday to 6 a.m. Monday, making these good times to run or bike. The best playgrounds are at 11th Street on Prospect Park West and Lincoln Road at Ocean Avenue. "A Walk Through Prospect Park," a sixteen-page brochure, is available from the Prospect Park Alliance, 95 Prospect Park West, Brooklyn, NY 11215.

A & S Fishing Contest. (Lullwater Pond, near Wollman Rink, near the Parkside–Ocean Avenue entrance, 287-3400 [Urban Rangers]. July.) ✳

If your child loves to fish, make note of the annual July Abraham & Straus fishing contest in Prospect Park. A&S provides fishing poles, or you can bring your own. Prizes are A&S gift certificates. Kids age fifteen years and under are eligible.

Boat House and Visitors Center. (Near the Lincoln Road entrance, 287-3474.)

A regular schedule of art and sculpture exhibits are shown here in warm weather. Call for information on current offerings.

11th Street Playground. (11th Street and Prospect Park West.)

There's something for everyone here: sprinklers in the summer, climbing equipment and swings for grade-school kids, a sandbox and kiddie swings for preschoolers. Located near various ball fields and a five-minute walk from the Picnic House, where the **Hot Prospects** series is held (see the following entry), this is a popular spot in all seasons.

Hot Prospects. (Picnic House, 3rd Street entrance, 788-0055. Suggested donation is $5.)

Performances on Sundays in July or August can make a hot, steamy day pleasant. Hot Prospects performances run the gamut from rock and roll to jugglers to Chinese dancers. Come early to get a seat.

Pelican Pedal Boats (Lullwater Pond, near Wollman Rink, 287-9824. Open May–Oct., weather permitting. Mon.–Fri., 11 a.m.–6 p.m., Sat. and Sun., 10 a.m.–8 p.m. Cost is $7 an hour for a two-person boat.)

For a nominal fee, you can take a pedal boat out in the Lullwater, a calm lake in Prospect Park. Kids under sixteen must be accompanied by an adult. This is good fun, and it's open daily. Call to confirm hours.

Prospect Park Carousel. (Near Empire Boulevard and Ocean Avenue, 965-8951. Call for hours of operation.)

A relic from the past, the Prospect Park Carousel reopened in 1990. For a mere 50 cents you can ride on this beautifully restored masterpiece, which cost more than $500,000 to bring back to life. There are fifty-one Coney Island–style horses, lions, giraffes, goats, and chariots, all restored according to the designs created in a Boerum Street shop around 1912. The Wurlitzer organ has been rebuilt, too. And how's this for exotic: the first-ever carousel in Prospect Park, installed in 1874 and long gone, was originally powered by wind and sailed on Prospect Lake.

Prospect Park Stables. (East 8th Street and Cullmit Place, near Park Circle–Coney Island Avenue, 851-9230.)

It may seem incongruous to ride a horse in Brooklyn, but for years there's been a stable of about twenty horses and gorgeous trails through Prospect Park. Call for information.

Prospect Park Tennis Center (PPTC). (305 Coney Island Avenue, corner of Parkside Avenue, 438-1200. Daily, 7 a.m.–10 p.m. Call to reserve courts.)

The city runs these courts during the summer, but from late October through April the PPTC erects a bubble and manages the nine high-quality tennis courts. Lessons (and babysitting) can be arranged. There are pee-wee tennis programs for three- to six-year-olds and junior programs for kids from seven years and up.

Prospect Park Zoo. (Flatbush Avenue, near Empire Boulevard, 965-8900.)

Now closed for renovation by the New York Zoological Society, the Prospect Park Zoo is scheduled for reopening by 1993 at the earliest.

Wollman Rink. (Near Parkside Avenue, 965-6561. Open Thanksgiving to March, Mon.–Thurs., 10 a.m.–6 p.m.; Fri.–Sun., 10 a.m.–9 p.m.) ✳

This outdoor skating rink draws a friendly crowd of kids and adults. Admission is $2, or $1 for children under fourteen. Skate rentals are $2.50, and instruction is available. There's parking right next to the rink, and pizza, hot chocolate, instant soups, and hot dogs are available. Weekdays are the quietest and least-crowded times. A shuttle bus circles the park about once every fifteen to thirty minutes. Call for the bus schedule.

There are two houses within Prospect Park that have been designated as historic landmarks: **Lefferts Homestead** and **Litchfield Villa**.

Lefferts Homestead. Flatbush Avenue, near Empire Boulevard, 965-8951. Wed.–Sun., by appointment, plus special programs. ✳

The Dutch were the first European settlers in Brooklyn. Outstanding among the several extant homesteads of this wealthy farming community is this 1777 traditional Dutch house which belonged to Peter Lefferts. Situated in Prospect Park, the house has period furniture and a garden planted with the herbs used during colonial times. To keep tradition alive, Lefferts Homestead offers terrific free holiday programs in the arts and crafts of yesteryear: sheep shearing, coopering, rag-rug making, broom and basket making, floorcloth painting, and more. Call the above number for the schedule, or get a Prospect Park calendar of events by calling 788-0055.

Litchfield Villa. Prospect Park West, between 4th and 5th streets, 287-3400.

Ah, for the good old days when one's mansion had a commanding view! Built between 1855 and 1857 for land baron Edwin Clarke Litchfield by architect A. J. Davis, this lovely stuccoed mansion was only one of many estates built in "rural Brooklyn" by wealthy industrialists as a getaway from Manhattan. Shortly after the villa was completed, the city of Brooklyn paid the Litchfield family about $4 million for the more than five hundred acres that now constitute Prospect Park and acquired the mansion itself in 1892. The villa is now the Parks Department headquarters. You can wander inside, but to get a full sense of Park Slope's early history, the best bet is to take a guided tour (see page 213).

POINTS OF CULTURAL INTEREST

Visitors will find it convenient to go to two major cultural institutions—**The Brooklyn Museum**, and the adjacent **Brooklyn Botanic Garden**—in the same trip. Both are a fifteen-minute walk or a five-minute car ride from the heart of Park Slope. This section lists The Brooklyn Museum and Botanic Garden first, then some of Park Slope's more immediate architectural sights, galleries, and other points of interest.

The Brooklyn Museum. 200 Eastern Parkway, corner of Washington Avenue, 638-5000. Daily, 10 a.m.–5 p.m.; closed Tues. Admission is $4 for general public, $1.50 for senior citizens, and free to members and children under 12. *

The Brooklyn Museum is the seventh largest museum in the nation, but until recently it was something of a sleeper. In the mid-1980s it finally began to receive its just recognition when the new director, Robert Buck, inaugurated an aggressive exhibition program. "The Brooklyn" boasts a fine collection of Egyptian artifacts, one of the premier collections in America along with Manhattan's Metropolitan Museum of Art and Boston's Museum of Fine Arts. Scholars come from all over the world to use the Wilbour Library of Egyptology. The museum also has a fine collection of European paintings, including some by Degas, Corot, Monet, and Cezanne, along with an extraordinary survey of nineteenth-century American painting and sculpture. To get an idea of how Americans lived in the eighteenth and nineteenth centuries, check out the nation's largest display of period rooms—twenty-eight in all—and the costume gallery.

Not to be missed are the sculpture installations by contemporary artists in the Grand Lobby and the garden of architectural sculpture that has been "saved" from New York City buildings headed for demolition. The museum also has collections of Asian art, North American Indian art and artifacts, and Central African sculpture. In fact, in 1923 The Brooklyn Museum was the first in the nation to exhibit African objects as art rather than as ethnological artifacts.

The museum building itself is a Beaux Arts landmark designed by McKim, Mead & White in 1893. The Brooklyn Museum has embarked on a $31 million renovation and expansion, designed by the internationally acclaimed architects Arata Isozaki & Associates and by James Stewart Polshek & Partners that will eventually double the size of the museum. Three new floors of galleries are scheduled for completion by 1993. Don't miss the two excellent gift shops here.

Shuttle buses to and from Manhattan can be arranged for groups through Singer Tours, (718) 875-9084. Parking is available at the Washington Avenue entrance. Take the 2, 3, or 4 train to the Eastern Parkway–Brooklyn Museum stop, or the D or Q train to the Prospect Park stop.

Brooklyn Botanic Garden. 1000 Washington Avenue, along Eastern Parkway, 622-4433. Tues.–Fri., 8 a.m.–6 p.m.; Sat and Sun, 10 a.m.–6 p.m.; closed Mon. Free admission. *

Strictly speaking, the garden is in Crown Heights, but most visitors end up in Park Slope either before or after a trip here. There are more than fifty acres of carefully designed and meticulously maintained environments: lilac and daffodil hills, rose gardens, a blossoming cherry orchard, a children's garden, a fragrance garden, and a garden for the blind, complete with Braille signs. A favorite is the enclosed Japanese garden, with foot bridges, paths, and a Shinto shrine. Kids will love feeding the ducks and fish or running along the walkways, including the Celebrity Walk, which has names of famous Brooklynites inscribed on it.

The new and architecturally acclaimed **Steinhardt Conservatory** is a must-see. It houses the Trail of Evolution, the Aquatic House, a bonsai pavilion, and tropical, desert, and temperate environments. If you want to take some of this home with you, the well-stocked **Botanic Garden Gift Shop** (see page 228) sells houseplants, gardening supplies, and lovely gift items.

Call for information about tours, concerts, classes, and festivals. Parking is available at the Washington Avenue entrance. Take the 2, 3, or 4 train to the Eastern Parkway–Brooklyn Museum stop, or the D or Q train to the Prospect Park stop. See page 241 for information on the Children's Gardens.

Places of Architectural Interest

Ansonia Clock Factory Cinderella Project. 420 13th Street, along 7th Avenue, 788-2574.

This four-story red brick apartment building was once an abandoned clockworks factory that had employed many Polish and Irish immigrants in the nineteenth century. It is one of five hundred projects undertaken since the 1960s by the Brooklyn Union Gas Company through its "Cinderella" program to help revitalize Brooklyn neighborhoods. The program is still active in up-and-coming neighborhoods along 5th Avenue, and in Greenpoint, Fulton Ferry, Coney Island, and other Brooklyn locations. It has an impressive track record in aiding the revitalization of neighborhoods.

Montauk Club. 25 8th Avenue, corner of Lincoln Place, 638-0800. Not open to the public.

One of Park Slope's finest old buildings, the Venetian Gothic palazzo is surrounded by a thin moat of neatly trimmed green grass. The brass rails up the steps to the entrance are usually well buffed. Built in 1891, the Montauk Club is still a private social club today and is often used as a set by film crews in need of a beautiful manor house interior. In true Victorian tradition, the club once had a private parlor and separate entrance set aside for the female set.

Park Slope Civic Council House Tour. 729 Carroll Street, 636-8736. Fourth Sunday in May, noon–5 p.m. Cost is about $10.

Park Slope is one of Brooklyn's finest brownstone neighborhoods, an activist community, and the heart of the brownstone revival—so it's no surprise that the area's house tour, popular since 1959, is the oldest of its sort in all of New York City. Up to eight hundred people, many seeking ideas for their own renovations, sign up for the tour of the interiors of brownstone homes. History and architecture buffs are also big participants. Each of the ten to fifteen homes on the tour is staffed with knowledgeable volunteers to answer questions.

Prospect Hall. 263 Prospect Avenue, between 5th and 6th avenues, 788-0777.

Built before the turn of the century, this old opera house, restaurant, and speakeasy gradually fell into disrepair until its new owners recently restored it as a catering hall. They don't advertise it, but if you call ahead you may be able to convince them to take you on a tour. If not, walk in for a quick peek at the main staircase just inside the front door. The Grand Ballroom, complete with two balconies, holds up to fifteen hundred people and was the scene of a wedding celebration in the film *Prizzi's Honor*. The Men's Card Room, a former speakeasy, appears in the film *The Cotton Club*. The hall also contains the first elevator ever installed in Brooklyn (it still works). If ever there were an ideal place to throw a *big* party, this is it.

Soldiers and Sailors Memorial Arch. Flatbush Avenue, at Eastern Parkway, 788-0055. Sat. and Sun. only.

Known as America's "Arc de Triomphe," this imposing structure was built at a cost of $250,000 and unveiled in 1902 to celebrate the fallen heroes of the Civil War. From the top you'll get an idea of the urban vision that park designers Olmsted and Vaux had in 1860 for bringing European-style greenery and airiness into cramped city life. The view includes the landmark entrance to Prospect Park, the Manhattan skyline, the monumental **Brooklyn Central Public Library** (see page 215) and the first few blocks of Eastern Parkway, built in 1870 as the first American tree-lined promenade with benches and plantings. The six-story spiral staircase to the "Quadriga," the horse-drawn chariot sculpture at the top of the arch, is a fairly easy climb. Look for the bas-reliefs of presidents Lincoln and Grant on the inner sides of the archway.

Woodward Park School. Prospect Park West, corner of 1st Street, 768-7890.

Want to get an idea of how the true pioneers of Park Slope lived? Looking over Prospect Park, this fabulous 1883 Romanesque Revival mansion has a double outdoor staircase and turret windows and was originally the home of

Henry Carlton Hulbertx, the vice president of the South Brooklyn Savings Institution. Today it houses a private school, so plan to appreciate it mainly from the outside. As you walk the half dozen blocks from Grand Army Plaza to Woodward Park School, you will pass a number of elegant mansions built in the same era.

Other Points of Interest

Brooklyn Tabernacle. 290 Flatbush Avenue, near 7th Avenue, 783-0942. Sunday services are at 3:30 p.m. and 7:30 p.m.

Known for its contemporary gospel music, Brooklyn Tabernacle's non-denominational Sunday services have a huge 180-person choir with musical backup equipment that is so high tech it looks like a recording studio. The clergy are white, the congregation is multiethnic, and the service is, to say the least, spirited. Come early; seats fill up fast.

Brownstone Gallery. 76 7th Avenue, corner of Berkeley Place, 636-8736. Wed.–Sat., 10:30 a.m.–6 p.m.; Sun., noon–5 p.m. Major credit cards.

Located on a sunny corner, the Brownstone Gallery sheds the best possible light on the works of Brooklyn artists. Openings are neighborhood events as adults and kids spill onto the street. The gallery owner also will do appraisals, restorations, and framing. Auctions are held each month. The gallery is open five days a week, and you can make appointments for private viewings on Tuesday. Ask to be put on the mailing list.

Chassidic Art Institute (CHAI). 375 Kingston Avenue, between Carroll and Crown streets in Crown Heights, 774-9149 or 778-8808. Sun.–Thurs., noon–7 p.m.; Fri., closes early; closed Sat.

Not just Jewish, but specifically Hasidic folk art and paintings are shown in this unusual gallery located in nearby Crown Heights. Like Hasidic prayer, the art is fervent and emotional, exploring a Hasidic view of Jewish history, rituals, family life, and Jewish travail in the European ghetto. The nonprofit gallery was founded by community leaders after a 1977 **Brooklyn Museum** (page 211) show on Hasidic art drew ten thousand visitors. More than sixty artists are represented, including increasing numbers of Russian emigrés, who were prohibited from depicting religious themes in their work while living in the Soviet Union. Prints start at $10; paintings go up to $2,000.

Gowanus Arts Exchange. 295 Douglass Street, between 3rd and 4th avenues, 596-5250.

Once a soap factory, the building now housing the Gowanus Arts Exchange (so named for the nearby industrial canal) was recently renovated into a center for avant-garde dance and artistic innovation. Performances by **Spoke the**

Hub (see page 207) take place in the seventy-five-seat theater upstairs. The building also houses studios for artists and performing companies. It is located between Park Slope and Carroll Gardens in the area known as Gowanus.

Tiger Sign Company. 245 Flatbush Avenue, corner of Bergen Street, 783-4192. Daily, 9 a.m.–7 p.m. ✻

You can't miss the one-man show of unusual, high-quality commercial art at the Tiger Sign Company on Flatbush Avenue. Tiger is located in a distinctive building that stands alone on a small island of property, set apart from other stores by the rapidly flowing traffic. The walls and windows of the building—and in fine weather, the sidewalk outside it—are crammed with realistic signs that will tickle and delight: three-foot-high ice-cream sundaes, fish, and cornucopia of fruit. If you stop by for a peek, you may decide on the spot to commission a piece for yourself or for a gift. Tokyo University–educated graphic artist Mori Tiger can copy a picture or develop an original design; the bare minimum is $100.

Libraries

Brooklyn Central Public Library. Grand Army Plaza, corner of Flatbush Avenue and Eastern Parkway, 780-7722. Call to check hours. ✻

With fifty-eight branches in the borough, Brooklyn's library system is one of the largest in the country, and this is the center of it all. Built as part of a WPA project in the 1930s, the beautiful and imposing structure was completed in 1941. The librarians here are excellent; there's even a Brooklyn history specialist. Kids love it, too: there's a large reading room for preschoolers, plus frequent movies and readings. A library card entitles you to listen to and take out recordings. Videotapes can be taken home overnight for free. There is also a cafeteria, which is useful, since the nearest shops and delis are a few blocks away.

Brooklyn Public Library. 431 6th Avenue, corner of 9th Street, 768-0593. Call to check hours. ✻

There are plenty of worthy selections and programs here for children, and you're only three blocks from Prospect Park's **11th Street Playground** (see page 208), one of the biggest in the area. Combine a library and park visit with a little shopping on 5th Avenue and make a day of it.

NOTABLE RESTAURANTS

Adele. 510 11th Street, near 7th Avenue, 788-4980. Mon. and Tues., 6–10:30 p.m.; Wed.–Sat., 5–9 p.m.; Sun. brunch, 11:30 a.m.–3 p.m. Major credit cards.

Elegant, expensive, and almost Manhattan, Adele is the place to go if you want excellent French-American cuisine in a charming setting—a chintz-decorated nineteenth-century carriage house, complete with fireplace. Adele is just right for special occasions or a little romance. Average dinners cost about $45 per person without wine, and the restaurant gets high marks for service, quality, and ambience. The chef, a veteran of Manhattan's well-known Chanterelle restaurant, varies the menu periodically.

Aunt Sonia's. 1123 8th Avenue, corner of 12th Street, 965-9526. Daily, 5:30–10:00 p.m.; Sun. brunch, 11:30 a.m. Major credit cards.

The warm atmosphere, simple decor, and wonderful food at this small nouvelle cuisine restaurant make it a popular local spot. The regular menu changes every three months, and you can count on nightly specials as well. Don't miss the Sunday brunch—it's a knockout. By the way, Aunt Sonia's takes its name from the nearby Ansonia Clock Tower, now renovated into cooperative apartments. Weekend reservations are recommended.

Aunt Suzie's Kitchen. 247 5th Avenue, between Carroll Street and Garfield Place, 788-3377. Sun.–Thurs., 5–10 p.m.; Fri. and Sat., 5 p.m.–midnight. Major credit cards. *

The *New York Post* called this "one of the best under $15" meals in New York City. Not only is the Italian fare home-cooked, but the place feels like home. Specials change but are likely to include several fish dishes and items such as spinach manicotti. The high-ceilinged dining room is filled with wooden tables of different sizes and shapes. A small table at the front has a selection of plate-size games and kiddie books for the picking, making this a good place to take little ones. A new take-out shop, Suzie's Pantry, is located at 171 7th Avenue (788-2868).

Cousin John's Bakery. 70 7th Avenue, between Berkeley Place and Lincoln Place, 622-7333 or 768-2020. Sun.–Thurs., 7 a.m.–11 p.m.; Fri. and Sat., 7 a.m.–1 a.m. Checks accepted. *

Chocolate lovers will think they've gone to heaven, and the smell of croissants, scones, and muffins will make your mouth water. The fruit pastries, such as kiwi and blueberry cream tarts, are both beautiful and tasty. Homemade ice cream and sorbet—try the cassis or champagne flavors—are sinful. Late hours on the weekend makes this a busy place after the movies or a show at BAM. There's also another café at 347 7th Avenue, between 9th and 10th streets (768-2020).

El Gran Castillo de Jagua. 345 Flatbush Avenue, corner of Carlton Avenue, 622-8700. Daily, 7 a.m.–midnight. *

There's almost always an urbane, working-class crowd at the take-out counter for the authentic Dominican food at rock bottom prices. You can also eat in at the restaurant section, which, with a jukebox and red plastic table-cloths, is unpretentious and fine for families. Food includes plenty of rice dishes, fried green plantains, shrimp soupy rice, fried chicken and chips, and paella. Breakfast specials are under $3, and average dinner entrées range from $5 to $12. It is conveniently located across from the **Plaza Twin movie theater** (see page 207). Free delivery is available.

Kar Chinese Cuisine. 428 5th Avenue, between 8th and 9th streets, 965-1010 or 965-1011. Mon.–Sat., 11:30 a.m.–10:30 p.m.; Sun., 1–10 p.m. Major credit cards. ✱

Appearances are deceptive: here is one of the best Chinese restaurants in all of brownstone Brooklyn, innocuously tucked away among neighborhood shops. While most Chinese restaurants seem to share the same menu, Kar has its own variations, plus some wonderful specials, like onion fritters and numerous seafood dishes. Brown rice is standard fare here, and the vegetables are fresh as can be. Entrées start at about $7. No MSG is used, either. (Kar has a second shop, takeout only, in Sheepshead Bay, at 2212 Avenue X, 891-6868.)

New Prospect Cafe. 393 Flatbush Avenue, between 7th and 8th avenues, 638-2148. Mon.–Thurs., 11:30 a.m.–10 p.m.; Fri. and Sat., 11:30 a.m.–11 p.m.; Sun., 10:30 a.m.–10 p.m. Major credit cards.

A very small restaurant with a homey atmosphere and good food, this is a favorite of many locals for dinner and Sunday brunch. It can be a little claustrophobic and pricey for small children, with dinners ranging from $9 to $16 per entrée. The menu tends toward fish, chicken, and vegetarian dishes. Reservations are recommended for three or more.

Raintrees. 142 Prospect Park West, corner of 9th Street, 768-3723. Daily, 5–11 p.m.; Sun., 11:30 a.m.–3:30 p.m. Major credit cards.

Located across from the 9th Street entrance to **Prospect Park** (page 207), this is a lovely place for a special occasion, particularly in the autumn, in spring, or right after a snowstorm. Sunday brunch is popular. It's slightly pricey, but the atmosphere is relaxed and vaguely European.

Santa Fe Bar and Grill. 60 7th Avenue, corner of Lincoln Place, 636-0279. Mon.–Fri., 5–11 p.m.; Sat. and Sun., 3 p.m.–midnight. Major credit cards. ✱

Frozen margaritas, cold beer, and chips with salsa make this a popular hangout for young Slopers on weekends and after work. On cool nights the doors and windows are flung wide open, making the street scene almost a part of the dinner scene. The food is average Mexican, the atmosphere is lively.

Tartine. 426A 7th Avenue, between 14th and 15th streets, 768-2764. Wed.–Sun., 5:30–10:30 p.m.; Sun. brunch, 12:30–3 p.m. Major credit cards.

You wouldn't expect to find such excellent food hidden away on such a nondescript block of Park Slope, but take note. At this small and spare yet romantic restaurant, the nouvelle cuisine and the selection of wines are excellent and the service is pleasant. The menu includes a small selection of approximately five appetizers, five entrées, and five desserts. Entrées run from $12 to $18 and include bouillabaisse, filet mignon, tile fish in olive oil with peppers and herbs, chicken, and daily specials.

Two Boots. 514 2nd Street, just off 7th Avenue, 499-3253. Mon.–Thurs. and Sun., 11 a.m.–10 p.m.; Fri. and Sat., 11 a.m.–midnight. Major credit cards. *

Following in the footsteps of its fabulously popular Manhattan location, this zany, eclectic restaurant caters to the young at heart. It combines excellent, moderately priced food with kiddie accoutrements: coloring books and crayons, kid-level tables and coat hooks, and a pizza decorated like a face. It's not just a kids' place, though: items such as sweet potato and scallion omelettes with salsa verde will appeal to adults. The colorful outdoor patio is an extra plus. Sunday brunch is a steal at under $10.

Two Toms. 255 3rd Avenue, corner of Union Street, 875-8689. Tues.–Sat., 5–9:30 p.m.; Sun., 3–7 p.m. *

Some people love it, others hate it, but Two Toms is an undeniably Italian working-class, family-oriented, no-nonsense restaurant. With huge portions of steak and chops, the meat dishes get raves. Ditto for the enormous antipasti. Good for kids, large groups, and low prices. Drive here if you can, since it's located in a somewhat isolated area between an auto body shop and a launderette near the Gowanus Canal. Weekend reservations are recommended.

Restaurants Within a Fifteen-Minute Walk or a Five-Minute Car Ride of Park Slope

Brooklyn Museum Cafe. 200 Eastern Parkway, corner of Washington Avenue, 638-5000. Wed.–Mon., 10 a.m.–4 p.m.; closed Tues. *

Sunday brunch has become something of an "in" thing to do here. This little café is so bright, clean, and quiet that it makes a wonderful lunch stop even if you don't have time for the museum exhibits. The salad bar is fresh and diverse, and there's a wide selection of soups, sandwiches, hot meals, and desserts. This is a good place to bring children, but it's pricey.

Farrell's Bar. 215 Prospect Park West, at 16th Street, 788-8779. Daily, 11 a.m.–1 a.m.

Farrell's, which reputedly was one of the first bars to reopen after Prohibition was repealed, has survived population shifts in the neighborhood not by catering to changing tastes but by staying the way it is: an old-fashioned Irish saloon. Its decor is polished wood, mirrors, and brass, and it's strictly standing room only. Run by second-generation Farrell family members, the place echoes with many a good story told. It is home-away-from-home to local retirees and is a favorite with firemen and cops from the neighborhood as well as with nurses from the local Methodist Hospital. At 16th Street, it is closest to the South Slope.

Garden Cafe. 620 Vanderbilt Avenue, corner of Prospect Place, 857-8863. Tues.–Fri., 6–9:30 p.m.; Fri. and Sat., 6–10:30 p.m.; closed Sun. and Mon. Major credit cards. ✳

In Prospect Heights, just a couple blocks across Flatbush Avenue from Park Slope, is this small neighborhood bistro with just eight tables—a nice, low-key spot for a quiet dinner for two or four. The owner-chef cooks in the nouvelle style while his wife handles the clientele. The food is fresh, cooked and spiced with flair, and the wine list is substantial, so it is no surprise that this is a neighborhood favorite. The menu changes, but figure on spending about $12 for an entrée.

Laura's. 1235 Prospect Avenue, corner of Reeve's Place, 436-3715. Mon.–Fri., 1–10 p.m.; Sat. and Sun., 1–11 p.m. Major credit cards.

Locals return time and again to this cozy, intimate restaurant for what the chef calls "original Italian" food. The quality can vary, but when it is good it is excellent. Soups and pasta dishes are best bets. Entrées range from $9 to $15 and include grilled chicken, flounder in three or four guises, stuffed calamari, various pastas, and more. Bring your own wine and beer or cross the street to a strategically located liquor store.

Terrace Cafe. 1000 Washington Avenue, along Eastern Parkway, 622-4433. Open April to Oct., Tues.–Sun., 10:30 a.m.–4 p.m.; closed Mon. ✳

Not only is this one of the most pleasant settings in New York for an outdoor café—the middle of the Brooklyn Botanic Garden—but the food is way above average. Besides burgers and sandwiches, the menu includes some good, hearty soups and salads at moderate prices. There's room here for kids to run around.

Tom's Restaurant. 782 Washington Avenue, corner of Sterling Place, 636-9738. Mon.–Sat., 5 a.m.–4:30 p.m. ✳

Just three long blocks past Flatbush Avenue is a former ice-cream parlor located in Prospect Heights that harbors one of the best breakfast eateries around. Since 1936 Tom, and now Tom's son Gus, has been serving up inexpensive, wonderfully tasty and filling breakfasts (they also do lunch). Three enormous apple pancakes cost just $3.50, a big bowl of grits is $1, and the French toast is made from *challah* bread. The muffins are huge, as are the bagels; the eggs and home fries are first rate. The setting here is 1950s-style, warm and friendly. Gus is a charmer, making sure the kids are okay and the food is to your liking. Tom's also makes a mean egg cream. *Note*: Washington Avenue is fairly run-down.

SHOPPING

Specialty Food Shops

A. S. Fine Foods. 274 5th Avenue, between 2nd and 3rd streets, 768-2728. Mon.–Sat., 7:30 a.m.–6 p.m.; Fri., 7 a.m.–7 p.m.; closed Sun.

For those seeking genuine Italian provisions from rolled veal with garlic to chicken stuffed with mozzarella and prosciutto, the people at A. S. have been perfecting the art of Italian cooking for more than forty-five years. This is strictly a market; there's no seating. If you go on the weekend, pick up a couple of the *focaccia*, a small southern Italian pizza that's available only on Saturdays. This is one of twenty-one locations in the greater New York metropolitan area. Two others are 8614 5th Avenue in Bay Ridge and 361 Avenue X in Gravesend near Sheepshead Bay.

Eagle Provisions. 628 5th Avenue, corner of 18th street, 499-0026. Daily, 6 a.m.–7 p.m. Major credit cards.

This small, ultraclean supermarket with its international flavor and large selection of high-quality eastern and western European items seems to belong in Manhattan's Yorkville section instead of largely working-class Latino 5th Avenue in Brooklyn. In addition to fresh produce, there are smoked meats made on the premises, from juicy hams to no-preservative sausages and oven-ready fresh stuffed chicken breasts and brisket. The store carries newspapers in Arabic, Spanish, and Polish alongside *Barron's* and the *Wall Street Journal*. The delicious breads are imported from a Lithuanian bakery. Other merchandise includes jars and jars of Hungarian red currants and gooseberries, Italian sour cherries, poppyseed filling for pastries, French chocolate and hazelnut sauce, Scottish soups, Italian polenta, German herring, imported chocolates, and so on. Conveniently located, it is a block from both **Aaron's** discount clothing (see page 223) and **Morisi's Pasta** (opposite).

Faith's Bakery. 169 Lincoln Place, between 7th and 8th avenues, 499-8108. Tues.–Fri., 8 a.m.–7 p.m.; Sat., 9 a.m.–6 p.m.; closed Sun.

If you've ever been to Manhattan's Cafe Des Artistes for dinner or Dean and Deluca for takeout, you may have tasted Faith's cakes. Chocolate addicts who make the pilgrimage here will go wild. Try the chocolate mousse cake, chocolate sour cream cake, tarts, and pies—simply taste one of everything! There's a second shop at 1112 8th Avenue, between 11th and 12th streets (499-8108).

Fifth Avenue Fish Market. 157–161 5th Avenue, corner of Lincoln Place, 638-8083. Mon.–Fri., 8 a.m.–7 p.m.; Sat., 8 a.m.–6:30 p.m. Checks accepted.

In business since 1914, this fishmonger used to sell mainly wholesale. Retail clients trooped in amid the sawdust and freezers for some of the freshest fish in this part of Brooklyn. Bowing to a booming retail demand, the store recently opened a sparkling clean retail shop that rivals the best in Manhattan and has a host of condiments, fish cookbooks, and other goodies to help make a meal complete. You'll find excellent prices and they'll pack your fish in ice if you have a ways to travel. They will deliver anywhere in Brooklyn for a minimum order.

Hot Bird. 665 Vanderbilt Avenue, between Prospect Place and Park Place, 468-2473 (HOT-BIRD). Daily, 11 a.m.–10 p.m. Delivery, noon–9:30 p.m.

Hot Bird will deliver a hot dinner to your doorstep (within half an hour of ordering) in Park Slope, Cobble Hill, Clinton, Fort Greene, Prospect Heights, or Ditmas Park. The menu includes great marinated barbecued chicken, ribs, Black Forest ham steak, plus vegetable pâté, corn on the cob, salads, semolina bread, soft drinks, and cheesecake or brownies. The store's motto is "no oil, no fat, no frying." The minimum order is about $10.

La Bagel Delight. 252 7th Avenue, corner of 5th Street, 768-6107. Mon.–Thurs., 6 a.m.–7 p.m.; Fri.–Sun., 6 a.m.–10 p.m. ✳

It isn't hard to find bagels in Brooklyn, but finding really *good* bagels is more of a challenge. Although there will always be those who disagree, many locals consider these baked-on-the-premises bagels the best around. You can pick up picnic fixings here before heading to nearby **Prospect Park** (page 207).

Morisi's Pasta. 647 5th Avenue, between 18th and 19th streets, 788-2299. Mon.–Sat., 8 a.m.–6 p.m.; Fri. and Sat., open later. ✳

No pasta lover will ever turn away from Morisi's. The inside of this old-fashioned pasta shop is ablaze in pastas of all colors, shapes, and sizes. More than two hundred varieties of pasta, from artichoke cavatelli and apple rotini to tomato *fusilli* and sesame elbows, grace the shelves here. Don't miss the fantastic ravioli and marinara sauce in the rear refrigerators; both freeze wonderfully. Once you've found Morisi's, you'll keep coming back. By the way, Morisi's pastas get their shapes from molds manufactured by the largest pasta diemaker in the United States, Maldari and Sons, located less than a half mile away on 3rd Avenue.

New Prospect at Home. 52 7th Avenue, between Lincoln Place and Sterling Place, 230-8900. Mon.–Fri., 7:30 a.m.–9 p.m.; Sat. and Sun., 8:30 a.m.– 8 p.m. Major credit cards.

When you don't want to sit down at the **New Prospect Cafe** (see page 217), head over to its take-out shop. It's a good place to pick up picnic supplies; choose from a wide variety of prepared dishes, including pasta and vegetable salads, fresh bagels, breads, and other baked goods. Many cheeses and natural juices are available as well.

Park Slope Food Co-op. 782 Union Street, between 6th and 7th avenues, 783-8819 or 622-0560. Mon.–Thurs., 5–9:45 p.m.; Sat., 9 a.m.–7:30 p.m.; Sun., 9 a.m.–5 p.m. Checks accepted.

You can't shop here unless you are one of the more than twenty-five hundred members that belong to this unique institution. This is one of the country's largest food cooperatives, in existence since 1973. Members do 90 percent of the work (paid employees handle the rest). The co-op caters to a wide range of tastes but specializes in healthy, natural foods. A big attraction is the extensive produce section, which includes many organic items, and low prices (just 16 percent above cost). Handwritten signs explain environmentally sound foods and staples to buy and to avoid.

Park Slope Seafood. 170 7th Avenue, corner of 1st Street, 832-2465. Mon.–Sat., 10 a.m.–8 p.m.; Sun., 10 a.m.–6 p.m.

You'd only buy fresh sushi from someone who knows what he's doing, right? Joung Un Tak is your man. With one store in exclusive Greenwich, Connecticut, and another in Greenwich Village, plus a master's degree in business, he runs a tight ship. You won't find a more immaculate fish store anywhere (in fact, you may not find take-out sushi at any other store in Brooklyn). If you take home this delicious sushi, dinner for two runs about $15. The store also features a beautiful selection of fresh fish to cook at home.

Small Feast. 447 1st Street, just off 7th Avenue, 788-9449. Mon.–Fri., 7 a.m.–8:30 p.m.; Sat. and Sun., 9 a.m.–6:30 p.m.

The red awning may say "catering," but Small Feast does a nifty retail business as well. Typical take-out fare includes green bean salad and roasted new potatoes as well as a large selection of fresh breads and whole-wheat baguettes. The garlic sticks—about sixteen inches long and laden with garlic and herbs—are delectable.

Catered entrées, for parties of two to fifty or more, include blackened Cornish hens, Milanese veal chops, and four kinds of pizza. Particular parents will like the "Mommy Made" baby foods, both vegetable and fruit purées and prepared foods in small servings.

Clothing and Shoes

Aaron's. 627 5th Avenue, near 16th Street, 768-5400. Mon.–Sat., 9:30 a.m.–6 p.m.; closed Sun. Major credit cards.

Their slogan says it all: "You won't do better unless your husband's in the business." Inside Aaron's innocuous, windowless storefront, you'll find discounts on leading designer sportswear, dresses, and coats at 25 to 50-percent savings. Look for labels like Harvé Bernard, Albert Nipon, Blassport, and Henry Grethel. There's parking across the street and the salespeople are quite attentive.

City Casuals. 223 7th Avenue, between 3rd and 4th streets, 499-5581. Mon.–Fri., 10 a.m.–7 p.m.; Sat., 10 a.m.–6 p.m.; Sun., noon–5 p.m. Major credit cards.

Some working women will love this shop for its relaxed yet professional fashions. The specialty here is outfitting those women whose jobs don't call for suiting up and wearing a bow tie around the neck. Among the store's loyal customers are dentists, doctors, lawyers, writers, professors, and therapists. The dresses and two-piece outfits start around $130. The shoes are good-looking and comfortable, with many imports ranging from $45 to $125.

Jamila's. 271-75 Flatbush Avenue, between Prospect Place and St. Marks Avenue, 398-6463. Mon.–Fri., 11:30 a.m.–7 p.m.; Sat., 10 a.m.–6 p.m.; Sun., noon–6 p.m. Major credit cards.

Beautifully displayed, fashionable casual wear is sold at this new shop run by one of a handful of African-American women entrepreneurs in the area. Prices are moderate, given the strong sense of style here. Often the store has brochures on hand for various cultural events of interest, such as dance performances and concerts.

Sneaker Factory. 47 Lincoln Place, between 5th and 6th avenues, 857-4474 or 857-4477. Mon.–Sat., 9:30 a.m.–6 p.m.; Sun., 10 a.m.–4 p.m. Major credit cards. ✳

Behind the unassuming brick exterior of this store is an enormous selection of sneakers, some at discount prices. Converse, Nike, Oshkosh, and other popular brands are all here. When everyone else had run out of Batman high-tops, the Sneaker Factory still had them. Great bargains are available on discontinued lines and overstocks, plus a few inexpensive no-name brands. You'll also find work boots, some dress shoes, T-shirts, laces, and other accessories.

Sumo. 169A 7th Avenue, between Garfield Place and 1st Street, 768-1847. Daily, 11 a.m.–7 p.m. Major credit cards.

This is the first retail location for wholesaler Chris Zuroski. His splashy graphics grace almost everything from T-shirts ($12) to cotton cardigans ($45), polo shirts, pants, socks, and bags. He's even got a few funky string ties, if that's your thing. Bloomingdale's and Macy's sometimes carry these items, but this is the source.

Triangle Clothing. 182 Flatbush Avenue, corner of 5th Avenue, 638-5300. Mon.–Fri., 9:45 a.m.–6:30 p.m.; Sat., 9:45 a.m.–5:30 p.m. Major credit cards. ✳

In business since 1917, Triangle is a potpourri of sporting goods, work clothes, and sports clothes. There's such a huge inventory that you may have to ask for help to find what you want—but you *will* find it. Prices can be very reasonable—last year's $100 ice skates were going for $59. The store is on the edge of Park Slope; to get here you can ride the 2, 3, 4, 5, or Q train to Atlantic Avenue, or the B, M, N, or R train to Pacific Street.

Vintage Antique Clothing. 111 7th Avenue, between President and Carroll streets, 638-7451. Mon.–Fri., 11 a.m.–7 p.m.; Thurs., 11 a.m.–8 p.m.; Sun., noon–5 p.m. Major credit cards.

It may be surprising that this tiny second-hand shop has survived the massive gentrification of 7th Avenue, but its secret of success is a constantly changing inventory, great window displays, and low prices. Standard items include coats, dresses, and jackets from the 1930s to the 1960s; interesting hats and accessories; and a wide range of new and old jewelry.

Shops for Children

Al's Toyland. 209 7th Avenue, near 3rd Street, 768-2414. Mon.–Sat., 10:30 a.m.–6:30 p.m.; closed Sun. Major credit cards. ✳

Imagine a Toys "Я" Us store squeezed into a rabbit's warren of rooms—that's Al's. You may have to ask for assistance, but this place has just about everything in toys. Many prices are discounted. Don't look here for fancy foreign stuff; you'll find that down the block at **Penny Whistle** (opposite). Al's stocks good old American games, toys, school supplies, and the like.

Little Things. 166-168 7th Avenue, between Garfield Place and 1st Street, 768-1014. Mon.–Fri., 10:30 a.m.–7 p.m.; Sat., 10 a.m.–6:30 p.m.; Sun., 11 a.m.–5 p.m. Major credit cards. ✳

The purple and yellow storefront is startling enough, but once inside Little Things, you may be so overwhelmed by the eclectic inventory that you miss the shop's best features. Forget the costume jewelry and T-shirts that crowd the front. Instead, head to the back for a good range of children's and babies' toys, educational toys, crafts, and knickknacks for party bags.

Our Children's Enterprises. 34 Garfield Place, between 4th and 5th avenues, 788-4400. Mon.–Fri., 7 a.m.–4 p.m.; closed Sat. and Sun. ✳

For basic educational toys—the kind you'll find in schools—this is one of Brooklyn's best-kept secrets. Primarily a wholesaler, this sizeable store has a wide selection of puzzles, blocks, beads, paints, books, tapes, and name-brand toys geared to children of all ages. The selection is exclusively no-nonsense, durable equipment favored by teachers. Prices are not discounted, but many of the items here cannot be found in traditional toy shops.

Penny Whistle Toys. 203 7th Avenue, corner of 3rd Street, 965-6680. Mon.–Sat., 10 a.m.–6 p.m.; Sun., noon–5 p.m. Major credit cards. ✳

Following in the footsteps of its highly successful Manhattan flagship store, the Brooklyn shop carries top-end toys, including many hard-to-find imported kiddie basics: beautiful books, blocks, bikes, art supplies, and even some cute cards. Kids love their "specials": the bubble-blowing bear outside, the weekly story hour, and a free present on every child's birthday (if you're on the mailing list).

Suzy's Circus. 200 7th Avenue, between 2nd and 3rd streets, 499-8184. Mon.–Sat., 10 a.m.–6 p.m.; Thurs., 10 a.m.–7 p.m. Major credit cards. ✳

As upscale as the neighborhood and owned by a local resident, Suzy's Circus carries one of the best selections of fine children's footwear in Brooklyn, plus a variety of stylish children's clothing from infant up to about size 7. Prices for shoes start at $10, and outfits start around $25. Many items are 100 percent cotton, such as Vermonter Jeanie Mac's line. There are also lots of exuberantly colored, well-designed seasonal accessories: flowery little Easter hats, mittens with puppet fingers, and so on.

Interesting Neighborhood Shops

Booklink. 99 7th Avenue, near Union Street, 783-6067. Mon.–Sat., 10 a.m.–9 p.m.; Sun., 11 a.m.–8 p.m. Major credit cards. ✳

Though small, Booklink packs a diverse selection onto its shelves, including a number of foreign and alternative journals you may not expect to find in a local bookstore. Not only is the children's section a good one, but it's in the back, where Junior won't disturb the peace. If you can't find the book you want, the owners will order it for you.

A second store recently opened at 7th Avenue and 8th Street.

Clay Pot. 162 7th Avenue, between Garfield Place and 1st Street, 788-6564. Mon.–Fri., 10:30 a.m.–7:30 p.m.; Sat., 10:30 a.m.–6:30 p.m.; Sun., noon–5:30 p.m. Major credit cards.

It's unusual to find a ceramics shop selling more than just the typical mugs and honey pots. Clay Pot carries real ceramic art (signed, hand-crafted pottery) as well as jewelry, glass and wood crafts, and some furnishings created by a wide range of nationally known artisans. Miniature ceramic scenes such as the 1950s diner cookie jar and cups, are fantastic. Prices range from about $30 to over $200.

Eclipse Studio. 180 Lincoln Place, between 7th and 8th avenues, 783-7313. Mon.–Sat., 10 a.m.–7 p.m. Major credit cards.

With all the stained glass that adorns homes in Park Slope, it's no wonder that Paul Solomon, Eclipse's owner and artist-in-residence, is busy. Customers come from far afield; one couple hired him to fix a broken window in a Long Island mausoleum. When Paul isn't repairing windows he builds beautiful hanging and standing lamps. The smallest cost around $150 and can be shipped—he guarantees—without breaking.

Eifel Antique Furniture Warehouse. 571 Carroll Street, between 4th and 5th avenues, 783-4112. Tues.–Fri., 10 a.m.–4 p.m.; Sun., 10 a.m.–5 p.m. Major credit cards.

You never know what you'll find in unlikely places. Located at the far end of Carroll Street, one of Park Slope's prettier residential brownstone blocks, this two-story space is filled with interesting bits and pieces of Americana from the 1930s to the 1960s, such as tables, desks, and chairs. There are some architectural elements, such as moldings and doorways, upstairs as well.

Fine Period Furniture. 239 Flatbush Avenue, between 6th Avenue and Park Place, 789-9091. Mon.–Sat., 11 a.m.–7 p.m.; closed Sun. Checks accepted.

Amid a number of antique shops on this stretch of Flatbush Avenue, this store stands out for its tasteful, well-restored pieces. The owners specialize in mahogany, circa 1910 through 1930. The prices are reasonable, and delivery is available.

Gaslight Time Antiques. 823 President Street, corner of 7th Avenue, 789-7185. Wed.–Fri., 4:30–7 p.m.; Sat., 1–6 p.m.

Catering to the neighborhood's love affair with Victoriana and renovations, this second-story shop packs a lot of lighting into a small space. Starting at $80 and going up to hundreds of dollars, the selection is particularly good if you're looking for converted chandeliers or reproductions. Originals are available as well.

Growingthings. 81A 7th Avenue, between Union Street and Berkeley Place, 638-0918. Mon.–Sat., 10 a.m.–7:30 p.m.; Sun., 11 a.m.–7 p.m. Major credit cards.

You don't have to buy anything to appreciate the tranquil beauty of this hole-in-the-wall flower shop. The owner, a young woman named Fonda, has turned the tiny space into a floral wonderland. She and her staff can choose, arrange, and wrap one of the most elegant bouquets you'll ever buy. The flowers are always fresh and often unusual.

Guitarcraft. 386 1st Street, between 6th and 7th avenues, 768-6735. Tues., Fri., and Sat., noon–6 p.m.; Thurs., noon–9 p.m.; Wed., 3–9 p.m.

Tucked into a residential block, this custom guitar shop builds guitars and repairs all fretted instruments. They've also got a selection of used guitars and can arrange lessons. Based in Manhattan for more than seven years, Guitarcraft moved to Brooklyn in the early 1980s.

Leaf 'N' Bean. 83 7th Avenue, between Union Street and Berkeley Place, 638-5791. Mon.–Sat., 10 a.m.–6 p.m.; Sun., 11 a.m.–6 p.m. Major credit cards.

Like its parent store in Brooklyn Heights (see page 118), this is a tastefully displayed shop selling a wide range of coffee beans and teas, plus attractive modern kitchenware, from cappuccino makers to oven mitts, mugs, tablewear, and more.

Nkiru Books. 68 Saint Marks Place, between 5th and 6th avenues, 783-6306. Mon.–Sat., 11 a.m.–7 p.m.; Thurs., 11 a.m.–9 p.m.; Sun., noon–5 p.m. Major credit cards.

A terrific resource, this tiny, densely packed bookstore is filled with the intellectual treasures of contemporary African-American and third world cultures. The selection is a rare compilation of American, Latino, Caribbean, South African, and African writers. Titles range from Afrocentric cookbooks and marvelous kids' books to novels by Achebe, biographies of Miles Davis, how-to career advice for minorities, and sociological studies of the Rastafarians. Some titles are in Spanish and other foreign languages, such as Vietnamese. If you're looking for books with a nonwhite perspective, a browse here is a good place to start. Gregarious Brooklyn-born owner Leothy Owens creates a welcoming environment. Meet-the-author events are held every couple of weeks; call for information.

Winston and Company. 97A 7th Avenue, near Union Street, 638-7942. Mon.–Fri., 11 a.m.–7:30 p.m.; Sat. and Sun., 10:30 a.m.–6 p.m. Major credit cards.

Beautiful handmade wood and metal furnishings and craft pieces along with fine weavings and an assortment of jewelry make this tiny shop sparkle. Objects are chosen from the works of some of the most promising artisans in the United States. Some furniture can be custom ordered.

Note: Winston's lease runs out sometime in mid-1991, but the owner has promised to stay in Park Slope. Call to check the address before making a special trip.

The following shops are within easy reach of Park Slope.

Brooklyn Botanic Garden Gift Shop. 1000 Washington Avenue, along Eastern Parkway, 622-4433. Tues.–Fri., 10 a.m.–5:30 p.m.; Sat. and Sun., 10 a.m.–5:30 p.m.; closed Mon. ✱

Even if you don't have a green thumb, you'll find something attractive in this spacious, bright new gift shop located next to the **Steinhardt Conservatory** (page 212). There are plants, seeds, flowerpots, and some garden implements, of course, but you'll also find plenty of interesting and heavily illustrated coffee table books, unusual stationery, toys, books, and stuffed animals for kids, and even kitchenware with a floral motif. This is a wonderful place to find unusual souvenirs or small touches to make a place feel like home. Prices range from under $5 to $75.

Brooklyn Museum Gift Shop. 200 Eastern Parkway, corner of Washington Avenue, 638-5000. Daily, 10 a.m.–5 p.m.; closed Tues. Major credit cards. ✱

Unusual among museum shops for its large collection of handmade items and antiques (rather than reproductions), this is a wonderful source for gifts. You'll find a stunning array of both contemporary and antique jewelry here, plus handmade African masks, quilts, rugs, and textiles, Japanese porcelain, and items that reflect the work shown in current exhibits. Among the extensive line of art books are some unusual remainders, often discounted. With plenty of items under $20, this is the place to shop for the holidays. A $40 museum membership entitles you to 25 percent off at the annual pre-Christmas sale.

There is also a special shop for children, ActSmart.

HOTELS

175.00

Bed and Breakfast on the Park. 113 Prospect Park West, between 6th and 7th streets, 499-6115. Open daily, year-round. Major credit cards.

One of New York's few European-style bed and breakfasts, this treasure of a getaway is tucked away in a row of 1890s landmark brownstones along what used to be called Brooklyn's Gold Coast. The wood-paneled bedrooms are decorated in lavishly feminine Victoriana. One has a canopy bed, another an outdoor patio with a breathtaking view of the Manhattan skyline, and a third has an old-fashioned dressing room. Breakfasts of homemade bread, homemade jam, fresh orange juice, and coffee, plus a main course of Belgian waffles, German pancakes, or stuffed omelettes are served in a beautiful Victorian dining nook. The entire house is homey and immaculate. Prices start at $100 per couple per night.

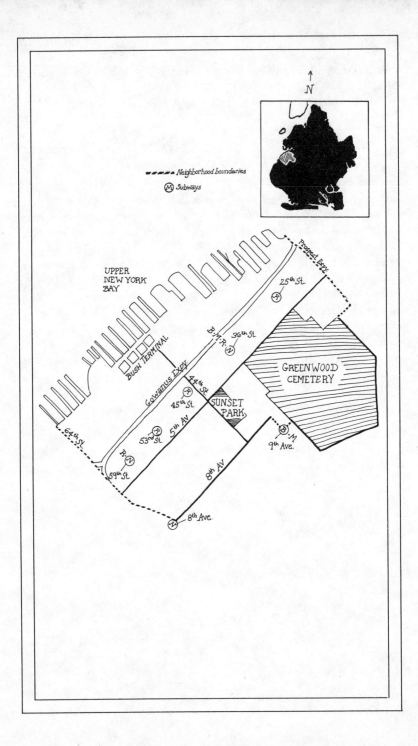

N

Neighborhood boundaries

Ⓜ Subways

UPPER
NEW YORK
BAY

Prospect Expy.

25th St. Ⓡ

B.M.R. 36th St. Ⓝ

GREENWOOD
CEMETERY

Bush Terminal

Gowanus Expy.

44th St. Ⓡ

45th St.

5th AV

SUNSET
PARK

53rd St. Ⓡ

Ⓑ·M
9th Ave.

R. Ⓝ

8th AV

64th St.

59th St.

Ⓝ 8th Ave.

SUNSET PARK AND GREENWOOD CEMETERY

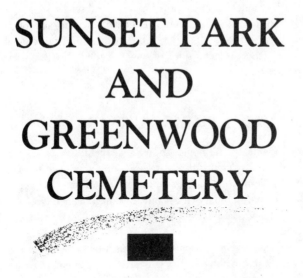

Where it is: Bounded by 65th Street to the south; Prospect Expressway to the north; 8th Avenue and Greenwood Cemetery on the east, and New York Bay on the west.

What's nearby: Park Slope, Bay Ridge, and Borough Park.

How to get there:

By car: Take the BQE (also known in this area as the Gowanus Expressway) to the 38th Street exit and proceed along 38th or parallel streets to either 5th or 8th avenues. To leave the area, re-enter the BQE on the Prospect Expressway or at 65th Street and 3rd Avenue.

By subway: R train to any stop between 25th and 59th streets, or the N train to the 36th or 59th street stop. For Greenwood, use the 25th Street stop.

Cab services: Apple Car Service (363-9000) or Harborview Car Service (748-8800). Cost is about $15 from Brooklyn Heights, $20 from Grand Central Station.

Special events: Chinese New Year is celebrated with a parade, costumes, and firecrackers along 8th Avenue. Chinese restaurants are closed during the celebration. Finnish Celebration (June); Swedish Santa Lucia Festival (November).

How it got its name: The area now known as Sunset Park took its name in the 1960s from a local park, which sits high above surrounding streets and commands a view of New York Bay. This area was previously known as part of Bay Ridge (the southern side) or simply called "South Brooklyn" (the shorefront area).

ABOUT THE NEIGHBORHOOD

Greenwood Cemetery (although the official spelling includes a hyphen in Green-wood, most references leave it out) is reason enough to make the trek to Sunset Park. From a culinary angle, hungry visitors may be happily surprised to discover a small Chinatown as well as some remarkably good and inexpensive Norwegian, Polish, and Latino restaurants in this unassuming slice of Brooklyn.

Fabulous, historic Greenwood Cemetery is a peaceful urban retreat set in 478 acres of rolling parklike hills. It is privately owned; you can take your chances on casually wandering in, but it's better to arrange a visit by calling in advance (see page 235). Your efforts will be rewarded. It is the burial site of the nineteenth and early twentieth century's rich and famous—actress Mae West, William Colgate of soap fame, Boss Tweed of Tammany Hall, abolitionist Henry Ward Beecher, and entrepreneur-philanthropist Peter Cooper, among others. Its elaborate Victorian mausoleums, obelisks, sculpture, and wonderful inscriptions offer an unmatched look at the history of old New York. Of Brooklyn's many historic sites, Greenwood Cemetery is the most evocative of the borough's patrician heritage.

Contemporary Sunset Park, on the other hand, is an American melting pot par excellence. Built more than a century ago by working-class immigrants, it is still a first stop for many newcomers. About half of Sunset Park's 100,000 residents are Hispanic. They include Dominicans, Ecuadorians, Nicaraguans, and Puerto Ricans. Asians represent over two-fifths of the community, and their numbers are growing. Immigrants from Poland, India, Jordan, and Yemen as well as a contingent of fourth- and fifth-generation Norwegian-Americans— descendants of Sunset Park's earliest nonnative settlers—round out an almost global cast. Since the 1970s a number of young professionals also have moved into the area and renovated many of Sunset Park's fine nineteenth-century row houses.

Ethnic diversity is the watchword for explorers of Sunset Park. You can have octopus, fried plantains, and *morir sonando*, a fruit drink, at **El Tipico**; or feast on Chinese food at the **Ocean Palace Seafood Restaurant**. Within blocks there is a Buddhist temple, a mosque, and Brooklyn's largest Roman Catholic church, Our Lady of Perpetual Help. There are Chinese acupuncturists, Latino botanicas, and *halal* butchers. Vestiges of previous waves of immigration are evident in shop signs bearing Irish, Italian, and Scandinavian names. And don't miss the view of the **Verrazano-Narrows Bridge** any time you're crossing 8th Avenue.

Historical Notes

Irish Catholics fleeing the potato famines of the mid-nineteenth century were among the earliest European pioneers to settle this part of Brooklyn. Polish immigrants followed in the 1880s, forming a community near the Czestochowa Church on 25th Street—now the site of a new wave of Polish immigration—and laboring in Greenwood Cemetery and Park Slope's Ansonia Clock Factory. Scandinavians found work at the shipyards in the late nineteenth century and created a "Little Norway" from 45th to 60th streets, where many of their descendants still live. The Finns here were the first in the nation to create cooperative housing, when in 1916 they joined together to build themselves affordable apartments, which are still in use today. Many of the Irish and Scandinavians moved into Bay Ridge by the 1920s. However, the slack was taken up by the huge Italian immigration that populated so much of Brooklyn and first settled in this waterfront area around the turn of the century. Saint Rocco's Chapel, at 27th Street, was a focal point of Italian life.

The neighborhood went into decline during and after the Depression. Like Carroll Gardens and Red Hook, Sunset Park's economic base suffered as construction of the Gowanus Expressway in the 1940s cut a swath through the neighborhood and again in the 1950s when a shift to containerized shipping rendered the Brooklyn waterfront facilities obsolete. The suburbs lured residents, and housing prices plummeted. Sunset Park's recent revival has been led by community activists and the local Lutheran Medical Center. It remains a working-class neighborhood, and the housing stock has largely been repaired and refurbished, the 5th and 8th avenue commercial strips are vibrant, and even the waterfront area is rebounding.

Kidstuff

Bring quarters—Sunset Park may earn a place in the record books for having the greatest number and variety of musical kiddie rides on its sidewalks of any urban neighborhood. You are as likely to meet an elephant playing Chinese tunes as you are to find a bucking bronco doing an old American ditty. The WPA-era **Sunset Park Pool** (see page 234) is big enough to accommodate your entire extended family, but try to come at off-peak hours.

ENTERTAINMENT

NY Harbor Lines. 204–207 Van Dyke Street, Pier 41, 857-5722. Mid-April–Oct.

For a smashing, adventuresome party, rent this sixty-five-foot boat for a tour up the East River, around the island of Manhattan to Sandy Hook, or even to West Point or Tarrytown. The forty-five-year-old boat, originally called *The Little Bear*, has been completely renovated, but it's not as fancy as the popular floating restaurants. The minimum is fifty people, or $1,600 for a four-hour trip. Groups as disparate as the Girl Scouts, business executives, and birthday revelers have enjoyed this trip. Catering, a bar, and live music can be arranged separately.

Swingaway. 6023 7th Avenue, near 60th Street, 439-3094. Mon.–Fri., 1–10 p.m.; Sat., 1 p.m.–midnight; Sun., 10 a.m.–midnight. Major credit cards. ✳

If a rainy day with the kids has you down, how about trying eighteen holes of miniature golf indoors? If golf's not your cup of tea, try one of five batting cages, where $1 will buy you twenty hardballs or softballs, tossed at any speed, right over the plate. Parents may be put off by the grime and smell of french fries, but kids love this place.

PARKS AND PLAYGROUNDS

Sunset Park Pool and Recreation Center. 7th Avenue, between 41st and 44th streets, 965-6579 or 965-6533. Call for hours. ✳

This enormous Olympic-size pool run by the New York City Parks Department is located inside an elegant old building, which also houses a community center that holds arts and crafts and aerobics classes. The quietest time for a swim is early on a weekday; it is extremely busy during weekends. Lockers are available, but bring your own locks. You'll find a friendly urban crowd from the surrounding neighborhoods.

POINTS OF CULTURAL INTEREST

Bush Terminal and Brooklyn Army Terminal. Along the waterfront, between 28th and 65th streets.

Bush Terminal. Use your imagination if you visit this large industrial site. Irving T. Bush first opened this area to industrial development in 1890. It had once been the site of Wild West shows, and later it was the location of

Irving's father's oil business. With some foresight, Mr. Bush anticipated the development of the huge shipping industry and related heavy industry and manufacturing jobs that would keep Brooklyn's economy going for decades. The waterfront declined after World War II. Today the area including Bush Terminal and the new Harborside industrial complex is again being marketed as a viable area for small and large businesses.

Brooklyn Army Terminal. The whole story here is in its original name: the New York Port of Embarkation and Army Supply Base. The terminal was built in 1918, after World War I, but in time for World War II. In fact, if you know someone who fought in Europe in World War II, he most likely left from this terminal.

Carl's Bar and Grill. 5609 8th Avenue, near 56th Street., 438-9737. Daily, 4 p.m.–11 p.m.

Here's history on a smaller scale. Even if you're not thirsty, take a look inside this small, unrenovated turn-of-the century bar. Long, dark, and cool, the wood bar and booths evoke another era. Don't miss the ornate carved sailing ships above the bar's mirrors or the reindeer heads along the other wall.

Greenwood Cemetery. The main entrance is on 5th Avenue, at the end of 25th Street, 768-7300. Call in advance for permission to visit.

World-famous Greenwood Cemetery is a vast parklike and entirely man-made environment of rolling hills, paths, and lakes. The Victorian Gothic gate at 5th Avenue and 25th Street is just one of the architectural masterpieces here, along with enormous mausoleums and ornate Victorian monuments. You can roam the serene setting or hunt for the tombs of the rich and famous. The roster of Greenwood's nineteenth-century inhabitants goes on and on: pharmaceutical giants Edward Squibb and Charles Pfizer; *New York Times* founder Henry Raymond; James Merritt Ives of lithographers Currier and Ives; Henry E. Steinway of piano fame (whose mausoleum has room for more than one hundred bodies); Charles Tiffany, founder of the Tiffany store; Louis Comfort Tiffany, the stained glass artist; Charles Ebbets, after whom the Dodger's ballpark was named: Samuel Morse, of the code by the same name; plus the inventors of, respectively, the safety pin, carbonated water, the sewing machine, and the steam locomotive. Also buried here are the following: James Renwick, Jr., architect of the Smithsonian Institution; Richard Upjohn, architect of Trinity Church in Manhattan; Peter Cooper, inventor of Jell-O and founder of Cooper Union; Henry Bergh, founder of the American Society for the Prevention of Cruelty to Animals (ASPCA); Lola Montez, companion to composer Franz Liszt, novelist Alexandre Dumas, and others; and William Marcy Tweed, also known as Boss Tweed. Plain folk also are buried here, as told by tales like the following on simple, old headstones: "Nelly, age 2, leaving an empty hearth and broken hearts."

Still a lovely place to roam today (and quite safe, due to extensive security), the 478-acre Greenwood was used as a park in the 1850s by locals and tourists, according to historical accounts. In fact, the popularity of Greenwood's open spaces was one of the reasons used to justify the creation of Manhattan's Central Park in 1856.

If you want a tour, your best bet is to call the **Brooklyn Center for the Urban Environment**, 788-8500, or the **Brooklyn Historical Society**, 624-0890.

Sunset Park Restoration Committee Tours and Digs. P.O. Box 288, Brooklyn, N.Y. 11220, 871-8340. Call or write for a schedule.

A volunteer organization, the Sunset Park Restoration Committee runs free one- and two-hour tours of Sunset Park and Greenwood Cemetery. It also organizes small-scale excavations in abandoned lots and open areas near the waterfront during the spring and summer. The area literally is littered with artifacts from the Gowanee Indians, early Dutch settlements, and even a major confrontation in the Revolutionary War. If you're lucky, you'll find some glass fragments or maybe a metal tethering ring for horses. Kids are allowed, but they must be supervised by an adult.

NOTABLE RESTAURANTS

El Tipico Restaurant. 4615 5th Avenue, near 46th Street, 439-7538. Daily, 8 a.m.–11 p.m. ✳

Nestled between shoe and clothing shops, this tiny, immaculate Latino restaurant serves excellent shrimp dishes in tasty sauces, a great pepper steak, fried plantains, a delicious orange juice shake called *morir sonando*, and lots of lobster, fish, octopus, pork, and chicken dishes. The beans and rice are also superb. Dinner entrées run from $5 to $10, breakfast specials are under $3, the service is friendly and informative, and there is also a menu of old standards, such as burgers and grilled cheese sandwiches.

Eva's Coffee Shop. 4902 8th Avenue, corner of 49th Street, 854-2700. Daily, 7 a.m.–9 p.m. ✳

Cheap, clean, and delicious, this Polish-American coffee shop is one that locals hope will stay undiscovered. One side of the menu offers the standard coffee shop fare: eggs, pancakes, bagels, and so on. But even these have a special touch: the banana pancakes, for instance, are studded with whole slices of banana. The other side of the menu is a mix of wonderful ethnic treats.

The potato pirogi are subtly spiced; also try the cabbage soup, borscht, noodles with cheese, apple fritters, goulash, or kielbasa.

Ocean Palace Seafood Restaurant. 5421 8th Avenue, near 55th Street, 871-8080 or 871-8081. Daily, 7:30 a.m.–11:30 p.m. Major credit cards. ✳

One of two big Chinese restaurants on either side of 8th Avenue, the Ocean Palace serves the full complement of dim sum specialties, ranging from pork buns for 40¢, up to spare ribs at $5 a helping. Even early on a Saturday morning the place is already half full of hungry local residents.

Ocean King Seafood Restaurant. 5418 8th Avenue, near 55th Street, 633-8580. Daily, 8:30 a.m.–11:30 p.m. Major credit cards. ✳

Ocean King specializes in Cantonese cuisine, from egg custard and dumplings to rolls and pineapple buns, and the menu is extensive. Dim sum rolls out of the kitchen here all day long—and you could probably eat it all day, the prices are so low. You'll know you've found the King, not its across-the-street competitor, by the ornate gold, red, and green sign across the facade.

SHOPPING

Birlik Oriental Food/Halal Meat Market. 5919 8th Avenue, near 60th Street, 436-2785. Daily, 8 a.m.–10 p.m.

Turkish, Middle Eastern, and Asian foods make for an eclectic mix at Birlik's, which covers almost half a block along 8th Avenue. Feast your eyes and taste buds on the olives, cheeses, and more than fifty fresh herbs and spices.

Bright Bakery. 5612 8th Avenue, near 56th Street, 492-1953. Daily, 7 a.m.–9 p.m. ✳

A bagful of fortunes, and the cookies that go with them, are only $1 at this Chinese bakery. Try the lucky walnut shortcake cookies, coconut cookies, and chicken cake with sesame, peanuts, and roast pork.

CD Deli. 5706 7th Avenue, near 57th Street, 439-3324. Daily, 10 a.m.–6 p.m. Major credit cards.

You can get rock-bottom prices ($9 to $13) on a good selection of both new-release and classic rock and jazz compact discs. The Telarc and DNP label recordings as well as other classical imports are about $16 here. Don't be put off by the store's exterior: there is no display window, only a gated door. Inside, though, it's a small, orderly second-generation business run by a Samoan family that provides knowledgeable, friendly service. Phone orders can be delivered within a week, COD.

Empire Gun and Coin. 5524 8th Avenue, near 56th Street, 438-4090. Mon.–Sat., 10 a.m.–8 p.m.; Sun., 10 a.m.–3 p.m.

Camouflage gear and other military paraphernalia is sold here, along with collectibles from baseball cards to comic books and tin toys. You also can order complete sets of Topps, Score, and other trading cards at the Empire.

Kolawster Bakery. 5804 8th Avenue, near 58th Street, 439-8545. Daily, 7 a.m.–8 p.m. *

The selection is vast and prices are low at this Chinese bakery. Mixed nut rolls, mini mooncakes with lotus seed paste, yellow egg bean cakes, and shrimp chips fill the windows. Try one of the enormous walnut or almond cookies for just 50¢, or grab a bag of red bean curd chips for just $1.25.

La Gran Via Bakery. 4516 5th Avenue, between 45th and 46th streets, 853-8021. Daily, 8 a.m.–8 p.m. *

You can't miss this spot. The display window is chockablock with reasonably priced decorative kiddie birthday cakes featuring Mickey Mouse, Superman, and other favorites, as well as three-tiered, triple-towered wedding cakes. Unless you're shopping for a whole cake, try one of the traditional Latino specialties, like coconut pudding or the pastries and sweet breads made of corn and coconut.

Luen Sing Seafood and Meat Market. 5613 8th Avenue, near 57th Street, 871-5283. Daily, 7 a.m.–8 p.m.

The fish sold here aren't special, but check out the fish tank built into the front display window. The crowds of carp make rush hour on New York's subways seem positively placid.

Nada Halal Meat. 5813 8th Avenue, near 59th Street, 435-5848. Daily, 8 a.m.–6 p.m.

This small Middle Eastern shop is filled with dozens of fresh spices, Turkish pastries, fava beans, feta cheese, olives, and fig marmalade. If you're looking for a large, ornate hookah, peruse the top shelves.

Reyes Music. 4818 5th Avenue, between 48th and 49th streets, 492-9665. Mon.–Fri., 9 a.m.–7 p.m.; Sat., 9 a.m.–5 p.m.; Sun., noon–5 p.m.

Tons of records and tapes are available here from a dozen Spanish-speaking nations. Styles and pop stars tend to change more slowly on the Latin scene than in American rock and pop music, so you are likely to be right with the beat—merengue, salsa, or bolero—if you get the latest releases from three exclusively Latino labels: T. H. Roven, WEA Latina, and Global. Try Louis Enrique, El Gran Combo, and Tito Puente for salsa, or Johnny Ventura and Wilfredo Vargas for merengue.

Signe's Imports. 5906 8th Avenue, near 59th Street, 492-5004. Mon.–Sat., 10 a.m.–6 p.m.

Push your way through the crowded, dusty bric-a-brac and thoroughly uninteresting wares for a look at a wide range of imported Norwegian knit sweaters and wools. That's the secret at Signe's. If you're looking for cassettes featuring Norwegian music you'll find a good selection here as well. The owners are charming.

Thoralf Olsen Bakery. 5722 8th Avenue, near 58th Street, 439-6673. Mon.–Sat., 8 a.m.–7 p.m.; closed Sun. ✳

This is an Old World Scandinavian bakery filled with tempting treats. Breads, cakes, muffins, and even ice-cream cakes are available. Try their sweet teatime rolls.

Off the beaten track but of interest are two discount stores:

Frankel's Discount Store. 3924 3rd Avenue, near 39th Street, 768-9788. Tues.–Sat., 10 a.m.–7 p.m. Major credit cards.

Baby-boom generation Europeans go crazy for cowboy boots and boating moccasins, so why not bring them to this most unlikely place for a shoe shopping spree. This industrial area is safe, with parking right under a constantly rumbling BQE. Specializing in overruns and closeouts, Frankel's sells Nike and other brand-name sneakers, as well as Timberland shoes, for at least 20 percent off the retail price. Frye, Dan Post, and El Paso cowboy boots for men and women also are discounted. You'll find discounted jogging suits, brand-name sunglasses such as Vuarnet, outdoor gear, hiking boots, and more.

Quiltex. 168 39th Street, on the waterfront, 788-3158. Mon.–Thurs., 10 a.m.–3 p.m.; Fri, 10 a.m.–1 p.m.; closed Sat. and Sun. Major credit cards. ✳

Over the decades, Brooklyn's waterfront factories have produced everything from soap to men's hats. Quiltex makes snowsuits and other outerwear, colorful quilts, and juvenile bedding. You can buy it here at a considerable discount from department store prices. There are also racks of clothing made by other manufacturers, also sold at a discount. Take the B, M, N, or R train to the 36th Street stop.

BROOKLYN'S BEST BETS FOR CHILDREN

Brooklyn offers great outings for kids, from museums to parks to fishing boat trips. Here we've listed some highlights. We've included a few outstanding attractions on nearby Staten Island as well, because it is so easy to reach from both Manhattan and Brooklyn. In this section you'll find museums, zoos, parks, special outdoor fun, live entertainment, places to see how things are made, and more. (For tips on what Brooklyn Heights, Park Slope, and other neighborhoods offer children, see individual neighborhood chapters. For listings of child-friendly restaurants, and toy and clothing shops, refer to Where to Find It (pages 258–281).

ESPECIALLY FOR KIDS

Bank for Kids. (800) 522-5214 or (212) 221-6056. The Williamsburgh Savings Bank in Fort Greene, at 1 Hanson Place (270-4247), or at 2301 86th Street (946-3600). The Republic National Bank in Park Slope, at 325 9th Street (499-4500); in Bay Ridge, at 6614 Bay Parkway (256-9700); or Bensonhurst, at 8603 21st Avenue (373-0707). Call for special hours.

Remember standing in line when you were a kid to deposit your allowance? Almost no commercial banks in New York City do this anymore, but at the

Bank for Kids your under-seventeen-year-olds can open a savings account with a minimum of $2 and earn 5.5 percent interest. They bank during regular hours and special times once a week when the bank is open just for kids. The Bank for Kids gives parties during the year, sends out a newsletter, and will schedule tours so kids can see where the tellers sit and what the vaults look like from inside. There are no fees or minimum balances to maintain, but to open the account, kids must be able to write their own names and have a social security number. Call for an application or drop by a participating bank.

Brooklyn Botanic Garden and Children's Garden (see full description on page 212). 1000 Washington Avenue, along Eastern Parkway, 622-4433. Tues.–Fri., 8 a.m.–6 p.m.; Sat. and Sun., 10 a.m.–6 p.m.; closed Mon.

There's plenty to do here, from wandering the Japanese garden to feeding ducks to serious nature study at the Steinhardt Conservatory (page 212). From April to August more than a hundred school-age children tend their own garden plots in the Children's Garden. Call early in the season to reserve a plot for the little green thumbs in your household.

Brooklyn Children's Museum. 145 Brooklyn Avenue, corner of St. Mark's Avenue, 735-4432. Wed.–Mon., 2–5 p.m.; weekends and holidays, 10 a.m.–5 p.m.; closed Tues. The suggested contribution is $2 per person.

Founded in 1899, the world's first children's museum has always been dedicated to hands-on learning. It is exuberantly interdisciplinary, multiethnic and multimedia—kids absolutely love it. Larger than the Manhattan Children's Museum and much more whimsical, the Brooklyn Children's Museum has wonderful, curiosity-provoking exhibits of cultural and technological artifacts; ethnomusicological instruments; and concepts of space, measurement, and weight. At the entrance, there is an unusual corrugated steel tube through which a constant stream of water flows. The current museum, rebuilt on its original site but partially underground to preserve park space above, opened in 1977 and recently was renovated to include new exhibits. Weekend concerts or special performances are held frequently. The only flaw in this marvelous, inventive place is that there is no cafeteria for lunch.

Coney Island (Astroland Amusement Park; see full description on page 85). Surf Avenue, at West 12th Street, 372-0275 or 265-2100. Daily, noon–midnight.

You'll find plenty of rides, noise, and hot dogs here; the famous Coney Island boardwalk and the New York Aquarium are nearby.

Nellie Bly Amusement Park (see full description on page 44). 1824 Shore Parkway, near Toys "Я" Us, 996-4002. Easter to Halloween, from noon to dusk.

This petite, relatively clean amusement park is just a couple minutes' drive from Toys "Я" Us. Not only is it a little bit of heaven for toddlers and preteens, it's also pretty easy on parents.

New York Aquarium (see full description on page 85). Surf Avenue, at 8th Street West, 265-3474 (265-FISH). Mon.–Fri., 10 a.m.–6 p.m.; Sat. and Sun., 10 a.m.–7 p.m. Admission is $3.75, or $1.50 for children under twelve.

Located along the boardwalk in Coney Island, the New York Aquarium was the first public aquarium in the United States. Today it is a world-class educational center for environmental conservation, with more than twenty-one thousand living specimens, a popular dolphin and sea lion show, and spiffy new exhibits.

New York City Transit Museum (see full description on page 113). Schermerhorn Street, corner of Boerum Place, 330-3060. Tues.–Fri., 10 a.m.–4 p.m. Adults $1.15, children 55¢.

Built in an old subway station, this underground museum, with its full-size trains to look at and wander through, is perfect for children of all ages.

Prospect Park Carousel (see full description on page 209). Prospect Park, near Empire Boulevard and Ocean Avenue, 768-0227.

Few things are more fun for kids than a ride on an old-fashioned carousel.

Staten Island Children's Museum, Snug Harbor and Trolley. 1000 Richmond Terrace, off Snug Harbor Road, 448-6557. School year: Wed.–Fri., 1–5 p.m.; weekends, 11 a.m.–5 p.m. Summer: Tues.–Sun., 11 a.m.–5 p.m. Admission is $2; children under three are free.

This award-winning museum caters to kids from five to twelve. It offers three floors of interactive exhibits created by teams of educators and artists, plus workshops and occasional live performances. Located in eighty acres of park dotted with a duck pond, botanic gardens, outdoor sculpture, a gazebo and more than two dozen historic homes, it is a wonderful—and underutilized—resource for Brooklyn parents. Founded in 1801, Sailor's Snug Harbor was the nation's first military hospital for sailors. Since its purchase in 1976 by the City of New York, this national landmark district has nicely preserved its tranquil mood. Enjoy the ride on the Snug Harbor Trolley (or take the S40 bus) from the Staten Island ferry, just five minutes away. Half the fun of visiting is getting there.

Staten Island Zoo. 614 Broadway, at Clove Road and Martling Avenue, 442-3100. Call for directions. Daily, 10 a.m.–4:45 p.m., except Thanksgiving, Christmas, and New Year's Day. Admission is $1; Wed. is free.

Small, clean, and well-designed, this zoo-in-a-park has a miniature farm complete with pony rides, pigmy goats, and other animals. Kids love to feed their furry friends, so bring dimes for the dispensers, which resemble parking meters and spew out a small fistful of animal food pellets. Started in the mid-1930s as a WPA project, the zoo also has a modern Serpentarium, a small aquarium, thirty-three mammals (from panthers to Canadian otters), and a new South American tropical forest.

LEARNING HOW THINGS ARE MADE

Anchorage (see full description on page 135). Cadman Plaza West and Front Street, under the Brooklyn Bridge, 619-1955. Call for a schedule.

Kids will love the space, and parents will probably enjoy the art shown here. How often can you actually walk inside the mammoth structures that support a bridge?

Brooklyn Terminal Market (see full description on page 155). The main gate is on Foster Avenue, near 85th Street East. Daily, 8 a.m.–6 p.m. Cash only.

Show your kids where the store owners go shopping, at this bustling food and garden wholesale marketplace.

Cousin John's Bakery. 70 7th Avenue, between Berkeley Place and Lincoln Place, 622-7333. Open daily at 7 a.m. Checks accepted.

Watch the bakers at work here: just take a seat at a couple of small tables perched upstairs, almost in the kitchen.

Damascus Bakery (see full description on page 128). 56 Gold Street, near Water Street, 855-1457. Mon.–Sat., 8 a.m.–5 p.m.

Kids love pita bread—known around some homes as pocket bread. If they'd like to see how it's made, group tours on Tuesdays can be arranged at Damascus Bakery, located near the Manhattan Bridge. Groups should number between eight and twenty-five. Be sure to call in advance.

Lefferts Homestead (see full description on page 210). Prospect Park, Flatbush Avenue, near Empire Boulevard, 965-8951.

This historic homestead conducts terrific free holiday programs in the arts and crafts of yesteryear, such as sheep shearing, coopering, rag rug making, broom and basket making, and floorcloth painting. Call for the schedule.

New York Experimental Glass Workshop. 647 Fulton Street, near Flatbush Avenue, 625-3685.

Kids like to see things being made, and this nationally recognized stained and art glass workshop offers a perfect opportunity. Call to make arrangements for a visit; they frown on drop-ins.

LEARNING ABOUT BROOKLYN

Borough Hall Tour (see full description on page 111). 209 Joralemon Street, between Adams and Court Streets, 802-3700.

Bring a brown-bag lunch in the summertime, take a stroll through the nearby Greenmarket, and give your kids a Civics 101 course here.

Brooklyn Center for the Urban Environment Tours (see full description on page 244). 788-8549 (recording) or 788-8500.

Older kids may enjoy these tours of Greenwood Cemetery, the Brooklyn Bridge, and industrial sites, such as Bush Terminal, Water Tunnel 3, and the Coney Island subway repair yards.

Brooklyn's History Museum (see full description on page 112). 128 Pierrepont Street, between Clinton and Henry Streets, 624-0890. Tues.–Sun., noon–5 p.m.; closed Mon.

Although not specifically for children, this museum offers lots to discuss with school-age kids. The admission fee for members is $2.50 for adults; children under twelve, $1.

Brooklyn Historic Railway Association (see full description on page 124). Atlantic Avenue Subway Tunnel utility hole, intersection of Court Street, 941-3160. Reserved tours are usually on Saturday.

You need a group of about ten to tour this fantastic underground tunnel. Call to get on the waiting list.

Greenwood Cemetery (see full description on page 235). The main entrance is on 5th Avenue, at the end of 25th Street, 768-7300. Call in advance for permission to visit.

Peruse the tombs of the rich and famous here and let the kids happily run and jump among the rolling hills.

Soldiers and Sailors Memorial Arch (see full description on page 213). Flatbush Avenue, at Eastern Parkway, 788-0055. Sat. and Sun. only.

If you're ready for a climb, the view from the arch is fabulous.

Weeksville (Hunterfly Road) houses (see full description on page 35). 1968-1708 Bergen Street, between Rochester and Buffalo Roads, 756-5250.

The museum provides a chance to talk with your kids about the history of African-Americans in the United States or about urban archaeology. Either way, it's an unusual and enriching trip.

LIVE ENTERTAINMENT

"Family Time" (see full description on page 163). Brooklyn College Performance Center, Whitman Hall—Brooklyn College, intersection of Hillel Place and Campus Road, 434-1900.

From *Cinderella* to puppet shows to musical concerts, this is a wonderful program for children and parents. Subscriptions are available.

Hot Prospects (see full description on page 208). Prospect Park, Picnic House, 3rd Street entrance to Prospect Park, 788-0055.

Performances on Sundays in July or August can make a steamy day seem pleasant. Hot Prospects acts run the gamut from rock and roll to jugglers to Chinese dancers. Come early to get a seat.

Penny Bridge Players (see full description on page 180). 520 Clinton Avenue, between Atlantic Avenue and Fulton Street, 855-6346. Call for a schedule of performances. No credit cards.

Classic children's theater is performed by actors in a fabulous Victorian church setting. Plays are appropriate for ages four to eleven.

Puppetworks (see full description on page 207). 338 6th Avenue, corner of 4th Street, 965-3391. Sat. and Sun. only. Call for show times. No credit cards.

There are wonderful puppet shows here for preschoolers through sixthgraders.

Shadowbox Theater (see full description on page 110). YWCA—Memorial Hall, 30 3rd Avenue, between Atlantic Avenue and State Street, 875-1190. For a schedule call (212) 724-0677.

Shadowbox stages puppet shows with original scripts and contemporary themes from October through June.

Spoke the Hub (see full description on page 207). Gowanus Arts Exchange, 295 Douglass Street, between 3rd and 4th Avenues, 596-5250.

Call ahead for tickets to the popular "Groundhog" series. Six Sunday afternoon performances in January and February feature different professional artists, all of whom involve delighted children in the show. Past performers have included a drummer who drums on all parts of his body, a fabulous storyteller, and puppeteers. In addition, the Kid's Outback program features shows in which very young talent (eight- to eighteen-year-olds) produce their own choreography. The theater seats about a hundred.

Young People and Family Series at the Brooklyn Academy of Music. 30 Lafayette Avenue, corner of Ashland Place, 636-4120. Call for a schedule. Major credit cards.

From December through May BAM sponsors over twenty professional musical, acrobatic, and dramatic programs for children ranging from pre-kindergarten through high school. Programs are scheduled both for weekday and weekend family performances. Prices range from $3 to $12.

MUSEUMS

Brooklyn Children's Museum (see page 241).

Brooklyn's History Museum (see page 112).

The Brooklyn Museum (see full description on page 211). 200 Eastern Parkway, corner of Washington Avenue, 638-5000. Wed.–Mon., 10 a.m.–5 p.m.; closed Tues. Admission is $4; children are free.

The twenty-eight full-scale rooms on the museum's fourth floor are a child's delight. An outdoor sculpture garden, a good cafeteria, a special children's gift shop, and proximity to the Brooklyn Botanic Garden make this a super outing for children.

Harbor Defense Museum at Fort Hamilton (see full description on page 14). Fort Hamilton Parkway, at 101st Street, 630-4349. Mon., 1–4 p.m.; Thurs.–Sat., 10 a.m.–5 p.m.; Sun., 1 p.m.–5 p.m. Free admission.

If your child loves military stuff, at Fort Hamilton you'll find cannons, barracks, and a fortlike stone house that now encases a military museum.

Magnolia Tree Earth Center Grandiflora (see full description on page 34). 679 Lafayette Avenue, opposite Herbert Von King Park, 387-2116. Mon.–Thurs. and Sat., 10 a.m.–5 p.m.; closed Fri. and Sun.

The George Washington Carver gallery is worth a visit to teach kids about environmental issues. Hours vary, so call ahead.

New York City Transit Museum (see page 113).

Wyckoff House Museum (see full description on page 93). Clarendon Road and Ralph Avenue, at East 59th Street, 629-5400.

The craft sessions, kiddie story hours, and outdoor programs held on a large lawn area are excellent. Call for current programs.

OUTDOOR FUN

Fishing and Boating

A&S Fishing Contest, Prospect Park (see full description on page 208). Lullwater Pond, near Wollman Rink, off the Parkside–Ocean Avenue entrance, 287-3400.

For fifteen years the Urban Rangers have organized this July fishing contest sponsored by the A&S department store.

Fishing Boats (see full description on page 91). Emmons Avenue, between Ocean and Bedford Avenues.

You can just look at these boats, or actually go on a half-day fishing expedition in one. For older kids only.

Pelican Pedal Boats (see full description on page 209). Prospect Park, next to Wollman Rink, 287-9824. May–Oct., 11 a.m.–6 p.m.; Sat. and Sun., 10 a.m.–8 p.m. (weather permitting).

Take a pedal boat out in the Lullwater in Prospect Park. Kids under sixteen must be accompanied by an adult.

Horseback Riding

Jamaica Bay Riding Academy (see full description on page 92). 7000 Shore Parkway, between exits 11 and 13, 531-8949. Daily, 10 a.m.–4:30 p.m.

There are wonderful trails here spread over three hundred acres of bird watching country, including three miles along the beaches of Jamaica Bay.

Ice Skating

Wollman Rink (see full description on page 209). Prospect Park, near Parkside Avenue, 965-6561. Open Thanksgiving to March, Mon.–Thurs., 10 a.m.–6 p.m.; Fri.–Sun., 10 a.m.–9 p.m.

This outdoor skating rink has equipment rentals, a food concession, and parking on the premises.

Swimming

Pools. Open daily, from the last Saturday in June through Labor Day, 11 a.m.–7 p.m.

Try the **Red Hook Pool** (see full description on page 143) at Bay and Clinton Streets, corner of Henry Street, 965-6579; or the **Sunset Park Pool and Recreation Center** (see full description on page 234) at 7th Avenue, between 41st and 44th Streets, 965-6579 or 965-6533.

Beaches. Take your pick: **Manhattan Beach** (see full description on page 91); **Brighton Beach** (see full description on page 79); or **Coney Island Beach** near the New York Aquarium or Astroland Amusement Park.

Other Sports

Gateway Sports Center (see full description on page 92). 3200 Flatbush Avenue, across from Floyd Bennett Field, 253-6816. Daily, 9 a.m.–11 p.m.

The golf range, tennis courts, and batting cages, plus an eighteen-hole miniature golf facility, are open year-round.

PARKS

Empire Fulton Ferry Park (see full description on page 135). New Dock Road, by Water Street and the East River, (212) 977-8240.

There's a big grassy space here with views of the East River, Manhattan, fabulous Civil War-era industrial lofts, and both the Brooklyn and Manhattan bridges.

Marine Park (see full description on page 92). Between Flatbush and Gerritsen Avenues, exit 11 off the Shore Parkway, 965-6551 or 965-8973.

This huge park has tennis courts, playgrounds, kite flying, bird watching, biking, and the usual park-related activities, as well as summertime concerts and a golf course.

Owl's Head Park and **Shore Road Park** (see full description on page 13). Shore Road, between 68th Street and Colonial Road, 965-6524.

With almost thirty acres of green overlooking the harbor, this breezy point is a popular place for family picnics. Around 97th Street there are ball fields, two lovely playgrounds, and tennis courts (call 965-8993 for permit information).

Prospect Park (see full description on page 207). Main entrance is at Grand Army Plaza, at the intersection of Flatbush Avenue, Prospect Park West, and Eastern Parkway; 287-3400 for special events or 965-8900 for park information.

This park offers more than five hundred acres of rolling hills and meadows, plus playgrounds, a carousel, and facilities for pedal boating, biking, and wintertime outdoor ice skating.

Shore Parkway Promenade (see full description on page 14). From Owl's Head Park at 69th Street to Bensonhurst Park at Bay Parkway.

Take the kids for a bike ride or run along the waterside here. Along the route are several popular places to fly kites.

OTHER PLACES TO WALK AND WANDER

Boardwalk. Along the Atlantic Ocean, between Coney Island and Brighton Beach, 946-1350.

There's plenty of room to run, bike, and cavort along this forty-foot-wide boardwalk, which extends through Coney Island to Brighton Beach. The breezes are fresh, and the ocean views can't be beat. And it is a quiet zone, so loud radios are prohibited.

Brooklyn Bridge (see full description on page 134). The walkway entrance is at Adams and Tillary Streets.

Walk it or bike it for a good breeze and a spectacular view of Manhattan's skyline, the East River, and the Statue of Liberty.

Brooklyn Heights Promenade (see full description on page 110). Along the East River, access at end of Montague, Orange, and streets in between.

This is an ideal vantage point for observing harbor traffic, the Statue of Liberty, and various bridges. There's a beautiful little playground here as well.

PLACES TO GO IN BAD WEATHER

Brooklyn Public Libraries. It may seem old-fashioned in the age of Nintendo, but books are still a favorite rainy-day diversion for kids. Every neighborhood has at least one library, and each library has a special section for children. If you have a New York City library card, you can take books out and return them to any Brooklyn library. Some libraries also have movies, game times, and story readings for children. Call the neighborhood library for information.

Movies. See the listing for movie theaters located in neighborhoods included in this book.

Indoor Sports

Bowling. There are several places to take kids bowling in Brooklyn. Try **Lee Mark Lanes** in Bay Ridge, 423 88th Street between 4th and 5th avenues, 745-3200 (see full description on page 12), or **Maple Lanes** at 1570 60th Street, near 15th Avenue in Bensonhurst, 331-9000 (see full description on page 44).

Other. You can book a court during the winter at **Prospect Park Tennis Center**, 305 Coney Island Avenue, corner of Parkside Avenue, 438-1200 (see full description on page 209). While not at all spiffy, **Swingaway**, 6023 7th

Avenue near 60th Street, 439-3094, has indoor miniature golf and indoor batting cages (see full description on page 234).

UNUSUAL STORES FOR KIDS

ArtSmart. Brooklyn Museum, 200 Eastern Parkway, 638-5000. Wed.–Mon., 10 a.m.–4:45 p.m. Major credit cards.

A wonderful museum shop for children, ArtSmart is crammed with unusual toys, books, games, and art materials for toddlers to teens. The themes reflected in the merchandise are in sync with the museum's exhibits. If specialty items like books about the Great Pyramids or kits for backyard archaeological digs exist, you'll find them here—the museum has an outstanding Egyptology division—alongside tribal dolls, stenciling materials, and corn-cob doll kits. Neither stuffy nor esoteric, this is a shop that makes kids love going to the museum. Prices range from under $1 to over $50.

Brooklyn Gallery of Coins and Stamps (see full description on page 26). 8725 4th Avenue, near 87th Street, 745-5701. Mon.–Fri., 9 a.m.–5:30 p.m.; Sat., 9 a.m.–4 p.m. No credit cards.

Children as young as six can start collecting stamps, coins, and antique toys here.

Cousin Arthur's Books for Children (see full description on page 121).

This wonderful children's bookstore has special reading hours on Sunday and midweek toddler story hours.

Craft Cottage (see full description on page 26). 8818 3rd Avenue, near 88th Street, 745-7578. Mon.–Sat., 10 a.m.–6 p.m.; Wed. and Fri., 10 a.m.–9 p.m. No credit cards.

As wholesome as apple pie, the craft supplies you'll find here include rows and rows of things to "get creative" with for preschoolers to adults.

Train World II (see full description on page 69). 751 McDonald Avenue, near Ditmas Avenue, 436-7072.

You'll find hundreds of trains, pieces of scenery, miniature figures, and lots of track at this store.

Walt's Hobby Shop (see full description on page 27). 7909 5th Avenue, at 79th Street, 745-4991.

Walt's features do-it-yourself plastic racing cars, role-playing games and materials, and models.

Zak's Fun House (see full description on page 55). 2214 86th Street, between Bay Parkway and Bay 31st Street, 373-4092.

This store is full of costumes, magic tricks, and some toys.

U. S. Post Office. Brooklyn Central Office, 271-301 Washington Street, 271 Cadman Plaza, 852-2869. Mon.–Fri., 9 a.m.–5 p.m.

The terrific Philatelic Center (834-3600) has interesting displays of commemorative stamps and also offers a free booklet for kids on how to start a stamp collection.

CALENDAR OF FESTIVALS AND EVENTS

For up-to-date listings obtain the Prospect Park Calendar of Events (780-0055) and a listing of cultural events sponsored by BACA, the Brooklyn Arts Council (783-3077 or 783-4469). For information on specific festivals and events call the numbers listed below.

JANUARY

Chinese New Year, Sunset Park (438-9312).

FEBRUARY

Black History Month. For a schedule of events call the borough president's office (802-3800).

MARCH

Irish American Parade, Park Slope (768-6796).
Women's History Month. For schedule of events call the borough president's office (802-3800).

APRIL

SimchaThon, Borough Park (851-5300).
House tour of historic Flatbush (469-8990).

MAY

Big Apple Circus, Prospect Park (780-0055).
Cherry Blossom Festival (Sakuri Matsuri) at Brooklyn Botanic Gardens (622-4433).
Craft Series begins, Lefferts Homestead, Prospect Park (965-6505).
DanceAfrica Bazaar, Brooklyn Academy of Music (636-4119).
House tours of Brooklyn Heights (858-9193), Fort Greene (783-8454 or 857-9471), Park Slope (636-8736 or 788-9150), and Prospect Heights (284-6210).
Indoor/Outdoor Art Show, Brooklyn Waterfront Artists Coalition (643-3395).
Memorial Day Air Show, Coney Island (266-1234 or 266-3004).
Norwegian Constitution Day Parade, Bay Ridge (238-1100).
Outdoor Art Show (juried), Promenade, Brooklyn Heights (788-3077 or 783-4469).
You Gotta Have Park Day, Prospect Park (780-0055).

JUNE

Finnish Midsummer Celebration, Sunset Park (438-9426).
Fulton Art Fair, Bedford-Stuyvesant (462-9425 or 919-0740).
June Balloon, Brooklyn Children's Museum (734-4400).
Mermaid Parade, Coney Island (372-5159).
Midwood Mardi Gras, Midwood (376-0999).
Welcome Back to Brooklyn Festival (second Sunday), Grand Army Plaza, Park Slope (855-7882).

JULY

A & S Fishing Contest, Prospect Park (788-0055).
African Street Festival, Bedford-Stuyvesant (638-6700).
Coney Island Air Show (July 4), Coney Island (266-1234 or 266-3004).

Feast of Giglio, Our Lady of Mount Carmel, Williamsburg (384-0223).
Procession of Saint Fortunata, Bensonhurst (331-6532).

AUGUST

Brighton Jubilee, Brighton Beach (891-0800).
Weeksville Family Festival, Bedford-Stuyvesant (756-5250).

SEPTEMBER

Coney Island, Air Show (266-1234 or 266-3004).
Atlantic Antic, Atlantic Avenue (875-8993).
Flatbush Frolic, Flatbush (469-8990).
Great Irish Fair, Coney Island (403-2580).
Outdoor Art Show, Sheepshead Bay (338-2043).
Ragamuffin Parade, Bay Ridge (833-3399).
Santa Rosalia Festival, Bensonhurst (331-6532).
West Indian American Day Carnival, Eastern Parkway (773-4052).

OCTOBER

Great Pumpkin Festival, Prospect Park (788-0055).
Halloween Festival, Brooklyn Children's Museum (735-4400).
Halloween Parade, 8th Avenue, Park Slope (636-8736).
House tour, Bedford-Stuyvesant (452-3226).
Outdoor Art Show (juried), Promenade, Brooklyn Heights (788-3077 or 783-4469).

NOVEMBER

Swedish Santa Lucia Festival, Sunset Park (438-9426).

DECEMBER

New Year's Eve fireworks, Grand Army Plaza (788-0055).
St. Nicholas Day Celebration, Wyckoff House (629-5400) and Lefferts Homestead (965-6505), Prospect Park.

TOURS

TOURS RUN BY NONPROFIT ORGANIZATIONS

Brooklyn Center for the Urban Environment tours. 788-8549 (recording) or 788-8500.

This organization offers innovative bus, boat, and walking tours all over Brooklyn for adults and families interested in the quirks and grandeur of our urban environment. Tours are led by an interdisciplinary roster of experts: urban archaeologists, naturalists, cultural historians, urban studies specialists, ecologists, and architects. Favorite tours include Greenwood Cemetery, the Brooklyn Bridge, and interesting industrial sites, such as Bush Terminal, Water Tunnel 3, and the Coney Island subway repair yards.

Brooklyn Historical Society. 624-0890.

The Brooklyn Historical Society also organizes fascinating walking tours and lectures on a regular basis. No one knows more about historic Brooklyn.

Sunset Park Restoration Committee tours and digs. 871-8340.

This group organizes free one- and two-hour tours of Sunset Park and Greenwood Cemetery and small-scale excavations in abandoned lots and open areas.

HOUSE TOURS

Tour the interiors of beautifully restored nineteenth-century homes in several neighborhoods. Generally the tours take place only once a year. Call the following numbers for details.

Bedford-Stuyvesant. Brownstoners of Bedford-Stuyvesant House Tour, 452-3226.

Brooklyn Heights. Brooklyn Heights Association Landmark House and Garden Tour, 858-9193.

Flatbush. Flatbush Development Corporation house tour (May), 469-8890.

Fort Greene. Fort Greene House Tours, 783-8454 or 857-9471.

Park Slope. Park Slope Civic Council House Tour, 636-8736.

COMMERCIAL TOURS

Brooklyn Discovery Tours (Gray Line). (212) 397-2600.
Six-hour bus tours that visit the Brooklyn Museum, Brooklyn Botanic Garden, and high points in Brooklyn Heights are available for about $25. You also can arrange for guides that speak foreign languages from Russian to Spanish. Tours begin and end at Gray Line New York Tours' office in Manhattan.

Brooklyn Historic Railway Association. 941-3160.
Built in 1861 and then abandoned and sealed up in 1884, the Atlantic Avenue Tunnel was the world's first subway tunnel. Rediscovered in 1980, it is now listed in the National Register of Historic Places. Robert Diamond conducts tours—you enter through a utility hole—for groups of ten or more. Cost is $10 per person. Call to get on the waiting list.

The Middle East in South Ferry. 522-1916.
Local resident and cultural historian Mary Ann Haick DiNapoli gives ninety-minute Saturday morning tours of the century-old Christian Syrian-Lebanese community around Atlantic Avenue. The cost is about $10.

Museum and garden tour. 857-7811.
This tour takes visitors to the Brooklyn Museum, Brooklyn Botanic Garden, and then to lunch at the elegant nineteenth-century Montauk Club in Park Slope. Call for details.

Singer's Tours. 875-9084.

A real "Brooklyn character," Lou Singer has given a variety of lively, informative tours focusing on Brooklyn's brownstones, Tiffany glass windows, ethnic foods, and more for over twenty years. He'll happily tailor a tour to your specific ethnic or culinary interest. He caters to foreign tourists and can accommodate small groups, individuals, or bus tours. Call for information on prices and routes.

Tours of the City. 625-7413.

Well-known tour guide Justin Ferate can take you on walking tours of any part of Brooklyn, from the Heights to Greenwood Cemetery. He has conducted tours for such organizations as the Municipal Art Society, the National Trust for Historic Preservation, the Victorian Society, the New York Public Library, and Columbia University. He will tailor your tour to your specific architectural or historic interests and tastes. Rates are about $175 to $200 for half-day group or individual tours.

WHERE TO FIND IT

This index will help you find your way around in terms of: 1. Getting Oriented; 2. Culture and Recreation; 3. Restaurants; and 4. Shopping. An alphabetical index follows.

1. GETTING ORIENTED

Contemporary Brooklyn: "Oh, they have *that* there?"
Note: Some of these are chain stores that are not listed elsewhere in this book.
   Check a Brooklyn telephone directory for locations.
Barnes & Noble
Benetton
Century 21, 11
D'Agostino's
David's Cookies
Domino's Pizza
Gap
Haagen-Dazs Ice Cream
Lum Chin, 18
Macy's
Radio Shack

Two Boots, 218
TKTS, 110

Ethnic Brooklyn
See the chapters under the following headings.
African-American: Bedford-Stuyvesant; Fort Greene
Irish: Bay Ridge
Italian: Bensonhurst; Carroll Gardens; Williamsburg
Jewish: Borough Park; Flatbush (Midwood); Williamsburg
Middle Eastern: Atlantic Avenue; Midwood
Polish: Greenpoint
Russian: Brighton Beach
Scandinavian: Sunset Park; Bay Ridge
West Indian: Flatbush (East Flatbush)
White Anglo-Saxon Protestant: Brooklyn Heights; Cobble Hill (Carroll Gardens and Cobble Hill chapter); Clinton Hill (Fort Greene chapter)

Half-day Trips for Manhattanites
Any organized tour (see tours section, page 255)
Brighton Beach, Coney Island, New York Aquarium, 75, 83, 85
Brooklyn Botanic Gardens, 211
Brooklyn Historic Railway Association, 124
Brooklyn Museum, 211
Fishing in Sheepshead Bay, 91
Lunch or brunch in Brooklyn Heights or Park Slope, 104, 202
Walk across Brooklyn Bridge, wander in Brooklyn Heights, 104, 134

Lodging
Bed and Breakfast on the Park, 229
Park House Hotel, 73

Nostalgic Brooklyn: Holdovers From the 1940s
Abraham & Straus, 111
Alba, 49
Bamonte's, 196
Bari Pork Store, 49
Brennan & Carr, 95
Brooklyn Academy of Music (BAM), 178
Brooklyn Army Terminal, 234
Brooklyn Botanic Garden and Children's Garden, 211, 241
Brooklyn Central Public Library, Grand Army Plaza, 215

2. CULTURE & RECREATION

Art Exhibits (Commercial and Not-for-Profit)

Churches and Synagogues (Historic)

Gospel Choirs and Other Religious Music

Movies

Museums and Exhibits

Nightspots: Places to Go Dancing

3. RESTAURANTS

Cafés

Children's Best Bets

Dining and Entertainment
Entertainment is usually on weekends; call in advance.

Ethnic

Chinese

Indian

Irish

Italian

Mexican-Spanish-Latino

Middle Eastern

Nouvelle

Polish

Outdoor Seating

Pizza

Popular Social Scenes

Romantic

Seafood
Abbracciamento on the Pier, 95
Cafe on Clinton, 146
Castle Harbour, 93
Gage & Tollner, 116
Hunan Seafood King, 94
Joe's Clam Bar, 94
Maria's Restaurant, 94
Martini's Seafood Restaurant, 23
Ossie's Table, 62
Randazzo's Italian Seafood Restaurant & Clam Bar, 95

Steaks and Ribs
Al Hubbard's Steak House, 16
Embers, 16
Peter Luger Steak House, 196
Roll 'N' Roaster, 96
Short Ribs, 20
Two Toms, 218

Turn-of-the-Century Ambiance
Boerum Hill Cafe, 126
B. J. Carey Provisions, 126
Cafe on Clinton, 146
Camille's, 126
Gage & Tollner, 116
Monte's Venetian Room, 146

4. SHOPPING

Antiques and Used Furniture
Architectural Salvage Warehouse, 199
Atlantic Attic, 130
Bird Dog Antiques, 130
Circa Antiques, 130
City Barn Antiques, 129
Eifel Antique Furniture Warehouse, 226
Fine Period Furniture, 226
Gaslight Time Antiques, 227
Hall & Winter, 128

For Men

For Women

Food
Bakeries

Coffee

Take-out Prepared Foods

Furniture

Gifts

Toys
Al's Toyland, 224
ArtSmart, 250
G & Sons, 71
Laughing Giraffe at Monkeyswedding, 151
Learning Wheel, 101
Lilliput, 26
Little Things, 225
Mini Mansions, 53
Moby Dick Toys, 122
Our Children's Enterprises, 225
Teacher's Pet, 69
Toys "Я" Us, 54, 103
Whispers 'N' Whimsies, 73
Zak's Fun House, 55

Weddings
Finishing Touches, 52
I. Kleinfeld and Son, 25
Val Con's American Bridal Center, 54

INDEX

READER'S QUESTIONNAIRE

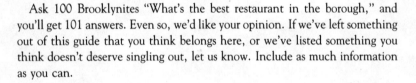

Ask 100 Brooklynites "What's the best restaurant in the borough," and you'll get 101 answers. Even so, we'd like your opinion. If we've left something out of this guide that you think belongs here, or we've listed something you think doesn't deserve singling out, let us know. Include as much information as you can.

Establishment name:

Establishment address:

Type of establishment (restaurant, park, shop, entertainment, etc.):

Neighborhood:

Who would be interested in it? (kids, bargain hunters, etc.):

Why it deserves to be listed (or unlisted) in this guide:

Your name:

Your address:

Mail your comments to: *Brooklyn: Where to Go, What to Do, How to Get There*, c/o St. Martin's Press, 175 Fifth Avenue, New York, N.Y. 10010.